Y0-BRN-803

IMMORTAL SLEUTH

Sherlockian Musings and Memories

Titles By The Author

Novels

Weep for Lycidas
Spring in Tartarus
All the Trees Were Green
Vernal Equinox
What Are We Waiting For?
Battered Caravanserai
So Linked Together
Treadmill
There's Glory For You!
Long Vacation
The Dividing Stone
The Brain
A Hansom to St James's

The "Rowcester" Novels

Higher Things
The House in Fishergate
Sinecure
The Darkened Room

Biography

Gambler's Glory (John Law of Lauriston)
Count Cagliostro: "Nature's Unfortunate Child..."
They Would Be King (Lambert Simnel, King Theodore, Bernadotte, Henry Christophe)
Prince of Hokum (Peter Cheyney)
Charles Dickens: A Sentimental Journey in Search of an Unvarnished Portrait
Rosa (Rosa Lewis of the Cavendish Hotel)
Lord of London (2nd Duke of Westminster)
Clarence (HRH the Duke of Clarence & Avondale)

Historical and Paranormal

Airborne at Kitty Hawk (The Wright Brothers)
The History of the Hat
London By Gaslight: 1861–1911
London Growing: The Development of a Metropolis

Mulberry: The Return in Triumph (Prelude to D- Day)
The London That Was Rome
Fanfare of Strumpets
The Roots of Witchcraft
Fire from Heaven (Spontaneous combustion)
Vanishings

The Sherlock Holmes Monographs

Theatrical Mr Holmes
Decorated Mr Holmes
Cynological Mr Holmes

The Sherlock Holmes Commentaries

In the Footsteps of Sherlock Holmes
The London of Sherlock Holmes
The World of Sherlock Holmes
I, Sherlock Holmes
A Study in Surmise: The Making of Sherlock Holmes

Philately

Mauritius 1897
A New Approach to Stamp Collecting (with Douglas B. Armstrong)

Cuisine

Beer Cookery

Short Stories

Transit of Venus
Exploits of the Chevalier Dupin (USA only)
Murder in the Rue Royale, and Other Exploits of the Chevalier Dupin

Advertising

Technical and Industrial Publicity

IMMORTAL SLEUTH

Sherlockian Musings and Memories

MICHAEL HARRISON

GASOGENE PRESS, Ltd.

Box 1041
Dubuque, IA 52004-1041

Publication Staff
Jean R. Starr, *Managing Editor*
Carlisle Graphics, *Composition*
Book Crafters, *Printing and Binding*

Library of Congress Catalogue Number: 86-083422

ISBN 0–938501–01–1

Printed in the United States of America

10 9 8 7 6 5 4 3 2 1

For
ANN BYERLY, ASH
enchanting Administratrix of the Red-Headed League
in all admiration and affection

THE HAT OF HATS

Where are the hats the Poet sings?
Where are the hats of yesteryear?
The Breton maids wore gauzy wings,
And Kalmuck peasants caps of fur
Like opened beech-nuts.

           Wired and starched,
Above elaborate *coiffure*,
Alsatians bows were quaintly arched,
And Grison girls wore caps demure
Of finest cambric, stitched and flow'red
With coloured thread.

           Mongolian priests
Wore hats of felt in Grecian shapes;
While Spanish girls, at solemn feasts,
Concealed their hair 'neath lacy drapes.

Korean hats were high and black—
As those of Welsh and Eskimo:
Not *quite* the same as, some while back,
Were seen each morn in Rotten Row.

The scarlet caps of Genoese,
The peaked and tasselled caps of Dutch;
The flat grey Spanish: all did please—
Yet made for difference quite as much
As charm.

           In hats' variety
Did human fancy richly thrive;
And hats were gay when men were free;
For, hatted, every man alive

Expressed his ego by his style
Of head-gear.

           Then undreamt-of were
Our modern days where, dreary, vile,
The Soft Felt rules from Monastir
To Valparaiso; from the Horn
To Tanu-Tuva.

           Sameness grey
Now robs of promise every morn;
And in Fedoras, Samurai
Regret the day that they were born.

Lock out Romance! The day is done:
The gonfalon of Gloom unfurled:
And, weary, every Mother's son
Fades in his baseball-hatted world.

With olden charm is Fancy fled;
And all that rich variety
She once bestowed on human head
Gives place to dim sobriety.

Hatless—uncovered—most now go;
Our present Age shews something rotten;
Sure Taste has touched an all-time Low
When hats and headgear are forgotten!

Yet stay! *One* famous hat survives,
As famous as the One who wears it;
Inseparable as any gyves;
Symbol of that Fame which spares it.

Twin-peaked, of tweed, and double-flapped,
A fashion that Time cannot kill:
A century of years have lapped—
Yet what he bought then's with us still.

Immortal Sleuth! no crown of gold,
Worn kingly-wise, e'er matched the fame
Of that tweed hat of fashion old,
Associated with thy Name!

Michael Harrison

*The "Deerstalker," from
c. 1875*

CONTENTS

ILLUSTRATIONS

I have sub-titled this, my sixth full-length 'Sherlockian' book, 'Sherlockian Musings and Memories'. That 'Memories' is, I think, not likely to call for any explanation: in eighty years, I have had, praise Heaven!, more than my fair share of passing through truly memorable times, and meeting many memorable people. Age alone (one need not to go adventuring) will fill the cup of Memory to overflowing—so that, of the 'Memories' in this book, I have been able to give but the smallest part of my huge store. But the 'Musings' in the sub-title does, I feel, call for a word of explanation here.

The now world-wide Sherlockian Cult stretches far, far beyond the activities of the many 'Scion Societies'—over two hundred in the United States alone—so that there is hardly a novel written to-day, in any language, which does not include at least a casual reference to Sherlock Holmes or Dr Watson, often by the simple reference to tricks of speech, universally known (or believed to be) idiosyncratically expressive of their twinned personalities: "Pass the cocaine, Watson!" is a non-Canonical but popular catch-phrase that seems as flourishing to-day among the light-hearted as when it was coined almost a century ago. At least—I pass now to the more serious side of these Holmesian references—three learned American judges have referred, in comment and legal judgement, to 'the Dog in the Night', and English-language writers as diverse as P.D. James and P.G. Wodehouse; as Scott Fitzgerald and Raymond Chandler; rarely write a book without at least one reference to the Immortal Sleuth of Baker-street and the companion who, in Britain's and America's more Classical days, was known as Holmes's *Fidus Achates*.

The Sherlockian Cult began, if not exactly in a joking, at least in a light-hearted tongue-in-cheek way, by seeking to explain the many—and many they surely are!—inconsistencies in the Watson-ian accounts of his friend's many cases. (An example: Dr Watson, in the case of *Silver Blaze*, tells us that the pair started for King's Pyland, in Devon, from Paddington Station, and then describes how they returned to Victoria Station, on an entirely different line.) Not hundreds, but thousands of books and articles have now been written, as further inconsistencies were detected, and attempts made to resolve them. All this vast literature is known generally as 'the Higher Criticism'; and the body of all the Sherlockian tales as 'the Canon' or, within the Inner Council of *Sherlockismus*, 'the Sacred Writings'.

This examination—this minute examination—of the corpus of Sherlockian tales has been no idle exercise; acute observation and true scholarship, in resolving the apparent or real inconsistencies; in attempting the dating of the stories; and— most important of all—in detecting, in the Sherlockian tales, the echoes of those true-life scandals and tragedies and crimes that so fascinated Conan Doyle, have 'paid off' handsomely. The result of all this dedicated scholarship has been, through the minute examination of his most famous character, to detect more and more the secret attractions, affections, principles, and prejudices of Sherlock Holmes's creator.

So this is what I mean by that word, 'Musings'. I have reflected on certain passages—certain references—in the many pages of The Canon, and given my own explanations of what, hitherto, have seemed obscure or even inexplicable.

HOVE, East Sussex
24 July 1986

SHERLOCKIAN MEMORIES

About the date of my first specific Sherlockian memory there is some dispute. My memory tells me—and has always told me—that the night on which my parents returned from a stage-performance of *The Speckled Band* fell in that most fateful year of 1914, when, though metaphorically, 'the lights went out all over Europe', within the theatres they went on blazing merrily enough. Still using that word 'specifically', I certainly—and how I now regret the omission!—never asked my parents at which theatre they had seen the play; and it is this omission that seems to have brought the memory of the *date* under suspicion. Or, rather, under the suspicion of that learned Sherlockian historiographer, my friend, Mr Peter Blau.

According to Mr Blau—and who am I to gainsay him?—there was no performance of *The Speckled Band* within an evening's accessibility of our house, a mere ten miles from London.

Against Mr Blau's assurance that *The Speckled Band* 'played' nowhere near London or its well-theatred suburbs throughout 1914, or even 1915, I have the most vivid memory of my father's 'white-tie and tails', and of a dress of my mother's, of which the elegant high-necked lace collar was edged with some brown fur. And though there was a Music-hall (an 'Empire', it was called then) at Lewisham, only some three miles away, I cannot believe that even with the (now considered excessive) formality of 1914, my father would have put on a dress-coat to sit in a stall at Lewisham Empire, though my mother might have dressed herself as elegantly as I remember her on that night made memorable for me from my having first heard the plot of *The Speckled Band*.

Again, though Mr Blau tells me—I have no doubt, correctly—that the play was revived, at the St James's Theatre, with Lyn Harding as 'Dr Grimesby Rylott'—name changed from Conan Doyle's 'Roylott' to suit some strange theatrical whim!—he adds that this revival took place, not, as I had 'distinctly remembered', in 1914, but in mid-1916—two years later.

But again, to counter that suggestion, there is yet another memory, and one less easy to dismiss. Lying in my bed, in a room in the front of the house; hoping that I would still be awake when my parents returned; I was heartened by the sound of a hansom's rattle and jingle and hoof-clopping: a sound which, if one have ever heard it, is among the most ineffaceable of all Memory's sounds....

Now, it is true that the hansom was, in 1916, by no means—even in Central London—quite obsolete; indeed, I recall that, the taxis seemingly all bespoken, we came back one night of a Zeppelin-raid from Woolwich (shades, though much later, of Cadogan West and the Bruce-Partington plans!) in a hansom.

All the same, that my parents should have taken a hansom, rather than a taxi, that night, smacks to me more of 1914 than of 1916. I still prefer to think that it was in 1914, rather than on some date two years later, that I first heard, from my father's lips, the story of the play that he and my mother had seen that night....

———

I mention here that my mother had seen *The Speckled Band*, for it was that fact that was the cause of the first...well, 'row' is too strong a word...'acrimony', then?.... Very well: the first acrimony that I had ever been permitted to hear. My mother had gone into her bedroom to (as the old phrase had it) 'slip into something more comfortable' and returned to say, in suitably 'horrified' tones: "*George! Really!* You don't mean to say that you've actually told the child the *plot*!"

Poor Father! Misled by my eager questions into indiscretion, my father had indeed told me the plot—in all its shuddersome details, not, of course, omitting the swamp adder....

Then my mother, as though a Sherlock-oriented Fate were rebuking her for her incomprehension, put it into her mind and mouth to do herself a singular disservice—for that coming night, at least.

Once started on her 'justified' denunciation of my father's folly, the rebukes came, as they say, 'fast and furious', but even did I remember them, there would be no profit in my recalling them. All women have access to the scripts that they use on these occasions; scripts which, I firmly believe, were composed by some indignant women even before the Ice Age, and which have come down, generation-after-generation, not by word- of-mouth, but by a means far more certain: by implant in the genes and chromosomes of all women, who never know when they will be called upon to express their justified indignation.

And what did my mother say that did her a singular disservice? This. The ages-old script, the tape of her wrath, having come to an end, my mother had to add the fatal last word: "*George!* I hope you *know* what you've done! Now the child will have nightmares and will keep us awake all night...."

All children respond eagerly to this sort of invitation. I don't know whether or not I had nightmares, but I certainly did what my mother had said was to be expected: I kept my parents awake that night....

———————

There had been, though I did not know it until 1926, a very close Sherlockian 'contact' between the Harrison Family and a certain tale in the Canon in 1911, a date about which there may be no dispute. I shall not describe it here, for I have given a separate chapter of this book to its detailed recounting.

I had, of course, after having had the tale of the Swamp Adder told to me by my father, taken out those volumes of *The Strand Magazine*, which had been in my father's possession since long before I was born, but which had, in some odd fashion been neglected by me. It was then the Golden Age of magazines, and ours, like most other families of our class, took most of them as a matter of course, if, indeed, not of unthinking habit. On the more 'intellectual' side, there were *The Illustrated London News* and (gone, alas!) *The Sphere, The Graphic,* and such now-forgotten—and, for a small boy, so wonderfully exciting— magazines as *Army and Navy, Black-and-White,* and *The King* (for all of which my father had been 'Our Observer at the Battle- front', during the Riff-Spanish war of 1904–6, into which he had happened casually as an idling tourist, going from Gibraltar to Ceuta).

For my mother, there was a plenitude of ephemeral reading-matter, that I find, on recent checking, to be far superior to anything offered to us to-day: *The Windsor, The Quiver, The Ladies Home Journal* (American), *Nash's* (with both 'science- fiction' and detective stories, besides the usual and expected love-stories, and with the prettiest of American girls, by the artist, Harrison Fisher, on each month's cover, a great favourite of mine). "Science-fiction" had not then received its modern Hugo Gernsback name; but of science-fiction in all the magazines, there was no dearth. A crop of 'flying saucers' had been seen over England in the years immediately preceding the death of the King on 6th May, 1910—predicting that death, said many—and in 1912, *Pearson's Magazine,* yet more of my mother's 'required reading', had run a serial, translated from the French: *The Sky People,* a strange and disturbing tale of very material but invisible visitors from Out There, who snatched luckless humans only in order to vivisect them. *The Red Magazine* ran a tale of the three Spider-women (gruesomely illustrated by Maurice Greiffenhagen) who glided down from Mars on their spider-filaments, landing by Lake Athabasca, intent on no good at all for Humanity. *Cassell's, The Blue Magazine,* (not at all 'blue'; in fact, a most respectable journal) and *The Century* (yet another American) are others that my mother 'took' regularly, and all, as I remember, ran what we should now call 'science-fiction' at one time or another. The boys' magazines, however—even the 'comics'—were full of science-fiction, though, as I look back, I see that it was of a simple, primitive, decidedly unsophisticated kind. Some of the boys' magazines were banned at home; Heaven knew why, since none was even obliquely obscene or subversive of the Established Order. My parents thought them 'trashy'—and I was forbidden to read them. Naturally, I bought them and read them, but well out of sight of my parents. What was permitted, and, indeed, recommended was the magazine of the type of *The Boys' Own Paper,* for which Conan Doyle had written in his beginner's days. (It literally bulged with what they now call 'fantasy fiction', besides 'stirring tales of adventure and derring-do', and not a year passed without 'our heroes' heading for a Lost City, if not for a Lost World. Permitted reading included *The Captain,* which had carried the school-stories and mock-Malory parodies of the just-beginning P.G. Wodehouse; and permitted, but almost not, was *Chums,* of which the Editor, Max (later Sir Max) Pemberton was himself a successful author, with such best-sellers to his credit as *Kronstadt* and *The Iron Pirate.*

I confess, with shame, that, with all this heady stuff about, I began to find the Conan Doyle of the Holmes stories dullish—though not the Conan Doyle of *The Poison Belt, The Lost World,* and 'Horror of the Heights' (all read by me in *The Strand Magazine*).

But a return to the spell of Holmes was at hand. In 1914, the year in which that Great War broke out that was to destroy most of the world as we (and Holmes) had known and loved it, *The Strand* began to serialize *The Valley of Fear,* though it was not until the following June (1915) that I was able to cadge the necessary six shillings from sympathetic or merely weary-of-importunacy adults to buy myself the hard-cover edition. From then on, I never lost my recovered liking and, indeed, reverence, for Holmes, despite all his imperfections.

One interesting (not Sherlockian, but Doylean) memory belongs to this sad period of savage warfare and mass-destruction, the more tragic as even before the war's official end (it is still going on, of course), it was acknowledged on all sides to have been 'a waste of time' in all possible aspects, from the destruction of human life to the destruction of human art and culture.

On Sunday, 21st May, 1916, at the height of the most terrible slaughter of the War, we children were permitted to sit out in the garden to enjoy the unprecedented wonder of a Spring day that continued a full hour longer than usual: Daylight Saving Time (at first called Willett Time) had arrived. Germany had adopted it a year earlier.

I was nine at this night of extended visibility, and well able to be talked to 'intelligently', and as 'intelligently', take in much of what was being said to me. And on this night, in a garden to which full Spring had come, my father told me how Conan Doyle, that great, tireless, and never-defeated Champion of Causes, had 'done his bit' (it was a popular war-time cliché) in securing that extra daylight that we were then so excitedly enjoying. In the year in which I was born, William Willett, a 'property developer' who had made a fortune in speculative (but structurally sound) building— he 'developed' the seaside village of Hove, two miles west of Brighton, into the pleasant town in which I now live—published a small pamphlet, *Waste of Daylight*—the first (at least, the first *modern*) plea for 'Daylight Saving', to which most countries of the Western world have since given their official allegiance. Willett's friend, Richard (later Sir Richard) Pearce, Member of Parliament, waited no longer than the following year to introduce a Private Member's Bill, the object of which was to get Daylight Saving made law, but the Bill was thrown out.

Willett, though, was not to be defeated by an initial set- back, and, as a self-made plutocrat, was certainly not lacking in 'push'. Through his parliamentarian friend, and by other means, Willett cleverly collected a committee of men, not only important and influential in themselves, but more important and more influential in that all—or most—of them bore names romantically and excitingly familiar to the Public: none more so than Sir Arthur Conan Doyle.

No need here for me to emphasize the pugnacious spirit of Sir Arthur—for one may be as pugnacious fighting in a good cause as in a bad; and for him, all the causes that he took up were mostly good. It was no hardship for him to add Daylight Saving to all the other causes to which he was giving his time and still undiminished energy. And, to cut this story short, seven years after the Daylight Saving Committee had been formed, there we were, sitting in the peace of a protracted—a miraculously protracted, it seemed to us children—Kentish twilight. The guns were far distant, and their murderous rumble, for all the legends, was too far off ever to have been heard....

There is yet another Sherlockian memory connected, not with that year of 1915, but with either the following year or the year after that; but in no case later than 1917. This particular memory has been vivid in my mind since the Autumn of 1984, when I found myself in the hall of Gillette Castle, in East Haddam, Connecticut, talking to that body of true Sherlockians known as 'The Men of the Tor', on (what and who else?) the Master and his work.

The memory: We lived in what was then, though less than ten miles from London, virtually 'country'. Opposite the house was Sparrow's Farm; to the right, a few hundred yards away, were the hop-gardens (*never* hop-*fields*!), which assured the tang and the mild narcotic quality to the fine Kentish beers of those days: Russell's *Shrimp Brand*, Leney's, Fremlin's *Elephant Brand*, Reffell's, Charrington's, and many others. (And a pillow filled with dried hops was considered a sovereign remedy against that familiar complaint of far-off days: 'stuffed-up nose'.)

There was, though, a fairly big town not many miles distant; and it was here, outside the Gem Electric Palace—its attractive name outlined in the glowing bulbs that gave it its name—that Memory finds me, a small, rather globular boy of ten, studying a large yellow poster, and asking that small boy's father what 'Presented by Essanay' meant?

Told that 'Essanay' was obviously one of those commercial words formed from, no doubt, the initials of the partners in the enterprise, one might confidently interpret the word 'Essanay' as 'S. & A.', further questioning shew no light on the identity of either 'S' or 'A'. The child then expressed a desire to see the film advertised, and, being in a compliant mood with nothing pressing to be done, the father paid his shilling and the boy's sixpence. Receiving two metal 'shapes' as proof of pre-payment, they were torch-guided through the darkened 'Palace'.

The film as promised by the bright yellow *Essanay* poster, was *Sherlock Holmes,* with 'the renowned American actor, William Gillette, in the title-rôle of Sherlock Holmes'. Age takes much away from us, but it has not yet taken away, in my affectionate memory, the magic of the moment when, at last, the Holmes of my so-familiar reading was here before me, incarnate in jerky black-and-white, but alive and excitingly real for all the imperfections of the early filming.

There were to be other Holmeses of stage and screen; indeed, the thespian rivals (perhaps poor imitators is the better phrase?) of Gillette had already appeared, and more were to come. Many, in the near future, were to prove themselves no inconsiderable successors to Gillette, and I saw most of them—at least, the better ones: Eille Norwood (like Conan Doyle, a star-cricketer), Arthur Wontner (by far the best of the older impersonators of the Master) and, of course, Basil Rathbone. I wish that honesty would permit me to include the elegant and pleasing Clive Brook within this notable company, but...alas!...there was nothing convincingly Holmes about Mr Brook; not even anything very Dartmoorish about the stage-sets of the spectral Hound's *milieu*. I liked—still like— Clive Brook and his acting; I must have seen *Shanghai Express* (with the incomparable Marlene Dietrich) six or seven times; and each time with even more enjoyment. So that I am driven to the con- clusion that, experienced actor as he was, if Clive Brook could not achieve a convincing Holmes, then it must require a very special sort of talent to play Holmes. That to *play* Holmes must be almost as difficult as to *be* Holmes.

But let's not forget the various Watsons, of whom (in my opin- ion) the very best to date is the—sadly, now dead— most talented British actor, Nigel Stock, whose one-man, two-hour show as the aging Watson revisiting the about-to-be rebuilt 221B, Baker-street, is a triumph of acting genius; such as, I think, no other actor, 'Sher- lockian' or not, could ever have even equalled, let alone excelled.

One of the dangers inherent in acting is that a well-known actor or actress will, by the very force of his or her personality, 'type' a part so effectively, that the Public will expect at least an echo of that archetypal 'interpretation' in all succeeding stage-pre- sentations of the part. It must be admitted that the shadow of Nigel Bruce, playing Watson to Basil Rathbone's Holmes has blighted far too many succeeding Watsons, who might have shone far more individually had they not acted with the 'classic' Bruce-devised Watson to 'live up to': the bumbling, almost half-witted caricature of the traditional stage-half-pay-English-major image. It took many years for post-Nigel Bruce Watsons to cast off his spell—though there were earlier Watsons rather closer to the original Canon. Arthur Wontner's was a 'quiet' Holmes, and his Watson was a 'quiet' interpretation, too. Indeed, there can hardly have been a quieter Watson than Ian Fleming's, in which, for the first time, we are asked to accept a silently pondering Watson, well able to think for himself, and neither offering nor being given the opportunities or the receipt of those Sherlockian ironies, sarcasms, and downright snubs, which, in the latest Sherlockian TV offering, seem to have returned even more plentifully and even more spitefully than they are to be found in the Canon, though one of the latest Watsons— David Burke's—is (thank Heaven!) reminiscent more of Ian Fleming's than of Nigel Bruce's. Looking back, I feel that Ian Fleming's presentation of a 'quiet' Dr Watson has not received the praise that it surely deserves. Here, stated in unequivocal, completely unambiguous, terms, was the theatrical presentation of a companion of Holmes's who appeared to be a reasoning, reasonable human being in his own right, with an innate dignity that would have responded to Holmes's 'needling' in the calmest of unruffled acceptances—but which 'needling', be it noticed, was never offered by Arthur Wontner's self-possessed, dignified Holmes. Some serious re-appraisal of the Fleming Watson is obviously long overdue.

The Nigel Bruce concept of Watson is, all the same, by no means dead, and is revived every now and then. The Watson nearest to Nigel Bruce's from a fairly recent period is that of the British actor, Thorley Walters, whom I saw only a few days before beginning this essay in a TV Agatha Christie whodunit. Mr Walters was a member of the cast. He was not cast as a detective, but sure as God made little apples, there, at one small remove, was our old friend Nigel Bruce, bumbling and all....

All this remembrance of things past (but, quite often, only just, or not even altogether past), brings me to a point now being hotly debated in Sherlockian circles, and, for all I know, outside those circles as well. The point is this. In dramatizing a written work— in the case of the Holmes dramatizations, the dramatizing is rather of two central characters than of the sixty stories in which, fictionally, they appear—how bound by artistic canons are the various dramatizers to 'stick to the original' in the matter of a meticulously faithful adherence to the letter and the spirit of the work or works to be dramatized? Well, if it be a *written* work that is to be transferred, as to its plot, its characters, and the *author's* description of how his fictional characters work out that plot, I may give here my firm opinion that this not only cannot be done, but that it ought not to be attempted to be done—for the undeniable reason that a tale told in a book and a tale told on stage or on film are told in very different ways. The first *serious* dramatization[1] of Sherlock Holmes, with William Gillette both writing the script and 'creating' the part of Holmes, took admirable and most financially profitable recognition of the dichotomy of story-in-book and story-on-stage.

William Gillette, already an experienced and successful playwright and producer, understood this truth so well that he entered into negotiations with Conan Doyle only on the strict condition that, so far as the theatre was concerned, Gillette should be in sole control.

Conan Doyle had already made several attempts—all, so far, unsuccessful—on the stage; the one partial success being his curtain-raiser, adapted from a short-story of his, but re-written for the stage by Henry Irving: *A Story of Waterloo* (originally, as a story: *A Straggler of '15*). But, undeterred by these successive proofs that his literary talent (like Tennyson's) did not lie in play-writing, Doyle, with typical Irish-Scottishness, bulled manfully on, coming up, at the century's very end, with a five-act drama about Holmes. What happened to this Doyle-written play demonstrates how the story told in a novel and the story told in a play must be, in all practical senses, quite incompatible. To be presented in convincing dramatic form, the story must be completely 'de-novelized'—that is, if it is to have the least chance of box-office success.

Gillette knew this well, and though Doyle was reluctant to have his own work 'interfered with', his agent, Watt,[2] persuaded him that, for his own good, he should let Gillette have his own way. Doyle, having agreed in principle that the play, re-written, should be produced by Charles Frohman, with Gillette playing the lead, made one last, but not more than half-hearted attempt to

---

[1] The first non-serious appearance of Sherlock Holmes on the stage was in the curtain-raiser 'skit'. *Under the Clock,* with Seymour Hicks (later Sir Seymour) in the principal part. It was staged at the Royal Court Theatre, Sloane-square, London, In 1894.

[2] And my agent, too, in later years.

retain control over 'his' play: "It will be perfectly all right, Mr Frohman. But I make one stipulation. You are a genius of the romantic production. There must be no love business in *Sherlock Holmes*." In the event, the play, for all its heavy revision, was to prove so unacceptable to Gillette, that he wrote (to his own satisfaction as an actor, fresh from a London stage-triumph in his *Secret Service*) a completely new play, the 'action' made up of bits-and-pieces from various Holmes stories, the whole mélange unified by the character of Sherlock Holmes.

Conan Doyle, sent this complete re-writing, was sufficient of a realist to know a good thing when he saw it, and the words in which he made his final, total, submission to Gillette are perhaps the best known of all Conan Doyle's utterances. To Gillette's cable from New York: 'MAY I MARRY HOLMES?', Conan Doyle had replied: 'MARRY HIM OR MURDER HIM OR DO WHAT YOU LIKE WITH HIM'. The Conan Doyle-Gillette collaboration had achieved perfection in that the inexperienced partner had gracefully deferred to the greater experience of the other, and had, in effect, become the sleeping partner. Doyle's was a wise decision: the play was an immediate success, making a fortune for Gillette (in whose Castle, built out of his wealth, I have thrice spoken), and Conan Doyle profited greatly—which brings me back to the question with which I began: How closely should—must—the dramatist 'stick to' the written original that is being 'adapted' for the stage or film? By *not* sticking to a written original—indeed, by picking and choosing from any number of originals, and *then* constructing an entirely new version out of the mix—Gillette, with his superb stage-sense, had created a runaway box-office success. Is, then, the accidental or deliberate getting away, for stage purposes, from the original written work an essential towards the realization of a stage-success?

I ask this because the latest of film—TV, rather—Sherlock Holmeses has had—*is* having—a very mixed reception precisely because, as I have shewn elsewhere, this obviously talented actor has, either by his own decision or by that of his director, abandoned the smoothness, which, in an ever-greater degree, has been characterizing stage-and-screen Sherlocks for decades, and has presented us with what is seen as a completely new interpretation of Holmes—a presentation that not all find either pleasant or acceptable. I refer, of course, to the Sherlock Holmes of Mr Jeremy

Brett, appearing with a very subdued, patiently enduring Watson in the not unattractive presentation— already noticed—of Mr David Burke. Mr. Edward Hardwicke, the new TV Watson, is subdued.

What is it that so many of my acquaintances and friends; so many professional and amateur film-critics find distasteful in Mr Brett's novel presentation? Well, mostly—I quote a percipient friend—that this new Holmes is 'unpleasantly abrasive', adding: "How the Public takes kindly—those that do— to the spectacle of his brash impatience and downright rudeness to everyone, especially to poor old Watson, beats me. How the Producer thought that people would like this new-type Holmes—and far too many of us don't—I simply can't imagine...."

But it was just this 'abrasive' Holmes that Vincent Price, introducing the first of the Brett-Holmes TV series, specifically promised, in these words (which, since they are mine, used without acknowledgment, I may accurately—and legally!—quote here):

> ...Holmes has some heroic qualities, but heroic qualities that are common to most decent, quite ordinary people. He is intensely prejudiced, often bad-tempered, irritable with the people who might look to him for a little kindness, capable of a quite unmerited snub, arrogant, grossly (and I don't mean the cocaine) self-indulgent, self-opinionated, and decidedly touchy about trivialities....[3]

Well, in using my words, Vincent Price certainly made an honest offer to the prospective viewer, if Mr Price was intimating that the Holmes that the viewer was about to see was the Holmes somewhat critically portrayed by me in the passage preceding. But that was, as one now knows, exactly the sort of Holmes that the viewer was about to see, and that he and thousands of others are still—with greatly varying opinions—seeing to-day.

What, then, is so 'novel', so striking, so (to many people) coldly repellent about Mr Brett's presentation of Holmes? Simply this: the Producer and script-writers of the new Holmes series have done what the undoubtedly successful Holmes-dramatist, William Gillette, firmly refused to do—and they have done it *for the first time*

---

[3]From my *Introduction*, as Editor, to the Sherlockian Anthology, *Beyond Baker Street*; Indianapolis/New York: The Bobbs-Merrill Co., Inc., 1976.

since Holmes appeared on stage or screen. It is this that makes Mr Brett's Holmes so unfamiliar. The nearly two hundred stage-Holmeses who have followed in Gillette's footsteps have, consciously or subconsciously, taken *his* Holmes as their master-model, and not Conan Doyle's. Whether this first-time-ever 'sticking to the book' will 'work' or not remains to be seen. If I don't care for the 'accurate' Holmes, so faithfully based on the written stories, then, as always, the box-office will pronounce the final, unarguable judgement.

It was at a roadhouse, some miles out of Columbia, Missouri, on Route 63, that the 'certain smile' of a waitress brought so vividly back to mind a bleak afternoon in London, when a gathering of Dedicated (this adjective surely merits the distinction of a capital letter) Sherlockians gathered on the 'down' platform of the Baker-street terminus of the Metropolitan Railway—'The Met'.

I sadden as I reflect that, to all the Great Sherlockian Names that I am about to recall, I must regretfully add the prefix, 'the late', though their faces, their mannerisms, their idiosyncrasies, their characteristics—are as bright in my affectionate memory as though all this had happened a bare week ago.

Of our select but, in that chill wind, slightly shivering company, I recollect the then President of the (London) Sherlock Holmes Society, Sir Sidney Roberts; my friend, Lord Donegall, the then Editor of the Society's journal; Philip Dalton, later to occupy half of that editorial chair; James Edward Holroyd, of what we then called the Board of Trade's establishment: he edited the *Board of Trade Journal* and was to write learnedly on Sherlockian matters until the end of his fairly long life. His *Baker Street Byways* (published in the Conan Doyle Centennial year of 1959) and his *Seventeen Steps to Baker Street* (1967), an anthology to which he contributed greatly, are landmark-rocks in the torrent of Sherlockian literature that has been pouring in a flood-tide for decades, but with quite irrepressible volume since the lapsing of the Conan Doyle copyrights in 1980. Of this unchecked (and, seemingly, uncheckable) flood of para-Sherlockiana, one or two steadfast monuments of Holmesian scholarship will—must, I think—remain. I would guess that my old friend, Holroyd's, will be among the respect-worthy survivors....

———

Well, that is the vivid image that memory brings back: I remember the others who were there on that Baker-street platform—there weren't many: hardly a dozen—but these four I remember well; and, as I regretfully observed above, they are all dead.

Why were we, the Dedicated, gathered there on the windy platform of a London suburban railway-station, watched by two almost disinterested black-leather-capped railway workers: the engine-driver and his fireman—his mate—for the diesel engine had not then come to power the Met trains; the motive force was the same as that which sent Stephenson's *Puffing Billy* rattling along from Stockton to Darlington in the 1820s: good old Steam? And, as in Stephenson's day, it was good old Coal that raised that steam: a fact that sufficiently accounted for a darkening of the two white railwaymen's complexions.

Why were we there? Well, in the 'machine-shops' of the Metropolitan, a long plate of blackened and polished bronze—long enough to span the distance between the protected heads of the two driving-wheels—had been attached to the side of the engine. The raised and polished bronze letters on this metal plate spelled out—

S H E R L O C K   H O L M E S

—and we were there formally to 'name' the engine, and to wish it Godspeed on its way to what the Railway's posters called 'London's Garden Suburbs'. Was it Sir Sidney Roberts who performed the 'naming' ceremony? I am not sure now, after the passage of so many years, but, as President of the Sherlock Holmes Society, Sir Sidney would have been the natural choice to speak the words of dedication; to have uttered the requisite *Salve atque Vale!* Yes...looking back to that chilly afternoon, I am sure that I can hear again Sir Sidney's academically-cultured tones pronouncing, with appropriate recognition of the moment's solemnity:

"I name this locomotive...the SHERLOCK HOLMES, and wish...,"
he hesitated for a second, aware that, perhaps, though 'her' would
have been appropriate had he been launching a ship, a locomotive
might properly have a less personal personal-pronoun: "...*it*...God-
speed on its lawful journeys...."

And Donegall, I remember, muttered, "...and all who travel
in h-...*it*!" He added, less solemnly: "Why on earth didn't *one* of
us remember to bring along a bottle of champers...?" (A remark
that was to acquire a sad significance within a matter of minutes.)

The two railwaymen had by now completely abandoned their
affectation of disinterest; they were now staring at us, locked in
the solemnity of this quasi-religious ceremony, with frank astonishment. As in a sort of trance of incredulity, the driver ('engineer'
in America) went about his mechanical work in a strikingly mechanical manner. His fireman was still gazing bemused at us as
Sherlock Holmes, its bronze name-plate shining bravely in the watery
sun, steamed out of Baker-street Station.

(That was not the last time that I was to see that name-plate.
When the Metropolitan Railway replaced its steam- by diesel- en-
gines, the name-plate was recovered, and was lent, by the late
Philip Dalton for the two-weeks Sherlockian Exhibition at their
Baker-street branch, arranged by Williams' & Glyn's Bank, of which
I was a customer. The exhibition, organized—and well organized—
by a professional Public Relations firm, was opened to mark the
simultaneous publication, in Britain and America, of my two books
(the revised) *In the Footsteps of Sherlock Holmes* and *The London of
Sherlock Holmes*. Since the name-plate was returned, on the closing
of the exhibition, to the late Mr Dalton, I have not seen it, though
I expect, as they say, that an article of such historico-Sherlockian
interest 'must be around somewhere'.)

———————

And now, what was it in the behaviour of a Missouri-roadhouse
waitress that recalled so vividly that chill afternoon on the platform
at Baker-street station? What did the pretty young Missourian say,
and what was the significance of that 'certain smile' that I have
mentioned...?

I shall explain....

But back to that Baker-street afternoon.

The *Sherlock Holmes* steamed smoothly away, the fireman still gazing back, as though reluctant to lose a single second of so eccentric a spectacle as we shivering Sherlockians must have presented to the horny-handed son of toil. Shivering...? Indeed. And with what relief did we open the doors of the Refreshment Room, as grimly unwelcoming as only the average British railway-buffet can contrive to be. But, thank God!, here—for all its grimness (of wall-colour, of seedy furniture, of unsmiling counter-hands, of marble counter chillier even than the blank faces of the waitresses)—was shelter from the more-or-less stormy blast. It was Sanctuary...and we gratefully welcomed it as such.

"And now," said someone, chafing his icy hands, "let's all have a drink to warm ourselves up...."

The forbidding person behind the marble counter let us all give our orders, before remarking, with a perfect composure that did nothing to hide her satisfaction in her being able to announce the fact: "It's *gone* three o'clock. No more drinks until the bar opens again at half-past-five. Or there's tea or coffee or cocoa...."

As we slunk out to get the tubes or buses or taxis that would take us home, I glanced back. Yes...she was smiling. She had triumphed.... She was one up on the Eccentrics....

I saw that same smile of warm self-satisfaction in that Missouri roadhouse; for, like that of the Mona Lisa, it is a smile of universal provenience, though a great deal more easily decypherable than that of Leonardo's inscrutably smiling lady.

We entered the roadhouse; we sat down, tired from the seemingly endless journey from St Louis, and even more tired at the thought of our completing the long trek to Des Moines. Weary, almost exhausted, I accepted the menu laid before me, but—

"I'll order later," I said; "first of all—above everything—please bring me a large Scotch. No ice. A little water on the side...and I shall bless you from the bottom of my heart...." I added: "You've no idea how I'm going to enjoy that Scotch...."

Yes..., you've guessed by now. I *had* seen that contented smile before. "Not," said the young lady, "in Missouri on a Sunday, you won't...."

My next Sherlockian memory involved less brushable-aside matters as the diabolic contrivances of Man-hating Authority to deny us our simple and innocent pleasures. This particular Sherlockian Memory came to mind as I saw Hesketh Pearson's *Conan Doyle* in my host's library and took it out to read in bed—remembering the last time that I had been in Pearson's company, and what had unhappily occurred on that *literally* memorable occasion.

The place ('venue' is the new word in the hotel- management's jargon): the big upstairs banqueting-room of the Charing Cross Hotel, still happily spared to us in all its Victorian amplitude, elegance, and—above all—unemphatic comfort by both Hitler and British Rail. The time: 7:30 on the night of 22nd May, 1959. The occasion: the Dinner given by the Sherlock Holmes Society of London to celebrate the Centenary of the birth of Sir Arthur Conan Doyle, whose daughter, Dame Jean, was, with Hesketh Pearson and me, and our respective wives, among the Guests of Honour. As they say in the theatre, there was 'a good turn-out', and the large room was full of Sherlockians—both men and women.

The Centenary Dinner followed the course usual to all such 'functions'; the various toasts were given and drunk to, until, at last, after the Loyal Toast had been proposed and given, smoking was permitted, and the company settled down to hear the two Guest Speakers, Hesketh Pearson and myself.

Paradoxically, Pearson, whose synoptic biography of Conan Doyle is certainly not at all free from sometimes sharp criticism of the Great Man, gave—possibly influenced by the consciousness of Dame Jean's proximity at the High Table—an eulogistic talk, entirely free from even the slightest suggestion that Conan Doyle was not a man about as perfect as this imperfect Creation could produce. Mr Pearson resumed his seat to predictably enthusiastic applause....

———

Then it was *my* turn to rise and give *my* talk.

Now, from the passage of mine quoted by Vincent Price in introducing the new Jeremy Brett TV adventures of Sherlock Holmes, the reader will have gathered what I have never hesitated to point out: the shortcomings that flaw the character of the Master Sleuth of Baker-street—though I have not, as yet, analyzed the character-defects, such as they may be, of the Master's creator. My talk that night to the assembled members of the Sherlock Holmes Society was strictly confined to an analysis of *Holmes's* character, as he is presented to us in the Canon.

There is no need here to recount all that I said of Holmes; but I did question that he had had the benefit of what we may call an upper-class education, not merely in the purely academic sense, but in—so much more importantly—the social. If Holmes had enjoyed the normal upbringing of a normal English boy and young man, how had he come to commit the grisly solecisms—his calling the butler, Brunton, 'Butler Brunton' seems the most inexplicable; and there are others—that Watson faithfully records as the very words of his hero. 'Lord St Simon', for instance....

"Of course," I commented, "it may be that Holmes never used such expressions as 'Butler Brunton' and the other solecisms and that Watson was, in fact, merely *reporting* the sense of Holmes's speech." That the solecisms reported were not Holmes's at all, but Watson's. "But," I instantly pointed out, denying my own suggestion, "Watson was no uncultured roughneck. He had been at school with the nephew of one of the most powerful peers—admittedly a *political* peer; but powerful for all that—in England, so that it can't have been a lower-class sort of institution. And even if, as has been hinted, Watson came from Australia, why, even a Digger from the Outback would have learned the conventional social graces—above all, the avoidance of solecisms—at even the most modest of English public-schools. So, if the reported words and phrases weren't Watson's," I mused, "then they *must* have been Holmes's.... But, in that case, how did the more obvious social graces come to have missed polishing him...."

There is no need to continue. Already, though I had not done with the mystery of a family-background or social upbringing which had permitted Holmes the unconscious indulgence in manners which would have earned the grim disapproval of Emily Post or Lady Troubridge, I would have been as pachydermatous as an armadillo had I not sensed—no: observed, rather!—that my audience was, as they say, 'not with me'. And, as they also say, 'I had lost them'. The atmosphere had grown heavy with disapproval; in the words of Edgar Allan Poe: 'suddenly the air grew denser', and—though without too obviously cutting short my talk—I brought my speculations about the mystery of Holmes's upbringing to a close.

The Chairman, as is always the case, thanked me, and another conventionally-minded Sherlockian rose to second the thanks ... when something decidedly unconventional came to make this evening the most truly memorable of all the Sherlockian 'occasions' that I or anyone else had ever attended.

Shaking with indignation; a biggish book in his hand, with an inserted thumb to mark an important place; a smallish man of chastely professional appearance rose from his chair, and said, in a voice, which like his body, was shaking, not merely from indignation but from a fear that only a driving recognition of inescapable duty was enabling him to face and to overcome. (Only later did I come to realize the bravery of this little man, and now, years later— nearly thirty years later—I, in all respect and humility, salute his shade...for what he was about to do that night was the next-but-last positive decision that his unhappy life was to shew....)

He rose, as I have said, from his chair, and, his voice half-choked from embarrassment, this is what he said: "Mr Chairman: I'm sorry—terribly sorry—to have to get up like this. I know that it's merely common convention to thank a Guest Speaker...but," gulping, "I cannot—I simply cannot—associate myself with the thanks just tendered to the second Speaker...."

The audience now waking up to what it was all about—or about to be all about—began to make little sounds of half-hearted disapproval, so that the Chairman felt that he might venture mild: "*Really*, sir...."

I took advantage of the pause that followed to say (I hoped that I should sound 'reasonable'): "No, Mr Chairman: please let the gentleman say what he wishes to say. He has," I added, "as much right to give his opinion as I think that I have...."

So, only a little less nervous now—but, judging by the signs, not all that much less—the Protester, still with a thumb in his book to mark a certain place, almost shouted: "I cannot stay silent...I simply *cannot* allow what's been said by the second Speaker to pass unchallenged. It's simply not fair to the Man (the capital letter was audible to all) whom we're here tonight to honour...." If any person present thought that the Protester meant 'Conan Doyle' when he referred to 'the Man whom we're here to honour tonight', that person was speedily to be disabused of the misconception. It was THE MAN—THE MASTER—Sherlock Holmes himself, and no other—whom my critic had risen, in defiance of all customary banqueting usage, to defend.

"We have heard the *Speaker's* opinion of Sherlock Holmes," he spluttered, as he opened his book and sought the passage that was to refute that opinion of mine, which had so roused his angry indignation.

"*Now*," he said, authoritatively, "now I'll read you the *real* opinion of Sherlock Holmes. And," he added, "we *can* accept it as the true picture—the true summing-up of all his unique qualities— because it's the opinion of a man who *really* knew him—perhaps the one man who did. Let me read you what *his* opinion of Sherlock Holmes was...." And, opening the book again, this is what he read out to the very silent company:

> "'I shall ever regard him as the best and the wisest man whom I have ever known....'

"And that, Mr Chairman, ladies, and gentlemen," he said, closing the book with a triumphant snap, "is a *real*—the only real— opinion of Sherlock Holmes...."

Then with some tardy realization that his behaviour had been, to say the least, a little out-of-the-ordinary, he made some sketchy bows, to include the High Table and the generality of the Banqueting Hall, adding in an oddly subdued voice: "I'm sorry, Mr Chairman, but it simply *had* to be said."

He sat down, and the Chairman, and, indeed, all of us, were happy that the 'scene' was over, though it was a subdued company which listened to the Chairman's closing remarks—none of which referred to the Defence of Sherlock Holmes.

———————

Afterwards, my wife asked me:

"What was he reading out from that book of his...?"

"What Dr Watson wrote, after he had believed that Holmes was dead...."

She pondered on this for a moment or two, then, puzzled, asked: "But didn't Conan Doyle *invent* Holmes and Watson...?"

"He did."

"They are just two fictional characters...?"

"Well...I don't know...."

"What do you mean: you 'don't know'? Are they, or are they not, just characters in a book? They didn't really live—have an actual existence, did they...?"

"Well...no: not really. Yes, I suppose we must call them fictional...."

"You don't sound very sure, I must say. But, as they *are* fictional, how could that man get up and quote made-up words to contradict yours...?"

I let it go. It's not easy to explain the mystical arcana of Sherlockismus to one untouched by the magic of the Inner Knowledge....

The Protester was a Dr Ascher—a biblical name if ever there was one—and he was, by profession, a psychiatrist, practising in London, with consulting-rooms in one of the better streets in the capital's Medical Quarter. (And, although, neither then nor since have I borne the least animosity towards Dr Ascher, I did think, when I heard what he did for a living, that I could have imagined a psychiatrist's behaving somewhat differently.)

As the dinner-party broke up, and the guests moved out into the public rooms, and several people approached me to proffer their quite unneeded expressions of sympathy, it was obvious that, on the whole, the Sherlockians had already decided to put the Ascher Affair well out of mind—and I am sure that most had done so, when two newspaper stories, both involving the name of Dr Ascher, not only brought the 'scene' in the Charing Cross Hotel back to all the participants' memory, but gave it a new and decidedly sinister interpretation.

The first news-story told how Dr Ascher's young actress daughter, Jane, had run off with a Beatle, and though no-one thought this entomological elopement of world-shaking importance, it was evident, from later news stories, that Jane's father had taken the trivial matter very much to heart—for now it was Dr Ascher who had vanished, and not until many days had passed was he found, alone in an empty house...dead by his own hand.

This tragedy of a most sincere, even if (as the facts seemed to shew) an unbalanced Sherlockian stirred many of us deeply, particularly those of the Sherlockians who had attended the Centenary Dinner. Of course, the question was asked—it was inevitable that it should be asked: Was that insanity that finally overtook Dr Ascher already revealed in that embarrassing outburst at the Dinner? Did Dr Ascher, in short, quote Dr Watson, in rebutting my opinion, because he did sincerely believe in the reality—the material, factual, historic *reality*—of both Holmes and Watson, and that when Dr Ascher triumphantly quoted Dr Watson's valedictory words against me, Dr Ascher was, indeed, acting under the delusion that he was quoting a real man's touching tribute to a once-living-and-breathing friend—and certainly not simply quoting an apposite passage from a work of pure fiction?

With the majority of Mankind, I share the ability to be impressed by coincidences, though, with a much smaller part of Mankind; a part headed most honourably by Carl Jung; I attach a significance to the Coincidence—that coming-together in time and place of two discrete events that Jung named Synchronicity—that, even when impressed by the 'oddity' of the coincidence, the average person does not attach to it.

Here, though, I shall tell of a Sherlockian coincidence without attempting any Jungian research into its real or assumed 'significance'. I shall simply give the facts as I remember them.

The coincidence—and all of us found it impressive, even startling, enough—occurred in what had been the upstairs writing-room of Conan Doyle's Sussex house (in which he died): 'Windlesham', near Crowborough, in the English county of Sussex.

I had been asked by an American Sherlockian friend, Jon Lellenberg of Washington, DC, to accompany Dame Jean Conan Doyle on a visit to her old home and to record that visit for the readers of *Baker Street Miscellanea*, a Sherlockian journal of which Lellenberg was, and still is at the time of this writing, the Joint-editor.

By letter and telephone, I had made the necessary arrangements to meet Dame Jean, who was to come by train, at Crowborough Station, and take her, in the car that a Sussex Sherlockian friend was kindly providing and driving, to the old house in which all the Doyle children of the second marriage had grown up.

'Windlesham'—the circumstances of its purchase were such that Doyle always thereafter facetiously referred to his 'white elephant' as 'Swindlesham'—is now substantially altered inside to provide more rooms than the Doyle family had needed. It now serves as a very—indeed, impressively—well-managed Rest Home for the elderly and the positively aged, and though not inexpensive, both Dame Jean and we two men were of the opinion that all the residents were receiving excellent value for their money.

Our visit had, of course, been arranged by letter with the Lady Superintendent; and it was she who took us around the house, of which a part of the drawing-room has been preserved as it was in the Doyle occupancy—but elsewhere in the house, the grim realities of commerce have caused the cutting-up of the rooms, or their conversion to more practical uses, as, for instance, in the turning of the big billard-room into the Home's common dining-room and the splitting of Doyle's upstairs study (from the windows of which he could clearly see—"Before the trees grew up," Dame Jean reminded us—all the way to Birling Gap; "Up from the Gap, my Father imagined the gas rolling up in *The Poison Belt*."). We were standing in one half of the now divided upstairs study as Dame Jean made these comments, and it was in this room that the coincidence startled us all.

But here, even at the cost of delaying this true story's dénouement, I must in all reverence for the truth, correct the very false impression of 'Windlesham' that Mr Charles Higham conveys in his excellent *The Adventures of Sherlock Holmes*. I quote part of Mr Higham's description of the house in which Dame Jean and I found ourselves in a sunny afternoon of 1983:

> Conan Doyle made arrangements to lease Undershaw [the house that he had built for his first wife at Hindhead, Surrey] so that [he and his second wife] could buy a house where they would be near Jean's family....
>
> [Windlesham] was a much more imposing residence than Undershaw.... A tremendous flight of stairs swept up to the first-floor landing....

This enthusiastic picture gives the falsest impression of what was—and still is—a comfortable, roomy but essentially unpretentious Sussex country-home. In the first place, it is not—and was never, even in Conan Doyle's occupancy—a 'much more imposing residence than Undershaw'; questions of comparison apart, Windlesham is not even imposing in itself. When Conan Doyle purchased the property, it had long been a Sussex farmhouse. He renovated and enlarged it, and, in all ways 'improved the property', though, as I have said, it was never 'improved' out of its original homely-country appearance—and (I don't think that this has been remarked-upon before) it stands as a testimony to Arthur Conan Doyle's essential modesty: the unpretentious home of a British country-gentleman—which was always his ideal of what the 'compleat' man should be.

When I arrived at Windlesham with Dame Jean, I looked in vain for the upward sweep of that 'tremendous flight of stairs'; indeed, the staircase was so narrow that I expressed my wonder to Dame Jean that the moving-men had been able to manoeuvre the heavier furniture up through so restricted a passage. So much for Mr Higham's picture of a semi-baronial magnificence; Windlesham lacks even that vast (and vastly pretentious) stained-glass window on the first-floor landing, containing 'many heraldic shields of the Doyle family'—an excusable innocent self-assertion of a young man who has been snatched from near-poverty to considerable wealth, *by his own efforts*, in less than a handcount of years. A decade later, when he was looking for a new home in which to install his new wife, he had passed beyond the need of ostentation; even of any overt self-assertion. He knew now that his works and his reputation would be his full and sufficient advertisement.... And now to the coincidence....

━━━━━━

The Lady Superintendent had, of course, made all arrangements for our reception; knew who we three were and why we were visiting Dame Jean's old home. But, as the lady led us around the now greatly-altered house, it was obvious that none of the guests had been apprised of our coming; none (until we were introduced as *Lady* Conan Doyle and her friends) seemed to know who we were and why the Lady Superintendent, knocking at so many doors, asked permission to 'let Lady Conan Doyle' see over their private quarters. What I wish to make clear is that *none* of the guests—all very old—had been told of our coming. (I am sure of this.)

But they weren't all old. When we got to the 'front' half of the divided Doyle upstairs-study and the Lady Superintendent had knocked on the door, and we had entered to her ritual, "May I shew Lady Conan Doyle over your room—she lived here many years ago?", we found ourselves in the presence of two extremely old people—obviously husband and wife, with a middle-aged lady, seemingly intelligent and alert. After we had thanked the occupants of the room for their courtesy in their letting us look over it, Dame Jean then explained what the room had looked like when it was undivided by the present party-wall. The old people seemed disinterested, but the younger lady was quite plainly taking a deep interest in all that Dame Jean was saying. Then, in a pause, this younger lady, with an air of great earnestness, asked: "Are you...I heard your name: Conan Doyle...are you the daughter of Conan Doyle, the author...? You *are*! His daughter...? Well, fancy that now! Tell me: did you ever read a book of your Father's called *Our African Winter*? Do you remember it...?"

"Of course. It came out in the year before my Father died. I remember it well...."

"Then, do you remember, in that book, how, when your Father and Mother arrived in Rhodesia, it was arranged that a Police-inspector should take them around...?"

"Well...."

The lady beamed—as indeed, she had a right to do. With the broadest of smiles, she explained her position in this Doyle reminiscence: "I am that Police-inspector's daughter...."

———

The strikingly coincidental element in this revelation is not at all simple. In the first place, the Police-inspector's daughter was there (as were we) on a quite fortuitously-chosen one-day visit. She had not been told that we were expected, and it was only on her hearing

Dame Jean's name mentioned that she remembered what must have been by then an honoured family legend: how the Rhodesian Police-inspector had had the privilege of guiding and protecting Sir Arthur and Lady Conan Doyle.

Well...there it was: 'just another' coincidence. But coincidental, too, in that we were all standing by the window through which, as Dame Jean remembered, her father had imagined the Death Mist rolling up to Windlesham from Birling Gap....

———

Apart from that coincidence, there was something more that makes that day memorable for me, notably as a Sherlockian.

The Lady Superintendent had invited us to eat luncheon in Windlesham, but Dame Jean declined, and we ate elsewhere; as it turned out, in a charming little country-inn, not too 'improved' by brewers' money.

Now, of all the events of the literary striving of the young Conan Doyle, none is more widely known than the story of how *A Study in Scarlet* came to be published in the year of Queen Victoria's Golden Jubilee—a tale, which, for all its subsequent life-altering influence on so many more than its author,[4] was sold *outright* to a London publisher for the derisory sum of £25 (then a fraction under $125). All the biographies, condensed or extensive, of Conan Doyle that I have read tell the same story, and all the authors stress that the small payment by the publishers, Ward, Lock & Co., included the copyright of the tale. As Hesketh Pearson, one of the more individualistic of Doyle's biographers, says: "Doyle never made a penny more than £25 out of *A Study in Scarlet*, which first appeared in 'Beeton's Xmas [sic] Annual' in 1887." (Strangely, another biographer, Charles Higham, states the sum to have been twenty-*four* pounds; I don't know why....)

Now, before I go on to present this 'outright sale of the copyright' in a different, and, I am sure, quite unprecedented, light,

---

[4] I refer here, of course, to all those hundreds who have been enriched by Conan Doyle's master-creation, beginning with his family, but notably including all who have published Holmes stories—the latest in the publishing-world even more enriched, now that the Doyle copyrights have expired.—M.H.

I should like to challenge a generally-held view that 'financial strin-gency' had impelled Conan Doyle to sell the story at any price, so that some needed money—however little—came into his distressed household. But the facts don't at all support this theory. In No-vember, 1886, when he assigned to Ward, Lock & Co. 'the Copy-right and all my interest in the book written by me entitled A STUDY IN SCARLET', Conan Doyle was by no means 'in a dis-tressed financial condition'. To the contrary, he was, as they say, 'comfortably off'—certainly by the standards of 1886. For consider: his medical practice was now yielding almost £300 per annum, to which, after his marriage to Louise Hawkins on 6th August, 1885, was added the modest income of some hundred pounds a year that his wife brought with her. This added up to about four hundred pounds a year, or eight pounds a week—the average salary, be it noted, of a British bank-manager, *forty years later*. One may well understand how it was that Conan Doyle, in alluding to this im-portantly formative period of his life, should comment that he and his wife could enjoy 'the decencies, if not the luxuries, of life'. No implication of straitened circumstances here....

Of all those who have written of Conan Doyle's accepting an outright twenty-five pounds for the copyright and all future earn-ings of *A Study*, a hint at the correct explanation of this 'derisory' sale is to be found—at least, I have found it nowhere else—only in Michael and Molly Hardwick's *The Sherlock Holmes Companion*, where the relevant comment reads: "He accepted £25 for the out-right sale of the copyright. He would have preferred a royalty basis, but the offer was the best he had had, *and the work would at least now reach the public*" (my italics). It is a pity that the authors did not follow-up their own hint; for it was *publication* that Conan Doyle desperately needed—not money. And he was prepared to pay for the privilege by accepting Ward, Lock's almost contemptuous offer.

Why was Doyle so anxious to see his book in print...? Well, it had certainly 'done the rounds' since he finished it (I have always thought that this finished copy was the last of several revisions) in April, 1886. James Payn, the Editor who had bought Doyle's 'solution' of the *Mary Celeste* mystery for *The Cornhill*, had turned *A Study in Scarlet* down; so had Arrowsmith, the Bristol publishers, who were later to make a fortune from *The Prisoner of Zenda*. (Ar-rowsmiths returned *Scarlet* unread—as did Frederick Warne & Co., for whom, too a fortune awaited: in the shape of the Beatrix Potter booklets.) The need of Conan Doyle to publish, *at any cost*, is explained, clearly and finally (in my opinion) by Green and Gibson in that monumental work of scholarship, *A Bibliography of Conan Doyle*. This is the relevant and fully explanatory passage:

> [Conan Doyle] tried on a number of occasions to find a publisher for his early stories, but was told that he would need to make his name known with a novel....

And now, in late 1886, he had at last an about-to-be-published novel...the essential first step, as he believed (and as events proved) towards the publication of his collected short-stories in volume form.

———

No: that seeming digression was a necessary one. I have not forgotten Dame Jean as she sits opposite me at the table, and I am expressing some indignation, not merely at the fact that Ward, Lock 'took unfair advantage' of a struggling young author—No man is an Island, entire of itself; and all authors resent an injustice suffered by another. I certainly echoed what I have quoted from Hesketh Pearson above: "Doyle never made a penny more than £25 out of *A Study in Scarlet*..."' and continued to enlarge on the speculation of yet another Sherlockian biographer, who mused: "Think how much that single copyright must have produced...," when Dame Jean said quietly: "They did return it later...."

This was said so quietly, as well as so matter-of-factly, that I hardly took in the words' significance. At last, after a full two seconds' absorption of what was probably the most unexpected news in my life, I managed: "Ward, Lock returned the copyright...?"

I said no more. What was there to say? All that indignation— my own; that of hundreds of others; Sherlockians and non-Sherlockians; authors and mere readers—all that indignation....

As I write, Sherlockian biographies are piled on my desk: Hesketh Pearson, Julian Symons, Charles Higham, Michael and Molly Hardwick, Pierre Nordon, John Dickson Carr, even those master-bibliographers, Richard Lancelyn Green, and John Michael Gibson.

All of them, and so many others; dead and living...and from *not one* that putting-right of the record....

No man was more stirred to both indignation and outcry by injustice; whether done to himself or others; no man exerted himself harder to put an injustice right; than Conan Doyle. So....

The inaccurate—indeed, grossly unjust—record must be put straight. It is never too late to admit error. Justice for the Ward, Lock of the past (the firm is still flourishing in its Baker-street offices) is surely too long overdue....

———

Finders, keepers.... The name of my prolifically writing friend, Colin Wilson, bobbed up in the conversation that I was having, in the fine old Philadelphian house occupied by the Rosenbach Foundation, with two young lady curators (curatrices?), when one of them, mentioning that she had come to Philadelphia from the University of Texas's riches-stocked Library, added that 'they' had quite a number of examples of my signature and work....

"Texas," I commented, "bought my stuff from the late John Gawsworth, an ardent converter of literary friends' gifts into Texan cash. I know what Texas has of mine, for I picked up, by chance, the record of the Texas literary holdings when I was waiting one day in the British Museum. But you were talking of Colin Wilson, who is, I'm glad to say, still very much alive...?"

The reply really did astonish me. Without, as we say in England, 'batting an eyelid', or, as they more forcibly say in France,'drôlement sans gêne', the young lady not only confirmed that Texas was rich in Wilson archives, but that the best of the papers held in Houston were 'those stolen from Colin Wilson's apartment when he lived in the Edgware-road...'. (And if this seems too unlikely a traveller's tale, I do have, as most competent witness, a Philadelphian professional man of excellent standing, who took me to see the Rosenbach Collection, and who was as startled as was I at this calm account of a world-famous Library's unhesitating receipt of stolen goods....)

———

If, as they often say, 'they do these things better in America', at least one highly-respected and generally-accepted-as-'respectable' public institution in Scotland seems to run Texas a close second in acquiring and retaining what it had no legal or moral right to acquire in the first place—yet another shameful example of the contempt in which an author and an author's work are held by non-writers in acquisitive authority. For, in the Green and Gibson *A Bibliography of A. Conan Doyle,* quoted above, I find this appalling entry (from the section D: 'Contributions to the Press'):

> 1883, December: ...An earlier story, 'The Haunted Grange of Go-resthorpe—A True Ghost Story', was sent to *Blackwood's Magazine* and neither published nor returned. It is now in the National Library of Scotland with the Blackwood Archives....

Where, in all justice, it has no right to be. It is *barely* possible to make out a case for *Blackwood's* editorial staff's having hung on to 'The Haunted Grange of Goresthorpe', in supposing that the author had omitted, in submitting his manuscript, to enclose a 'self-addressed stamped envelope' for that manuscript's return on its having been rejected. There is not the least justification for the National Library of Scotland's permanent retention of this discovery of a windfall Conan Doyle story amongst the Blackwood Archives. 'The Haunted Grange of Goresthorpe' should have been returned, by all the laws of honesty, no less than by those of courtesy, to the Conan Doyle family—at least to the Conan Doyle Estate.

The young lady formerly with the Texas Library had the candour to admit that Houston was prepared to hang on to the typescripts stolen from Colin Wilson's Edgware-road apartment in his absence. It would seem that the morality of childhood, expressed in the old, familiar excuse for opportunist annexation, 'Finders, keepers...' may still motivate and 'excuse' persons who have left their childhood far behind. But writers, it would appear, are fair game—have always been fair game—for those who hold them and their work in contempt....

SILVER BLAZE AND SILVER NITRATE

Canonical echoes of a Victorian super-scandal

The Canon (as its *afficionados* call it) of four long and fifty-six shorter Sherlock Holmes stories is full of echoes of those contemporary or just-past happenings that had interested and sometimes deeply shocked the author of those stories, Arthur Conan Doyle. In the latter category, none more interested nor as deeply shocked him, as the 'continuing story' of the racehorse-owning, crudely self-indulgent and all-round caddish friend of Albert Edward, Prince of Wales—Sir Frederick Johnstone, baronet.

Hero of the British mob—for his horses invariably won, particularly in the racing 'Classics'—Sir Frederick was no hero to any other of the rigidly-structured levels of the Victorian caste-and-class system: one and all, from the Queen downwards, held Sir Freddy (as the Prince called him) in horrified contempt; repelled, not merely by his total caddishness, but by his obvious desire to flaunt himself, as the Victorian Bounder *par excellence*, in an age and within a society not at all lacking in self-advertising and no-holds-barred cads. (Poor Princess Louise, the Queen's talented sculptress daughter, was handed over to one hardly less offensive than Sir Freddy—the sixth

Earl of Fife, who was promoted to a Dukedom on his marriage into Royalty—but then, Queen Victoria herself had a soft spot for un-couth persons, and she wished to keep the foul-mouthed Scotsman in the Family.) The Queen, however, strongly disapproved of Sir Freddy, as she disapproved of most of her eldest son's friends; but never had she deplored the presence of Sir Freddy in her wayward son's life than when, in 1869, the dreadful Mordaunt Scandal brought Sir Freddy's shameless sexuality into column- after-column of the newspapers...and the Prince of Wales into the witness-box of the Divorce Court. (Queen Victoria's letters to her daughter, Princess Frederick of Prussia, pay heart-moving testimony to the pain that the Prince of Wales's conduct was causing his Mother, the Queen.)

Sir Charles Mordaunt, English baronet of unsullied reputation, had married one of the eight beautiful daughters of the Scottish baronet, Sir Thomas Moncreiffe of Bridge-of-Earn, Perthshire, possessor of landed property even more extensive than that of Sir Charles.

There was, indeed, money on both sides of the families, and when the lovely and gifted Harriet Sarah Moncreiffe married Sir Charles Mordaunt, she brought with her more than her naturally endowed gifts of brilliant intelligence and beauty. She brought with her a dowry sufficient to ensure her full independence of her wealthy husband, and—even more important in Victorian estimation—she, as the daughter of a seventh baronet and the wife of a tenth, enjoyed a social position firmly based upon the standing both of her husband's family and of her own. All these tremendous social advantages she was to lose, in circumstances which, in an Age of Scandal, were to make her personal tragedy one of the most memorable of all Victorian *causes célèbres*.

Lady Moncreiffe, Harriet's mother, should have been at her daughter's bedside as Harriet swam dizzily into consciousness after the birth of Harriet's first (and, as it turned out, only) child. Unfortunately, the persons present were the nurse and Mrs Cadogan, wife of the local Rector. Blinking into semi- wakefulness, and almost certainly unaware of the identity of the two women standing by her bedside, Lady Mordaunt remarked to the clergyman's wife: "Everybody does it—so why shouldn't I? Besides," she added, with something the air of an afterthought, "I only did it once or twice in London. I'll soon make it all right with Charley."

When, sometime later, Mrs Cadogan made *her* appearance in the witness-box, no-one had the least difficulty in believing her when she said that Lady Mordaunt's words had shocked her. For Mrs Cadogan had known that 'Charley' was Sir Charles Mordaunt, and that Lady Mordaunt was confessing—and without any great show of repentance—her own adultery....

Nor was the repentance more in evidence when, summoned urgently by the Rector's wife, Sir Charles hurried to the Mordaunt Town house in Chesham-place to find his wife hardly recovered in health but even more candid than before.

"Charley," she greeted him, "I want to tell you something. I have been dreadfully wicked, and I have done very wrong.

"I have been unfaithful to you. I have committed misconduct with Lord Cole, and Sir Frederick Johnstone, and with other people as well.

"One of them was the Prince of Wales. It is Lord Cole," she added, "who is the father of my child."

The 'innocent child', as Lady Mordaunt weepingly called it, entered life with one putative and one established disadvantage: the first, that of bastardy; the second—about which there was no doubt whatever—was his having been born with the dreaded *ophthalmia neonatorum*: gonorrheal infection of the eyes.

After Lady Mordaunt had confessed to her husband that, "You are not the father of the child; Lord Cole is the father," she had added: "I am the cause of its blindness"—a statement that might have implied a superstitious belief in the punishment of an Avenging God, but to which a much more commonsense explanation may reasonably be conceded. But, in saying that she was the 'cause' of her baby's blindness, did Lady Mordaunt acknowledge that she herself had been venereally infected or that she had learnt, after the act, that the man with whom she had slept had been so infected?

The grave condition of the baby's eyes was not neglected; as soon after the birth that the abnormal condition was apparent, one of Britain's leading oculists, Mr Solomon of Birmingham, was called in for consultation, and his remarks breathe the very spirit of Victorian tact and reticence; tact and reticence that were no less apparent later, when he gave evidence in the Divorce Court, in the matter of *Mordaunt* versus *Mordaunt; Others intervening*, for, despite the contemporary prejudice against divorce, Sir Charles had really no option in the matter of his divorcing his wife.

Observing here that a Victorian euphemism for any venereal disorder was a 'specific' disease, we may quote the tactful Mr Solomon's evidence in Court: "I was called in to see Lady Mordaunt's child on the Saturday after her confinement. I found it labouring under ophthalmia. *There were no appearances which were diagnostic of specific or non-specific disease* [my italics]. I advised astrigent applications, and recommended that a wet-nurse should be engaged." [That is, for the child.]

Several years ago, in commenting on the Mordaunt case, especially in its legal aspects, I had this to say of those enquiries which centred about the possible presence of 'specific' syndromes:

> The Court needlessly concerned itself in seeking to prove—or disprove—that Lady Mordaunt had been suffering from a 'specific' disease before or at the time of the birth. All that [the Court] needed to prove was that Lady Mordaunt *believed that she was so suffering*. This would have proved that she believed that she had had good cause to consider herself infected with such a disease—and the matter of her guilt would have been self-evident.
>
> It would not have affected the issue one way or another to prove—as much of the evidence called tended to prove—that she had been mistaken in thinking herself the victim of some venereal distemper.

Yet the Court would not leave this business of suspected venereal disease alone. The Court called Mr Priestley, Fellow of the Royal College of Surgeons, and, apparently, a physician as well as a surgeon, to give *his* evidence.

> DR PRIESTLEY: I gave medicine for a discharge from which Lady Mordaunt was suffering.

SERJEANT BALLANTINE: Am I right in supposing that it must have been an innocent discharge, or was it the result of improper intercourse?

DR PRIESTLEY: It was innocent; it was not of a specific character.

SERJEANT BALLANTINE: Was there any time when you thought it might have been otherwise?

DR PRIESTLEY: No, I never thought it otherwise. As I have said, it was not of a specific character.

SERJEANT BALLANTINE: Was it of a character that would produce upon a child the same symptoms as a complaint of a specific character [i.e., gonorrhea]?

DR PRIESTLEY: Yes.

SERJEANT BALLANTINE: If of an innocent character, would you not have thought that it would have yielded sooner to your remedies?

DR PRIESTLEY: Not necessarily.... I saw the child shortly after its birth. It was then perfectly well, and the complaint from which it afterwards suffered could not have been of a specific character, seeing the rapidity with which it was cured. I examined Lady Mordaunt on several occasions, extending over a considerable period. I saw her during her pregnancy, and she was then suffering from the same disease in an aggravated form. The remedies I used would be applicable to disease of a specific character.... Though the treatment is the same, the complaints are totally different. I am quite certain this was not the specific complaint.

We must observe here that, though much of the evidence—especially the medical evidence—relating to the supposed venereal infection of Lady Mordaunt appears to be irrelevant, it must be emphasized that none of this evidence was so considered by Conan Doyle, for reasons that we shall examine later. Of the fate of Lady Mordaunt and her husband; of the Prince of Wales and Lord Cole—and of all but one of the men whose names had come to be associated scandalously with that of Lady Mordaunt—Conan Doyle took little notice; his whole attention being taken up, not so much with Lady Mordaunt, as with her suspected 'specific' complaint. And of the suspected or actually cited co-respondents, only the odious Sir Frederick Johnstone claimed Doyle's fascinated and all-absorbing regard—a fascination that was to be echoed nearly a quarter-of-a-century after Sir Charles Mordaunt had initiated the most scandalous of Victorian *causes célèbres*.

It was evident, from the recollections of both Nurse Hancock and Sir Charles Mordaunt of Lady Mordaunt's confession: "Charley, you are not the father of my child.... I am the cause of its blindness," that Lady Mordaunt *did* believe herself infected with a 'complaint of a specific character', and that, if she had not contracted this from her husband, then she had contracted it from someone other than Sir Charles—and so she must, in the opinion of the Court, have stood self-convicted of adultery.

But few Courts will deny the expert witnesses and Counsel their 'say'—and so the examination of witnesses continued:

> MR SERJEANT BALLANTINE: When did you become aware your wife was in the family way?
>
> SIR CHARLES MORDAUNT: I cannot recollect whether she told me she was in the family-way at the time.
>
> BALLANTINE: But when did you first become acquainted with the fact?
>
> MORDAUNT: I cannot recollect the precise date, but I remember that she told Mrs Cadogan [the Rector's wife] of it. The first time I heard, I think, was in the first week in August, before I went to Scotland. That excited no suspicion in my mind at the time. We returned from Scotland in the beginning of September, and went to Walton [*the Mordaunt country-house*]. I remember the November following that Sir Frederick Johnstone was on a visit to us. Previously, Lady Mordaunt had asked me why a man of Sir Frederick Johnstone's fortune and position had not married. I answered that I had heard there was a reason. She pressed me to tell her the reason. I told her that I had heard he had a disease. She pressed me to tell her the reason. I was reluctant; but, on her pressing me, I told her that I had heard he had a disease and that if he married it was possible such disease might be conveyed to his children. *Sir F. Johnstone had been on a visit to us on several occcasions.* When Lady Mordaunt went up to London in November, she told me she visited Dr Priestley previous to her confinement. *She did not tell me she had any disease* [my italics].

Of course, venereal infection of a wife might have come by means of her husband, and so, in the interest of 'fairness', Ballantine asked Sir Charles bluntly whether or not he had ever suffered from a 'disease of a specific character'.

Equally bluntly, and even more tersely, Sir Charles answered: "I never suffered from it in my life."

Now it was the turn of Sir Frederick. His reply was more explicit—and much more heated, so that Ballantine, that bright forensic star of the Victorian law-courts, pounced instantly on Sir Frederick's anger. Asked, in his turn, whether or not *he* had ever suffered from a venereal disease, Sir Freddy answered indignantly: "No more unfounded statement was ever made by any man to the prejudice of another behind his back!"

There was no refuge in indignation for Sir Frederick—not, that is, from Sergeant Ballantine's legal acuity. He began to press the indignant baronet, forcing him to qualify that first over-emphatic denial.

SERJEANT BALLANTINE: At this particualr period [i.e., when he was *seeing Lady Mordaunt*], were you suffering...?

SIR FREDERICK: No.... Nor for many years previously.

This admission produced a reflective quiet in the Court, as one and all pondered on the admission extracted from Sir Frederick (one of the several Top People co-respondents), each—no doubt—reflecting that what one had once contracted, one might, in pursuit of the same indulgences, easily contract again.

———

The appearance of the Prince of Wales in the witness-box undoubtedly provided the sensation-hungry newspaper-readers with their Thrill of the Century—even more of a thrill for those knowledgeable in Royal gossip, who knew that 'Bertie' had chosen to give evidence against the strongest protests of his Royal Mother.

There were, however, no revelations to come from that witness-box appearance: the Prince was handled by the Court with a delicacy far softer than that accorded by the proverbial 'kid gloves'—

and if there be an echo, in the future Holmes writings, of this Court appearance of the Prince's, it may possibly sound in Sherlock Holmes's refusal to accept a knighthood from that same Prince, now on the throne as King Edward VII. But Royal indiscretions and Royal witness-box appearances held, for Conan Doyle, little interest compared with that fascination that the introduction of venereal disease into the legal arguments had for him.

Both sides, it must be recorded, offered His Royal Highness a deference that did not halt this side obsequiousness, though it says much for the Prince's courage that he volunteered to enter the witness-box, and to give evidence on his supposed involvement with Lady Mordaunt; and this against the express commands of the Queen (though not, be it noted, against the advice of Lord Granville and Lord Hatherley, respectively Foreign Minister and Lord Chancellor).

As *The Times* reported: "A stir and buzz ran round the court. Then followed a dead silence, as H.R.H. entered and bowed respectfully to his lordship [i.e., the Judge, Lord Penzance]."

No very painful ordeal awaited 'Bertie' in the witness-box, and, had such threatened, Lord Penzance's welcoming words to his illustrious witness safely established the tone desired from Counsel. The welcome, however, though friendly and deferential, conveyed a warning.

"It is my duty," said the Judge, "to point out to His Royal Highness his position under the Act of Parliament that was passed last session. This provides that no witness, in any proceedings, whether a party to the suit or not, shall be liable to be asked, or be bound to answer, any question tending to shew that he or she has been guilty of adultery.

"Now, from the course that this case has taken, I think it is right to point out to His Royal Highness, and to tell him that he is not bound or required by law to submit to any interrogation on that subject."

Bertie, however, declined to avail himself of this plain offer of escape from the witness-box: he had every confidence that Dr Deane, examining, would take him as painlessly and as non-committally as possible, through the questioning. This, of course, and with the full acquiescence of both sides of the Court, Dr Deane did.

To accuse Dr Deane of having "led" his star witness would be unjust; nevertheless, Counsel for the Respondent so phrased—and restricted—his questions as to force the Prince to be as brief and as self-justifying as possible.

Sir Charles Mordaunt's butler had already told the Court how her Ladyship had given orders that, when the Prince called on her and was with her, no other caller was to be admitted. The butler added that when the Prince *did* call, he always came unattended by even one of his gentlemen, and remained closeted with Lady Mordaunt for a couple of hours.

Tactfully, Dr Deane made no reference to this unusual mode of paying social calls on a married lady; and, with equal tact, the Court expressed no wish to pursue the matter further.

Well aware on which side his bread was buttered—or about to be buttered—the Prince answered all Dr Deane's questions 'in a calm and undisturbed manner', recalling—rather than 'admitting'—that he had known the Moncreiffe family since before Harriet Moncreiffe's marriage; that he had written to her on her marriage, and sent her a wedding-present; that she had visited Marlborough House [*the Prince and Princess of Wales's London residence*], and that she had gone to the theatre with the Prince and Princess.

"In the year 1867, did you see much of her...?"

"I did."

"And in the year 1868?" (*That was the year preceding the Court action.*)

"I did also."

Now, before the Prince's examination, Lord Penzance had advised him that, 'under the Act of Parliament that was passed last session', there were certain questions that he would be absolved from answering. A question was now to be put by Dr Deane that the Prince certainly need not have answered. But, since the Prince had come voluntarily to Court, in order to appear as a witness for the defence, Dr Deane knew that he was on pretty safe ground, not only in venturing to ask an all-important question, but also in his expecting a satisfactory answer. (And the Prince knew that he might repose the utmost confidence in Dr Deane's knowing his way through the tricksy mazes of Court-practice.)

"Only one more question with which to trouble your Royal Highness. Has there been any improper familiarity or criminal act between yourself and Lady Mordaunt...?"

The brief answer came clear and firm in that tense hush. Said the Prince (on oath, of course): "There has not."

(What, then did they two do during those several 'couple of hours', behind locked doors in the Mordaunt house, of which the Court had only just heard: Talked of Art and Music and Literature...? That this thought was in many minds in Court that day, there can be no doubt. But the question was never asked. And the Other Side was as tender to the Most Distinguished Witness as Dr Deane had been....)

The witness was ready to be cross-examined.

"I have," said Serjeant Ballantine, rising, "no questions to ask your Royal Higness."

And though Sir Frederick Johnstone, called to the witness-box, admitted to a 'tête-à-tête' dinner with Lady Mordaunt in a London hotel....

"You knew that her husband was not with her?"

"Certainly."

"—And about this dinner. Was anybody else in the room at any time?"

"Yes."

"Ah! Who was that...?"

"The waiter." (*Who, by the way, was never sought or called.*)

...the witness was as firm in his denial of 'any improper familiarity or criminal act' between Lady Mordaunt and himself as, a few minutes earlier, the Prince had been.

———

The other male callers (in Sir Charles's absence) at the house in Chesham-place, London, and Walton Hall, Warwickshire—the Court heard of (some of) them: Lord Cole, Lord Newport, and Captain Arthur Farquhar, of the Guards, did not enter the witness-box. Lord Cole was invited to do so—for, in her 'confession', Lady Mordaunt had actually named him as the father of her child—but his lordship declined the invitation.

Not for six more years did the Divorce Court grant Sir Charles Mordaunt his freedom from a wife long since demonstrably insane. In the revived action, only one co-respondent—Lord Cole—was cited, and as no defence was entered, on behalf either of Lady Mordaunt or of Lord Cole, Sir Charles was granted his decree.

For all those concerned in the case—and expecially those many members of the Prince's 'Marlborough House Set' (including the Prince himself) who had cuckolded Sir Charles Mordaunt—that final decree must have seemed to close the case once and for all.

For all these men, including Sir Charles, it quite certainly seemed over-and-done-with. (In my Debrett of 1900—the classic guide to the British titled aristocracy—the marriage of Sir Charles to Miss Harriet Moncreiffe is not recorded, as 'better forgotten'.)

And so, for all the men involved in this sordid case, it probably was. But for one man, the case, which had so interested him on first reading, was not to be forgotten for many years—if ever. The case literally haunted his mind, consciously and sub-consciously; and, as I have said, the memory, the never-forgotten awareness, of the case was to ferment and nag and torment for years, until, at last—after nearly a quarter-century—the one man who, though not involved in the Mordaunt Scandal, had become obsessed with it, had to write about it, for all that the allusions to the case are veiled in his own very personal code.

That man was Arthur Conan Doyle.

What obsessed him about the case, and why; and how he wrote of it years later, we shall now examine.

———

Silver Blaze, the first of the stories in the collection grouped under the general title of *The Memoirs of Sherlock Holmes,* appeared, after publication in *The Strand Magazine,* in 1893, in the hard-cover collection of the following year: George Newnes's London edition and Harper & Brothers' New York edition—both of 1894.

Almost certainly written in 1892 or early 1893, this story (still one of the favourite and most-quoted of all the Sherlockian tales) appeared, then, twenty-three or twenty-four years after the divorce-case that it so patently echoes. What was it, then, in that dingy Mordaunt affair, which so fascinated Conan Doyle that, close on a quarter-century later, he *had* to 'recreate' it analogically and veiled in his own personal cypher as *Silver Blaze?*

The first and most important factor in that fascination with the Mordaunt case was that Conan Doyle had become, soon after his enrolling as a student at the Medical School of Edinburgh University, interested in—if not already fascinated by—Venereal Disease, a subject that was completely 'taboo' in lay circles and even in medical circles was by no means a popular or frequently-handled subject. Later, I shall suggest, but (lacking decisive proof) shall in no way affirm, what I believe first attracted Doyle's interest to the *lues Veneris.* His close study of the venereal diseases; of their origins and results; had its just reward when his brilliant thesis on the subject earned him his Edinburgh doctorate of medicine—one of the most impressive academic distinctions that Victorian scientific scholarship had to offer. In writing to me, to confirm the facts of Conan Doyle's doctorate, Dr J.T.D. Hall, the Sub-librarian of Edinburgh University, mentioned that 'the manuscript of Conan Doyle's doctoral thesis is on the desk before me as I write'. And added: 'I can confirm that Arthur Conan Doyle graduated from this University, first MB CM in 1881, and MD in 1885. The degree of MD was in fact the only medical degree awarded by the University of Edinburgh for many years.... Arthur Conan Doyle is an honoured and well-remembered alumnus....'

———

Now, although it was the central fact of venereal infection of Lady Mordaunt's new-born child that had made the case of her divorce memorable to Conan Doyle, he had not overlooked the possibility—and, to him, it was more than a mere possibility—that the source of that infection had been Sir Frederick Johnstone.

Lady Mordaunt, long since committed, as hopelessly insane, to a lunatic-asylum, had been as long forgotten by all but her family and a few, a very few staunch friends. Sir Freddy, on the contrary, had stayed prominently in the news, not only as one of England's most successful racehorse-owners, but as the friend of his fellow-witness in the Mordaunt divorce-case, Albert Edward, Prince of

Wales—though Johnstone's too-long-tolerated drunken arrogance was soon to end that friendship.

As I said earlier, Sir Frederick Johnstone was one of the darlings of that section of the English who turn first to the racing-pages of their newspapers—for Sir Freddy was a consistently 'lucky' winner and many a humble backer had cause to bless Sir Freddy for the small but welcome addition to his weekly wages.

Nor were Sir Freddy's turf-triumphs 'old-history'—he had already established himself as a winning owner even before the opening of the Mordaunt case, when Conan Doyle was barely eleven years of age, and he was still England's foremost race-winner in 1881, when Conan Doyle, newly-qualified medical practitioner, was twenty-two. In that year, Sir Freddy had brought off the 'classic hat-trick', that is, winning all three of the year's racing 'classics': the Derby, the Oaks, and the Ascot Gold Cup. The name of the wonderful racehorse that had achieved this triple triumph should be borne in mind, as it was ineffaceably borne in mind by Conan Doyle. The name of the horse was...*St Blaise*.

———

Now for the 'echoes'. Conan Doyle, always intensely interested in the world around him—not for nothing does he make Sherlock Holmes so assiduous a reader of the newspapers—is always 'echoing' in his stories, but never exactly re-telling, the hopes, the fears, the ambitions, successes, and failures of that Humanity whose active follies or achievements filled, day-by-day, the columns of reported fact.

Silver Blaze, in this respect, is no different from all the other tales of Sherlockian adventure. Conan Doyle did not set out to recount the sad story of Lady Mordaunt's frailty or of the many cads who took advantage of that frailty—though, through the *persona* of his creation, Sherlock Holmes, Conan Doyle registered his deep disapproval of the chief of those cads: Albert Edward, Prince of Wales.

No, *Silver Blaze* does not recount, as 'fiction', the Mordaunt Case: the tale is merely filled with so many 'echoes' of that case that it is clear that Conan Doyle had not merely not forgotten it; he was quite obsessed with it.

Take, to begin, the change of Sir Freddy's horse's name, from 'St Blaise' to 'Silver Blaze'. 'Blaise' and 'Blaze' have exactly the same pronunciation—in sound, they are (as Conan Doyle intended them to be) the same word. But why the change of 'Saint' to 'Silver'? Because the Mordaunt infant, who had been born with the dread *ophthalmia neonatorum*, gonorrheal infection of the eyes, would inevitably have been treated, as to those infected eyes, with *silver* nitrate, now for many years past mandatory in *all* cases of birth, and traditional since silver nitrate's invention and introduction by the Arabs in the 9th Century.

Again, observe how the 'eye-business' enters into the details of the story, even in what seem to be quite irrelevant ways. The trainer of the sure-to-win racehorse, Silver Blaze, John Straker, has been found dead, killed by a savage blow on the skull. Straker (named, in all probability, after a firm of chain-store stationers, from whom both Conan Doyle and I bought the paper on which we wrote our first stories) was in financial trouble, brought on by his being involved with an extravagant mistress, and he had agreed, for money, to lame the horse, in the interests of some who would be threatened with ruin in the (almost certain) event of Silver Blaze's win in the forthcoming 'classic', the Wessex Cup. Having agreed to make Silver Blaze incapable of winning the race, Straker visits the horse at night, and has hardly nicked the horse's sensitive skin with the point of the knife, when the frightened creature lashes out with its hoof, and—as Holmes convincingly deduces—kills the dishonest trainer.

And that is all of the story of *Silver Blaze*'s plot that need concern us here. What should interest us, as a *direct* echo of the Mordaunt case in particular, and of ophthalmology generally, is the unusual— and, in this context, almost inexplicable—*nature* of the knife that Straker intended to use on Silver Blaze. It was this unusual nature of the knife—at first supposed to have been used by Straker to defend himself against a murderous human assailant—which instantly engaged Sherlock Holmes's interest, as it surely must engage ours.

> ...an ivory-handled knife with a very delicate, inflexible blade marked Weiss & Co., London....

And let the reader observe that though 'Weiss', in German, means 'white', the pronunciation of the German word is identical with that of the English word, 'vice', a word which would spring instantly to the mind of anyone who was recalling the Mordaunt case....

> "This is a very singular knife,"said Holmes, lifting it up, and examining it minutely. "I presume, as I see blood-stains upon it, that it is the one which was found in the dead man's grasp. Watson, this knife is surely in your line?"
>
> "It is what we call a cataract knife," said I.
>
> "I thought so. A very delicate blade devised for very delicate work. A strange thing for a man to carry with him on a rough expedition, especially as it would not shut in his pocket."
>
> "The tip was guarded by a disc of cork, which we found beside the body," said the inspector. "His wife tells us that the knife had lain upon the dressing-table, and that he had picked it up as he left the room. It was a poor weapon, but perhaps the best that he could lay his hands on at the moment."

A very singular knife indeed, and one for which it is impossible to account, as in the normal possession of a racehorse-trainer.

And, indeed, we do not have to think of it as normally related to the dishonest trainer; the 'very delicate blade, devised for very delicate work' has been introduced by Conan Doyle into the tale of *Silver Blaze* to emphasize its connection with the true affair of Lady Mordaunt, her baby's ophthalmia, and the *silver nitrate* with which her baby's eyes had been bathed. (Nor had Conan Doyle forgotten how Sir Frederick Johnstone had, with masterly bad taste, named one of his finest racehorses...*Sore Eyes*.)

What 'triggered off' the recollections of the Mordaunt Case that are so plainly to be heard 'echoed' in the tale of *Silver Blaze*? Well, plainly, here—as in most other 'echoes'—several 'reminders' operated to recall the main theme of the Mordaunt Case. It may be well to list the most probable 'reminders':

1 Between the finishing of *Micah Clarke* and his beginning *The White Company*, in 1888, Conan Doyle, still intent on making a career of his sound medical degrees, began to study ophthalmology. His studies here cannot have failed to bring to memory the affair of Lady Mordaunt's baby—unless, perhaps, such a memory had turned his thoughts towards ophthalmology?

2 On the journey, with his wife, to Berlin, in January, 1891, to hear Dr Koch's lectures on his supposed cure for tuberculosis, Conan Doyle had encountered a famous dermatologist, Malcolm Morris, who had warmly encouraged Doyle to continue his ophthalmological studies.

3 On Morris's advice, Doyle went on from Berlin to Vienna, to take a specialized course in ophthalmology, before setting up a practice in London.

4 He did take consulting-rooms in Devonshire-place (near the 'Medical Mecca' of Harley-street, and put up his 'plate'/ 'shingle'—only to receive not one enquiring patient. NOTE that the action of *Silver Blaze* takes place in the county of Devon (Devonshire).

5 In 1890, in the disgraceful affair of *The Baccarat Scandal*, the Prince of Wales voluntarily entered the witness-box to testify to his belief that his friend, Sir William Gordon-Cummings, had been detected in cheating at cards. (For this the Prince, as he left the Law Courts, was wholeheartedly hissed and hooted by the mob—the first demonstration of unpopularity that he had experienced in England. It is impossible that this appearance cannot have recalled the Prince's *first* witness-box appearance, when he gave evidence in the Mordaunt Case.

6 Recollections of the Mordaunt Case would have been impossible without equally vivid recollections of the most caddish actor in that drama, Sir Frederick Johnstone, who, *as his horses were constantly winning, was as constantly mentioned in the newspapers.* Sir Freddy, despite his regrettable moral quality, was always good 'copy' for the newspapers, and so dedicated a newspaper-reader as was Conan Doyle could never have escaped the mentions of Sir Freddy and, so, the constant recollection of the Mordaunt Case.

7 Recollections of the venereal disease which was the principal theme of the Mordaunt Case, and without which disease there would, in all probability, have been no divorce-case to consider, troubled Conan Doyle more than

(apart from the self-revelation of the 'echoes' in *Silver Blaze*) he would ever have admitted even to his nearest. It was not only the Skeleton in the Family Cupboard, it was, more, Conan Doyle's own particular Skeleton: the suspicion that his father's insanity, which had committed him to an asylum in March, 1879, *was of venereal origin.* Perhaps the young Edinburgh medical-man, who had gained his doctorate with a thesis on Venereal Disease might have been on the look-out for evidence of the disease in any place: I think that he might well have found such evidence in his father's insanity.

———

And what of Albert Edward, pleasure-loving, self-indulgent Prince of Wales; fellow-witness with Sir Frederick Johnstone in the Mordaunt Case: is there no 'echo' of him in the tale of *Silver Blaze*?

Indeed there is. Conan Doyle makes him one of the racehorse-owners competing in the Wessex Cup, giving him the title of 'Duke of Balmoral' (on the grounds that, in real life, Queen Victoria used the title, when travelling 'incognito', of 'Duchess of Balmoral'). And that the Prince of Wales did not miss the 'echoes' of the Mordaunt Case in *Silver Blaze* had been confirmed for me in a curious fashion, ninety-four years after *Silver Blaze* was written in the early Spring of 1892.

I had written to the Royal Library at Windsor, to enquire whether or not *Beeton's Annual* for Christmas, 1887 (in which Sherlock Holmes made his first bow) had ever entered Queen Victoria's household. The letter that I received from Miss Bridget A. Wright, the Bibliographer, in answer to mine, contains the information that

> The Royal Library does not contain a copy of *Beeton's Annual* for Christmas 1887, nor is there any record in the Royal Archives of any member of the Royal Family subscribing to it. There is also no record of Queen Victoria's reading Sherlock Holmes stories.
>
> On the other hand, her grandson, later King George V, did read them, as they are listed amongst the books that he read in the 1880's and 1890's. Moreover, there are in the Royal Library two of the volumes of collected stories about Holmes, namely:

A. Conan Doyle: The Adventures of Sherlock Holmes 3rd ed. and The Memoirs of Sherlock Holmes

both published by George Newnes, in 1894, in the Strand Library series.

Both contain the bookplate of Queen Mary as Duchess of York. The Duke and Duchess of York were in the habit of reading aloud to each other, and may have read these in that way. The only other Holmes story is in a single number of the 'Strand Magazine', part of vol. 4, containing *Silver Blaze*.

A brief word here to explain the relationships of the Royal persons mentioned in Miss Wright's letter to me.

Queen Victoria's eldest son and Heir Apparent to the Kingdom of Great Britain (with its Colonies and Dominions) and the Empire of India, was Albert Edward, Prince of Wales: that very same Prince of Wales who had appeared twice in the witness-box: on the first occasion, in the matter of the Mordaunt Divorce; in the second, in the sad business of the Baccarat Scandal, twenty years later. The Prince was to become King, as Edward the Seventh, on the death of his mother, Queen Victoria, on 22nd January, 1901.

The elder son of the Prince of Wales, Albert Victor, Duke of Clarence & Avondale—himself, as his father's elder son, Heir Presumptive to the twin crowns of Britain and India—had died, in very mysterious circumstances, in February, 1892, a few weeks only before Conan Doyle (receiving, perhaps, yet another mnemonic 'triggering of echoes' in this widely-publicized Royal tragedy?) had written *Silver Blaze*. On Prince Albert Victor's death, his younger brother, George, Duke of York (whose Duchess pasted her bookplate into the Yorks' copies of *The Adventures* and *The Memoirs* of Sherlock Holmes), succeeded his dead brother as Heir Presumptive. The Duke of York was later, in 1910, on the death of King Edward VII—'our' self-indulgent Prince of Wales—to ascend the Throne as King George the Fifth.

Here, though, I am concerned only to make clear the relationship between 'our' Prince of Wales, Queen Victoria's eldest son and heir, and the Duke of York. They were, respectively, father and son. The son certainly knew his Sherlock Holmes; what I shall ask here is this: Did that son's father, the Prince of Wales, have—or acquire—a special interest in one particular Holmes story? Or, to be as precise as possible, did the Prince of Wales have reason to take a special interest in the story, *Silver Blaze*?

If he did not, how, then, may we account for the presence, in the Royal archives, of that 'stray' copy of *Silver Blaze* to be found in a single number of *The Strand Magazine*?

For consider: had any member of the Royal Household wished to read *Silver Blaze*, the story was immediately accessible in the bound volume of *The Memoirs*, belonging to the Duchess of York, the Prince of Wales's daughter-in-law. *But*—if the Prince had been privately informed that 'there was something in that Holmes story of *Silver Blaze* which might well interest your Royal Highness'— and if, further, he had had it hinted to him that what he might find in that tale might be disturbing as well as interesting...?

In that case, I suggest, he would have wished to study the story on his own. He would not have wished to ask his daughter-in-law to let him read *Silver Blaze* (provided he knew that she had it) in her bound volume of *The Memoirs*. ("Oh, Father, why do you wish to read *that* particular story...?") In any case, he would not have had to confide his interest in *Silver Blaze* to either his son or that son's very observant wife. The Prince had merely—and without giving reasons—to ask his Librarian, Sir Richard Rivington Holmes, MVO (a cousin of Shelock Holmes's, by the way, as well as having been lieutenant-colonel of the 1st Volunteer Battalion, Berkshire Regiment—Dr Watson's old regiment) to order up a copy of *The Strand Magazine* containing the story of *Silver Blaze*. (And what the Prince made of the Mordaunt allusions, we shall never know.)

But that, I suggest, is how that spare copy of *Silver Blaze* came to be ordered—and why, quite unaccounted for, it is still in the Royal Archives.

———————

Conan Doyle could always use a name which had interested him. The surname of the shocked Rector's wife, Mrs. Cadogan, turns up again in The Bruce-Partington Plans (1917).

LIGHT ON A CERTAIN LIGHTHOUSE

Which 'board-school' was it...?

Out of the many oft-quoted passages in the Canon, there is—apart from that reference to the Dog in the Night—no passage so familiar by quotation or better-known to all Sherlockians than the passage in which Mr Holmes, passing in the railway-train through Clapham Junction, expresses his admiration of the English[1] educational system.

> Holmes [wrote Watson] was sunk in profound thought, and hardly opened his mouth until we had passed Clapham Junction.
>
> "It's a very cheering thing to come into London by any of these lines which run high and allow you to look down upon the houses like this."
>
> I thought he was joking, for the view was sordid enough,[2] but he soon explained himself.
>
> "Look at those big, isolated clumps of buildings rising up above the slates, like brick islands in a lead-coloured sea."
>
> "The Board schools."

---

[1] I stress 'English' here, because the Scots have a different system.

[2] Alas! after a century, even more sordid.

"Lighthouses, my boy! Beacons of the future! Capsules, with hundreds of bright little seeds in each, out of which will come the wiser, better England of the future...."

Overlooking, as generations of Sherlockians have tolerantly overlooked, the very mixed metaphor ("Lighthouses" generating "capsules...of bright little seeds"!), those many generations have known some varied responses to Holmes's almost too-emotional reaction to the sight of the 'isolated clumps of buildings...like brick islands in a lead-coloured sea'. Some have seen in those Clapham Junction remarks—or professed to have seen—Holmes's interest in, and tenderness towards, the Young (an interest and tenderness not strikingly apparent in all the other tales of the Canon); others, with perhaps more justification, have interpreted Holmes's obvious approval of the Board-schools with the warmest approval of the English educational system, and others have gone even further in their speculative interpretation, and seen, in the Clapham Junction paean unmistakable proof of Holmes's 'Socialistic' sentiments—sentiments not at all uncommon among persons of Holmes's social class, at a time that saw the foundation of the Fabian Society and the publication of Wilde's *The Soul of Man under Socialism*. Others, of surely more 'practical' turn of fancy, have seen in Holmes's encomium only satisfaction at the sight of the handsome red-brick-and-Portland-stone Board-schools as a welcome aesthetic break in the desolate uniformity of that depressing 'lead-coloured sea'. All opinions may have something of validity in them; but I am concerned here with a more immediate 'triggering': What was there in the appearance of these (then cleanly new) 'brick islands in a lead-coloured sea' to bring the concept of 'lighthouses' instantly to Holmes's mind? I am concerned here to explain (at *first* reading, not merely metaphor-mixing, but decidedly catachrestic analogy: Does the average Board-school building instantly suggest the thought of a *lighthouse*?) which, of all the *six* Board-schools visible from the train at Clapham Junction, was the one catching Holmes's interested regard; the one—*and one only*—that fulfills *all* the conditions of having that special quality of being able to invoke immediately the remembrance, the image, of a lighthouse.

When, as I propose to do, we shall have seen which of the six Board-schools caught Holmes's eye and inspired his complimentary comments, we shall even be able to affirm that, as the train sped through the Junction, on its way, through Queen's Road Battersea and Battersea Park stations, to the terminus at Victoria, Holmes was sitting in the left-hand corner seat of the compartment, facing the engine—for that was where I was sitting when, after much memory-searching, I at last identified that one particular school that inspired those immortal comments; that one school that may be seen in its significant detail, *only from that single* position in the railway-carriage. (As, in Poe's story of *The Gold Bug*, the treasure-locating skull nailed to the tree-branch may be seen from one position—and one position only.)

———

The term, 'Board-school', once so well-known in Britain, but hardly known outside that country (so that the usually meticulously-informed William Baring-Gould confuses the English *boarding*-school with the English *Board*-school) has become almost as unknown in Britain. So...an explanation: What were the Board-schools? They were (and most of the buildings survive, for all that these schools are now known by a different term) the State—what in America are called the 'public'—schools established under the truly revolutionary *Elementary Education Act* of 1870, the building of the schools being entrusted to the School-boards organized by counties—hence their name of 'Board-schools''. Holmes was right: the system— attacked at every social level—was sound. It aimed to give the children of the lower working-class a solid grounding, in four years (the parents were violently antagonistic to the proposition that their potentially money-earning children should be kept 'uselessly' at school after age eleven years. Though step by hard-fought step, the school-leaving age was gradually extended, until, before the end of the Century, it released the children at fourteen).

———

As the railway-traveller approaches and passes, Londonwards, through Clapham Junction, no fewer than six Board-schools are plainly visible on a clear day; all, as they say, within 'spitting distance' of the multiple railway-tracks that bisect and dominate this part of seedy Clapham. Three of the schools lie to the left of the tracks; three to the right. The school that caught Holmes's eye and that (after far too long a memory-search) enabled me, first, to identify the particular building, and, second, to explain the choice and significance of Holmes's enthusiastic words about Board-schools, is the first of the three schools lying to the left of the railway-tracks and is seen a moment before the traveller comes into the Junction proper. (*See map in gallery section.*)

———

In all successful research, the successful researcher will—must, indeed—acknowledge (and always with just gratitude) that element of the fortuitous, the serendipitous, the 'plain lucky', which, almost always at the end of the search, and often when the discouraged researcher is minded to abandon the apparently 'hopeless' quest, quietly manifests itself to provide the long-sought solution of the problem.

So with my trying to identify the familiarity that the lantern crowning that 'first school on the left' had had for me, ever since I first saw it atop the school's steeply-pitched roof. (A 'lantern', in architect's parlance, is a relatively small ornament, almost always a multi-sided, glazed 'sentry-box' of generally more-or-less Gothic feeling, perched on the centre of a roof's ridge-pole. Originating in late Mediaeval times as a strictly functional skylight, the 'lantern' now serves only a purely decorative purpose—and each Board-school sprouted one, no two exactly the same.)

I had, as I have said, been noticing this particular 'lantern' for a long time—for several years, in fact, as I always sat in the left-hand corner of the carriage on my daily journeys up to London, and never, thus, missed my daily sight of the Board-school, or my daily recollection of Holmes's comments on schools of this type.

Now, though I could not remember where, in the distant past, I had seen the original of which the Board-school lantern was a copy, I did remember enough to be sure that the copy was an exact one, and that, to find the original (if I ever should hope to) I must familiarize myself with every smallest detail of the lantern, so as not to miss the recognition of the original, were I either to come across it accidentally, or—best of all— remember what that original really was. For I was certain now that, in my remembering—in my being able to identify—the original, I should (I was *sure* of it) find the reason why Holmes had spoken as he had....

━━━━━━

If a faithfully-pursued idea evade the ultimate capture, and 'luck' comes to end the quest, I maintain—I have always maintained—that the 'luck' is nothing 'chancy'; nothing fortuitous; nothing in the least 'mystical'—though, but in the purely literal meaning of the word, it is undoubtedly 'psychic'. For that seeming element of chance—seeming, *only*, be it well noted!—enters when, and because, the conscious mind has grown tired of the apparently unprofitable quest—at which point the subconscious takes on the abandoned duty and finds what obstinately stayed hidden from the deliberate and reasoned searching of the Conscious. My subconscious led me into the local newsagent's shop, to find out whether or not the latest edition of the British bi-monthly, *Private Eye*, was on sale?

It was. I opened it. Inside the front cover—a page of advertisements—was an advertisement for *Listerine*. (Through such strange agencies does the always-helpfully-active Subconscious work its wonders....)

The *Listerine* ad was decorated with a line-drawing, at which, let the reader well believe, I stared in momentarily uncomprehending wonder. For the line-drawing shewed the original on which the architect of the Board-school had so accurately based his lantern.

And that original had been...*a lighthouse.*

("The Board-schools...." ..."Lighthouses, my boy! Beacons of the future!")

━━━━━━

Were that Jung were still alive! Would that there were years ahead of me! That Jung and I might seek to map the circuitous and complex meanderings of a thought—any thought—making its way towards the light through the dark, hidden tunnels of the Subconscious. We know the purpose and function of the Subconscious, which is to absorb and store knowledge, as that knowledge is being absorbed by the Conscious (though storing it not half so efficiently as it is stored by the Subconscious), and to release that Knowledge when (for reasons that are still not understood of us) when—*and only when* the Conscious fails 'to come up with the answer'. As now.... It will hardly be believed—any yet I do ask the reader to accept that it is so— that, until I came to this part of the *true* account of how the Board-school of Clapham Junction triggered the image of a lighthouse in Holmes's subconscious, the implications of the name of the journal in which I found, at last, the answer to an old question, had never struck me. *Private Eye.* I had never thought of this magazine as any other than a source of news not normally handled by other newspapers, and though its Editor had hunted for, and made public, many a social scandal, especially in the worlds of Finance, Politics, and Foreign Relations, I had never thought of it as in any way a 'detective' organ. It was neither a *Black Mask* or a *True Crime,* and so it was that, until a few minutes ago, I had not realized that, doing some literary detective-work of my own, I had found my answer in a magazine bearing the colloquial (if now a little out-dated) American name for a Pinkerton-type investigator: *Private Eye.*

The Subconscious likes, I have found, the impressively apposite. That *Listerine* ad must have been carried by a number of other journals, some of which I must have habitually read. True, I 'took' *Private Eye* pretty regularly, but, then, I took some others as regularly. My Subconscious knew perfectly well that my Conscious hadn't noticed the semantic content of that magazine's name, *Private Eye;* hadn't related it to the nature of my present investigative activity. So what, as I have said, more apposite a place of final revelation than the page in a magazine named after a detective...?

———

The lighthouse, reproduced in minature as the lantern of a Clapham Board-school's roof, Sherlock Holmes recognized at once. It was the fantastically gabled-and-finialled timber lighthouse built by Henry Winstanley—mark the name!—on the Eddystone Rock, thirteen miles at sea beyond Plymouth. Erected in 1698, it was by no means the first of the world's lighthouses, but it was the first 'rock' light, built away—and, in this case, well away— from the mainland. It lasted—in its brief life, one of the world's wonders— a mere five years. The great storm of 1703 proved too much for its relatively frail structure, and its fussy wooden decorations served only further to catch the force of the terrible gale.

Now *why* should Holmes have recognized, in a lantern of one of the six Board-schools visible from a train passing through Clapham Junction, a small copy of Winstanley's, first of the four lighthouses that were to rise on the Eddystone Rock? Or, to ask the question more practically: Why did Conan Doyle cause Holmes (in *The Naval Treaty*) to recognize the original of the Board-school lantern? Which, of course, begs yet another question: How did Conan Doyle, coming up to Victoria from Hindhead on the London & South-Western Railway, know all about the Winstanley Lighthouse, so as to be able to recognize a miniature version of it as it topped a Clapham Board-school?

That question, fortunately, we are able easily to answer.

Three successors to Winstanley's lighthouse had been built on the Eddystone: the granite-filled timber light of the London silk-mercer, John Rudyerd, destroyed by fire in 1755; the granite light of John Smeaton, F.R.S., Engineer, completed in 1759, but which, though apparently of the strongest construction in solid granite, began, in the mid-1870s, to shew signs of fracture, and it was decided to rebuild. The top was removed and taken to Plymouth, to be erected on Plymouth Hoe, where it still stands as a memorial to Smeaton. The rebuilding of the Eddystone was entrusted to Sir James N. Douglass, Engineer-in-chief to Trinity House, and one of the most famous civil-engineers of his time. His Eddystone stands, as strong as ever, to this day.

The present light was completed in 1881; in the following year, its designer-builder died.

The Western Times, Devon's leading newspaper, not only gave the maker of the newest Eddystone a splendid obituary, but gave a history of the four Eddystone Lights, with line-drawings of each.

In 1882, when Sir James Douglass died, and he and the Eddystones were remembered lavishly in the pages of Plymouth's local press, Conan Doyle was living in that Devon city, enduring the painful experience of living and working with Dr Budd. Certainly Conan Doyle, if only from his reading of the history of the Eddystone in *The Western Times*, would have known of Winstanley's first lighthouse and been able instantly to recognize its miniature copy atop the Clapham Board-school. Conan Doyle's exceptionally retentive memory is a matter of record....

That the lantern topping the 'first Board-school on the left, as one enters Clapham Junction' resembles the Winstanley lighthouse by design, and not by accident I proved when I turned to Clapham Junction in the map of London. Instructed to build a Board-school at a certain location, the architect was surely inspired to decorate his design in the way that he did, when he was told where his new school was to rise; within the corner-site formed by the junction of Newcomen-road and...Winstanley-road.

Fearing, at the beginning of his literary career, that the acknowledgment of his debt to Edgar Allan Poe might impugn his claim to originality, Conan Doyle warmly denied Poe's influence; as warmly acknowledging it when, years later, Doyle had himself achieved both literary and worldly success.

But the undeniable influence of Poe on Doyle—strong even to the point, not merely of imitation, but of downright plagiarism— is to be detected in ways quite outside any normal business of literary influence; ways that seem to partake, in their essence, of what has now come to be called 'the Paranormal'.

For instance, how is it that Conan Doyle, born a half-century after Poe's birth, and educated under a completely different instructional system, by teachers of a different religious affiliation, should have developed a handwriting so like—so startlingly identical with—Poe's, that it is difficult to distinguish between the handwritings of both.

But, perhaps, the most striking of these unaccountable likenesses is to be seen in the subject of that tale of terror, of which

Poe wrote no more than six hundred words before death overtook him. A strange tale indeed, in which those surviving six hundred words *promises* so much of terror, from the skilled pen of a master of horror....

And the subject and title of this never-to-be-finished tale...? *The Lighthouse.*

THE ADVENTURE OF THE POLITICIAN THE LIGHTHOUSE, AND THE TRAINED CORMORANT

Or, rather, The Adventure of Winston Churchill, the Periscopes, and the Trained Seagulls...

In the preamble to *The Veiled Lodger,* Watson refers to 'the mass of material at my command'; he is referring to the notes that he had kept of Mr Sherlock Holmes's 'doings' during the seventeen years that Watson was 'allowed to cooperate with him'. Speaking of these notes, Watson adds that 'There is the long row of year-books which fill a shelf, and there are the dispatch-cases filled with documents, a perfect quarry for the student, not only of crime, but of the social and official scandals of the late Victorian era. Concerning these latter, I may say that the writers of agonized letters, who beg that the honour of their families or the reputation of famous forebearers may not be touched, have nothing to fear. The discretion and high sense of professional honour which have always distinguished my friend are still at work in the choice of these memoirs, and no confidence will be abused.'

But now a distinctly sharper note is audible. A sharper note, in which is to be heard the plainest of threats.

'I deprecate, however,' the text continues, 'in the strongest way, the attempts which have been made lately to get at and destroy these papers. The source of these outrages is known, and if they are repeated, I have Mr Holmes's authority for saying that the whole story concerning the politician, the lighthouse, and the trained cormorant will be given to the public. *There is at least one reader who will understand.*'[1]

I have italicized this last line because it was, for me, one of the main, though not quite the principal, clues to the decypherment of this most cryptic of all Watson's cryptic utterances.

More than two generations of Sherlockian exegetists have puzzled their brains in seeking to interpret the allusion to a Politician, a Lighthouse, and a Trained Cormorant. (One such exegetist of my acquaintance even claiming to have explained it, to his own satisfaction, as a rather catachrestic reference, on Watson's part, to his own position in the Baker-street situation—the literary situation, that is to say. "For 'politician', read 'any kind of superior, administrator, governor, overseer'.... In this case, Sherlock Holmes, obviously the dominant partner in the Holmes-Watson relationship."

"I see. And the lighthouse...?"

"Obviously, something which gives off a very bright light.... Which is a source of illumination. Surely it's not straining the meaning *too* far if we interpret 'illumination' as any sort of teaching, instruction, or—to come a little nearer to the point—a history, a recording. In this case: Watson's recording and *interpreting* Holmes's cases for the general reader.... In other words, *shedding light* upon Holmes's actions and methods.... In fact: *illuminating* the Holmes saga...."

"I see.... And the Trained Cormorant...?"

"You remember your *Coleridge*, surely?"

"Co...Coleridge...?"

Impatiently: "Surely you can't have forgotten what he called Publishers...? You *can't* have forgotten: He called them 'Cormorants nesting in the Tree of Knowledge'. Pretty good, eh...?"

---

[1]My italics.—M.H.

"I see. Yes. And the 'Trained Cormorant' is Watson's publisher...?"

I refrained from asking my Sherlockian exegetic friend why, if the allusion to a Politician, a Lighthouse, and a Trained Cormorant referred to Watson himself, why had burglars broken into Baker-street to steal *Watson's* records, and whom was Watson threatening...? But I knew better than to wish to prolong this dismal stuff. "I think you've got a point," I said—and left it at that. My other Sherlockian friends have frankly stated their inability to understand what all admit to be an allusion to...something; *but "what"*, in the words of another Sherlockian, "God knows!")

In this essay, I shall explain the entire significance of Watson's allusion. The title of this essay has already explained that the 'Politician' of Watson's allusion is Sir Winston Churchill (not then, of course, a Knight of the Garter: then merely plain 'Mr Churchill'), and, in due course I shall explain why Watson, to hide the facts, *but anxious to record his knowledge of them*, called a submarine's periscope 'a lighthouse', and trained seagulls a 'trained cormorant'.

I shall anticipate the final full explanation by making clear here that the hidden significance of the Politician-Lighthouse-Cormorant code—revealed by me for the first time—is much more than a secret memorandum of fact. It is, more, a regretful record of disappointment in an admiring trust betrayed; of the sick realization of contempt for inexcusable folly in others; of the self-reproach painfully inevitable in remembering what now seemed the most inexcusable self-deception.

Let the reader bear in mind that the allusion to 'the Politician, the Lighthouse, and the Trained Cormorant' was made by Conan Doyle in a spasm of bitter self-disgust, in which contempt for others is pretty evenly balanced with contempt for himself.

Bear, too, in mind, that Conan Doyle was a born Crusader. His biographies make, rightly, much of this element in his character. They dwell on his campaigns—they were never less in magnitude than that—for the wrongly-traduced British South African army; for Edalji, for Slater, for Divorce Reform, for Daylight Saving, for communicating with Our Loved Ones on the Other Side. Conan Doyle's 'interest' in warning his fellow-countrymen of the Submarine Menace has been treated by his biographers as no more than that...an 'interest'. True, those biographers all concede that

Conan Doyle 'worked hard to awaken Britain to the Submarine Menace'; that 'he felt very deeply about what the Germans might do with their submarines; that 'he did a lot to get the Right People interested in the Submarine Question'—but never have these biographers managed to see that Conan Doyle flung himself as passionately into the matter of the Submarine Menace as he had done, and was yet to do, many times, into other strivings after Truth and Goodness. That this preaching the Gospel of the Submarine Menace was not merely a fight to rank with the greatest of his Campaigns—it was, in his opinion (as it ought to be in the opinion of his biographers) the most important Campaign of all, since it vindicated him completely, for all that it failed utterly of its aim. His countrymen didn't heed his warnings, and the man whom he had trusted to take him seriously; to back him up in every way; who had (yes, this was the word!) led him on with more than a mere show of interest, and even, it seemed, of friendship; had rejected his message, his warnings. Not with indifference; not with scorn; not with Smart Aleck sophistries. No, not with those. But worse, infinitely worse: with the most soul- shattering rejection of all— with what, to an historian, from a distance of seventy years, looks like nothing less than laughingly insolent buffoonery.

The betrayer of Conan Doyle's trust was the Right Honourable Winston Spencer Churchill, then First Lord of the Admiralty. Not for nothing did the adjective 'impish' attach itself to Churchill's character....

———

Conan Doyle and Winston Churchill had been in South Africa together at the time of the Boer War; Churchill as war-correspondent, Doyle as director of the field-hospital provided, at his own expense, by John Langman, the philanthropist. Conan Doyle, who was to go on to write both a pamphlet defending the British Army against the accusations of 'atrocities' and a full- length history, *The Great Boer War*, returned home with better credit than did the twenty-six-year-old Churchill, whose 'daring escape' from a Boer prisoner-of-war camp was explained by the less romantic Boers as a breaking of Churchill's parole. This widely-believed story (circulating, to my knowledge, a good quarter-century later) did not, however, pre-

vent Churchill's being returned as Member of Parliament for Oldham in the 'Khaki Election' of 1900.

The first full personal contact between Conan Doyle and
Churchill came during and through one of Doyle's noisier cam-
paigns: this, in defence of the supposedly maltreated natives of the
Belgian Congo; a defence which involved a viciously personal at-
tack on the Belgian King Leopold II, accused of plundering the
Congo for his own profit. Letters to President Theodore Roosevelt,
the Kaiser, most of the world's newspapers, and lectures in many a
British city, culminating in a meeting of five thousand in the Albert
Hall, presided over by the Archbishop of Canterbury, were only
some of the activities with which Conan Doyle absorbed some of his
superfluous energy in speaking up for the darker inhabitants of
Darkest Africa. He also sent his book—for, in the conventional
Conan Doyle campaign-strategy, a full-length book followed the
ballon d'essai pamphlet as the night the day—broadcast to the Important of this world, and among the Important who received *The
Crime of the Congo* was Winston Churchill, now President of the Board
of Trade.

Board of Trade, Whitehall Gardens
5 Oct./1909/

Dear Sir Arthur Conan Doyle,

I am very glad you have turned your attention to the Congo. I
will certainly do what I can to help you as opportunity offers.
There are rumours in the newspapers to-day—I hope they are
well founded—that we are to have a British Consul General at
Berlin! In any case a change is being made.

Yours truly,
Winston S. Churchill

To Conan Doyle, the friendliness—indeed, the sympathy—of
this letter must have meant, to Doyle, the firm addition of yet one
more Influential Person to his list of such. To say that Conan Doyle

'used people' would (or, perhaps, might) convey the idea that he 'used' them for his own selfish purposes, when, in fact, he could, and did, persuade himself that he used the Influence of the Influential only from the highest of impersonal motives, and only from the noblest of aims—the Aim *always* being the success of any of his numerous Campaigns. In the furtherance of that Aim in the business of the Congo Atrocities,[2] Conan Doyle had tried to invoke the interest and practical help of many of the leading personalities of the day: such notable figures as the Duke of Norfolk, the Archbiship of Canterbury, the Earl of Cromer (whom Doyle had met in Egypt when Cromer was governing that country for Britain), Sir William Maxwell Aitken (later Lord Beaverbrook, and already a powerful Press Baron) with Ralph Blumenfeld, Editor-in-chief of Aitken's *Daily Express*. Winston Churchill was not, at this moment, to be added to the Pro-Congo lobby—Doyle was reserving the cynically opportunist Winston for possible use in some Campaign not yet envisaged—with what strange results I hope to make clear.

A word here is needed, I think, on the young Winston Churchill's rise to Influence (though not yet to Power), a rise to which only the newspaper *cliché*, 'meteoric' must properly apply.

Passing out of (that is, graduating from) Sandhurst Military College, Churchill was 'gazetted', as a subaltern, of course, to the 4th Hussars—not, by any means, as 'socially prominent' (to use an American expression) as the crack 11th Hussars, of which the recently-dead Duke of Clarence, Heir of the Prince of Wales (the regiment's Colonel-in-chief) was a major. With a Duke for an English grandfather, and a millionaire for an American grandfather, it is remarkable that Winston's relatives should not have arranged for his gazetting to the smartest of all Britian's cavalry regiments, but his father's death after years of complete mental and physical

---

[2]Alfred Harmsworth (later Viscount Northcliffe), most dynamic of the three Harmsworth brothers, who, all contributing, effected a revolution in the world of British newspaper and periodical publishing. Alfred Harmsworth didn't precisely 'support' Doyle's Congo Campaign—instead, like the sharp newspaperman that he was, he used the Doyle-inspired agitation to attack the Quaker chocolate-monopolists, with a costly law-suit as a result. Harmsworth's *Daily Mail* had accused the Quakers of using cocoa-beans imported from the Congo.

deterioration may have momentarily upset his mother's ambitious plans for her son's social advancement. And it is, perhaps, the sense of his regiment's relative social inferiority that made Churchill, after a single experience of warfare *as an officer*, resign his commission, to take part in three further wars—with General Kitchener in the Egyptian Sudan; with Theodore Roosevelt in Cuba; and with General Buller and his fellow military incompetents in South Africa—but in all three, as 'an attached former officer', and no longer as a 'serving regular'. In this free-lance capacity, he acted more as reporter than soldier; and it was as the war-correspondent 'hero' of his 'escape from the Boers' that he returned to England, long before the Boer War was over, to win, as I have said, the Oldham parliamentary seat in the 'Khaki Election' of 1900, standing, note, as a 'True Blue' Conservative.

Six years later, we find him again offering himself to the voters of Oldham—this time to be indignantly and ignominiously rejected, as—a 'traitor to his class'[3]—he had, since the last General Election, 'changed sides', and was now standing as a Liberal; now as passionately 'Radical' as, only a couple of years before (still as Conservative Member for Oldham), he had been as passionately Tory. However, a Radical seat was found for him—the Liberal voters of Manchester were prepared to accept the surprising sudden convert to Radicalism—they returned him to Parliament with what is still called, in Britain, a 'healthy majority', and the Liberal Prime Minister, Sir Henry Campbell-Bannerman, was so impressed by the convert's Ducal background, that—unprecedented in British parliamentary history—Winston took his seat as a Liberal...and with ministerial rank: Undersecretary for the Colonies. In that decisive year of 1906, the Liberals were to 'sweep to power'; a power that they were to retain, more or less, until their extinction as a political party in 1929. In 1906, they commanded, with their huge parliamentary majority, all the power of the House of Commons. From the purely opportunist point-of-view, Winston Churchill's 'scandalous' change-of-loyalties had everything to recommend it:

---

[3]As, to those of a generation who have survived two World Wars, he still remains—for all that they acknowledge and admire what he did for Britain in World War II.

could he, still within the Conservative Party, have hoped for an Under-secretaryship at his age? Whereas Campbell-Bannerman did not hesitate to accept the young Winston's proposition: an immediate Under-secretaryship in return for Winston's deserting his own Party ('All for a handful of silver he left us....') to join Campbell-Bannerman's.

And it says much for Conan Doyle's long-sighted appreciation of the future, more even than for his vaunted broad-mindedness, that he, a staunch Tory Imperialist, did not permit Churchill's 'treachery' to shock him. Despite Churchill's 'betrayal' of Party and social class, Conan Doyle sought the 'renegade's' acquaintance and interest—and it must have seemed to Doyle that his own unfashionable tolerance was about to be justified and most profitably repaid when, after a move from President of the Board of Trade to Home Secretary (in which self-advertising capacity he 'personally' led the world-publicized 'Siege of Sydney-street', an attack, by the Guards, on an empty house reported to be harbouring Russian anarchists), he became, a year later—1911—First Lord of the Admiralty, an appointment that, so it seemed, fitted Churchill and Churchill's authority perfectly into Conan Doyle's plans.

For the Congo Campaign was over—successful: "I do not think," said E.D. Morel, the professional agitator who had stirred up the whole Congo business in the beginning, "that any other man but Conan Doyle could have done for the cause just what Conan Doyle did at that time."

It was true. Almost single-handed, he had taken over, conducted, and finally won the Congo Campaign.

Now he had another, and much more important, Campaign waiting to be opened with all the traditional Doylean *brio*; a Campaign on behalf of, not abused Congolese Negroes this time, but on behalf of his own people; of Britain; of the Empire.

For the successful conduct of *this* Campaign, he needed a powerful friend both in the Government and at the Admiralty. In Churchill, so it seemed to the old Campaigner, he luckily had both....

One of the most honest of all Conan Doyle's autobiographical admissions he puts into the mouth of Sherlock Holmes: 'My mind is like a racing engine, tearing itself to pieces because it is not connected up with the work for which it was built.'

'My mind is like a racing engine....' For such human types, and for the never-to-be-tranquillized restlessness that must deny them even the possibility of repose, Aldous Huxley happily coined the description: 'adrenalin-addicts'—those who, if I may 'explain' Huxley, need the over-stimulus of (usually contrived) excitement in order to enjoy 'normal' peace of mind. These are what we may like to think of as the Red Queens of ordinary life: running twice as fast in order to stay in the same place....

To adapt an old phrase, had Worthy Causes not called Conan Doyle to vigorous supporting action, he would have invented those Worthy Causes. But let us not forget that, though he *needed* Causes (cricket, football, ski-ing, and other physical activities being insufficient to drain him of troublesome excess energy) the Causes that he did select to espouse were, by any standard, Worthy—and this newest of all his Campaigns would be for a Cause Worthiest of all.

This, of course, raises the matter of Conan Doyle's 'sincerity'. Granted that his *physical* make-up needed the perpetual stimulus of Activity-with-an-apparent-Purpose, one may justly ask the question: How 'sincere' was Conan Doyle in taking up and launching and throwing himself, 'heart and soul,' as they say, into any and all of his Causes? To be blunt: How genuine was the emotion behind all his impulses to Seek Justice, to Right Wrong, to Save from Peril...? Was that emotion always and purely the honest indignation that was, with his story-telling ability, the most notable legacy of his Irish blood?

My opinion...? My answer to these searching questions...?

I may say unequivocally that, in all his actions, Conan Doyle was never guilty of the least duplicity (save, as in the matter of his overlooking Churchill's 'apostasy', Conan Doyle could command a little prudence in a Good Cause); he truly felt the indignation that impelled him to take up arms on behalf of the Wronged. Over the spontaneous emotional reaction to the sight of, the awareness of, Injustice, he had no more conscious control than he had over his sympathetic nervous system. Indeed, it would hardly be an exaggeration to say that this instinctive response to the stimulus of Injustice-seen *was* a fully functioning aspect of that system. Injustice made his indignation froth up as the 'head' froths up in an Irishman's glass of Guinness's porter. He had simply no control over that frothing-up—and, more, it was so instinctive that he could never have exploited it to his own profit, as it came truly, not from his head but from his heart.

Self-advertising...? But what had he to do with publicity (in that respect, differing fundamentally from his fellow-Irishman, Bernard Shaw, not one of whose public statements was uttered without carefully-planned *arrière pensée*)? He did not need publicity. He had long enjoyed a fame which would have turned any less modest man's head. Comforting a gravely-wounded soldier in Langman's Hospital, during the South African War, Conan Doyle bent down to hear the man whisper: "I've read your books...."

No...Conan Doyle needed no publicity; but such publicity as he earned, he valued as help in his 'getting his Message across'.

Born in Scotland of Irish blood (on both sides), he could so easily have grown up, in a period when the English were disliked by the Scots and Irish more passionately than they are to-day, nursing a bitter hatred of England, and all that she stood for.

Rabid Irish and Scots Britain-haters must have considered Conan Doyle a 'traitor to his Blood', as others were classifying Churchill as a 'traitor to his Class'.

But Conan Doyle's loyalty was to Britain and her Empire; a loyalty that came from the heart; a loyalty without stint or limit. He knew the sort of romantic love of Britain—her Monarchy, her Institutions, her People, her vast Empire, her (to borrow a phrase from a future time) Manifest Destiny—which, in his day, was both popular and highly popularized. The British, then, were not only not ashamed of patriotism; they took a deep spiritual pride in their belonging to an Empire that covered a quarter of the world's land area (and, though this has been forgotten, a great deal more, by no ambiguous proclamation of ownership, of its sea-area as well). Aware of the very simple nature of his emotions, Conan Doyle was perfectly aware of the nature of his patriotism; aware, too, that it differed in no way from that of the Board-school children who, on Empire Day, mustered in the school-yard, to receive an orange, a paper bag of 'sweets' (candies), and a paper Union Flag to hold aloft while singing *Rule, Britannia!* and *God Save the King!* Except among the very Smartest of the Smart Set, this simple, unquestioning patriotic faith in the indisputable 'rightness' of Empire conditioned the thinking and feeling of every class of Society, from the very lowly to (perhaps all but) the very highest—and this was the faith that Conan Doyle unashamedly held and proclaimed. It was, in essence, no different from that simple, unquestioning patriotism implied and spelt-out that ran through the whole range of boys' magazines and adventure-books; magazines such as *The Captain, The Boy's Own Paper, The Boy's Friend Weekly*—all of which carried his writings—and the 'healthy' adventure stories of such popular authors as Percy F. Westerman, Captain R.E. Brereton, Herbert Strang, and, in his more juvenile moods, Rider Haggard.

The essence of this blind but, paradoxically, fully conscious acceptance of Patriotism, was perfectly caught, for Conan Doyle as for millions of others, in the words that A.C. Benson set to Edward Elgar's confidently triumphant music: *Land of Hope and Glory, Mother of the Free...Wider still and wider shall thy bounds be set; God, who made thee mighty, make thee mightier yet....*

And now that God-given might was threatened by the Enemy Without—and, he knew well, only Conan Doyle seemed to understand the danger. Only he could warn against the imminent and ever-pressing menace of German naval arming; only he fully understood the specifically anti-British threat of the Submarine. Only he had both the knowledge and the skills to awaken the Nation and those who governed it to a realization of the lowering peril; and to guide them out of peril's way, in arming them to combat it. So Conan Doyle, fired with Patriotism and alert to his beloved Britain's danger, flung himself, heart and soul, into the greatest Campaign of all....

———

The details of Conan Doyle's 'Wake up Britain!' Campaign must be so well known to anyone who has read one or more of the numerous biographies of the Great Campaigner that they need only to be touched on here in the most sketchy way.

With so many Campaigns behind him—all, be it noted, more successful than otherwise—Conan Doyle had come, by 1911, the year in which we may see his Campaign of Warning properly launched, to have evolved a pattern for any Campaign—and that begun in 1911 did not deviate in pattern from any of its successful predecessors. Once again came the familiar stages in the Campaign's unfolding: this particular Campaign opening with a 'powerful' article, 'Great Britain and the Next War', in the influential *Fortnightly Review*. Initiation of arguments and special-pleadings in the correspondence-columns of the more influential newspapers (beginning with *The Times*, of course) followed, and, of necessity, not this time a full-length book, but a long short-story in *The Strand Magazine*: 'Danger', in which Captain Sirius, commanding a flotilla of no more than eight submarines for a small country, 'Norland', makes Britain sue for peace. For, while the British Grand Fleet is completely destroying 'Norland's' fleet at its base, Sirius, ignoring any British man-o'-war, is torpedoing the merchant-ships that are bringing vital food-supplies to Britain.

That such prescience on Conan Doyle's part set him aside as a man of super-human vision will undoubtedly be agreed by any who were in submarine-beleagured Britain during two World Wars—and this prescience was acknowledged at its true value, and warmly praised, but not, alas!, by the British, least of all by those British at (as they used to say) 'the helm of the Ship of State'. This was how his full meed of praise came to Conan Doyle....

On 1st May, 1916—the year in which Britain was nearly starved out by her losses at sea—a special meeting, to discuss naval strategy, was called. The meeting, in the Reichstag, was addressed by Admiral Capelle, Secretary of the Imperial German Navy, and this is what Admiral Capelle said of the author of 'Danger!' and his ideas:

> "Admiral Gelster [of the German Navy] is generally accredited as the inventor of submarine warfare. *He never mentioned it.* The real and only prophet was Sir Arthur Conan Doyle."

The United States was not then at war with Germany, and Capelle's 'tribute' to the far-sighted and imaginative Briton was printed in *The New York Times*. Obviously, this unsought and embarrassing praise from the Enemy called for some comment from Sir Arthur. He called a press-conference, at which he said:

> "I need hardly say that it is very painful to me to think that anything I have written should be turned against my country. The object of

the story[4] was to warn the public of a possible danger which I saw over-hanging this country, and to shew it how to avoid that danger.''

It says much for Conan Doyle's self-control that he did not use this occasion to denounce the politicians, admirals, and generals who (unlike the Germans) refused to be alerted by his warnings; who, despite those warnings loud and clear, had sown the Wind Willful of Deafness, only (as in the natural order of things) to reap the Whirlwind of National Near-disaster....

———

But then, the rôle of a Cassandra is not, and never was, a popular one——and Cassandra, in the person of even so well- liked and well-listened-to a character as Conan Doyle, was no more popular than had been any of the numerous Warners-of-Doom who had preceded him.

For the Menace-of-the-Submarine Campaign was different from all his previous Campaigns in that it was not being conducted to achieve belated justice for this unjustly-convicted person (Edalji) or traduced body of men (the British South African Army) or en-slaved and tortured native population (in Brazil and in the Congo). It was—for the first time in Conan Doyle's Campaigning— a Warning...real enough, and justified enough, to the Campaigner, but (and here let us adopt the most practical point-of-view) a warning against a hypothetical danger, *possibly* to manifest itself in a war not yet declared and, in the opinion of the majority, unlikely ever to happen.

Besides: to whom was Conan Doyle addressing the warning...? All such warnings (and Churchill himself was to succeed Conan Doyle as a warner of the world against the Nazi menace in and throughout the decade following Conan Doyle's death) are sup-posed to be addressed to *a nation*—but this is mere brainless con-vention: no *people*, as such, ever had either the money or the power

---

[4] I.e. 'Danger!' Like Poe, Conan Doyle often indulged in somewhat juvenile puns, for his own enjoyment, not to be shared with the reader. It is possible to explain the odd name of 'Sirius' thus. *Sirius* is the Dog-star, and it is perfectly possible to re-spell 'Dog-star' as 'Dogs' Tar'—a sailor in the service of the German *Schweinhunden*.

to change the colour of a postage-stamp, let alone do what Conan Doyle was, supposedly, asking the British to do: *do* something to combat the menace of the German submarines....

Well, obviously, the British people, even were they to heed the warning—to take the threat to heart—were powerless to take effective measures to protect themselves. So that left those who had the money, the power, and—if they chose to exercise it—the will to take up the challenge of the German submarines, and to effect, if that would be possible, an adequate defence.

To a politician—any politician, of whatever race, colour, period of history; of a powerful empire or a tin-pot principality or banana-republic at the back-of-Nowhere—*all* criticism is hostile criticism, and *all* politicians respond to all criticism in exactly the same way: by seeking (as the saying goes now) to 'pull the rug' from under the Critic; to-day there are many ways of doing this effectively—demonstrate that his criticism is ill-judged and without validity; that he is urging measures of national protection that have already been considered (without *his* help!; without *his* advice!) and already put in hand. The opinion of the Amateur is *not*—and never was—welcome by those who, by one seedy ploy or another, have raised themselves, in the social pecking-order, above the citizen with no more 'right' to suggest reform—much less to direct affairs—than his standing as a taxpayer gives him.

The *practical* result of Conan Doyle's Submarine Warning Campaign was this:

1 As regards the Public, the Warning affected them, to use a homely saying, 'like water on a duck's back'. The consciousness of its having no power to effect changes, reforms, last-minute remedies is not altogether distasteful to the Public, whose complacency and trust that others will provide the needed last-minute remedy has always been pretty hard to shake.

2 As regards the Government, and particularly the Admiralty—but, in practical terms, the Establishment generally—all that Conan Doyle achieved was to raise a

bumper crop of powerful enemies, all well-entrenched socially and quite invulnerable in important official positions. Against his one Service supporter, Admiral Sir Percy Scott (not altogether socially acceptable, with brother who was a female-impersonating music-hall comedian), Conan Doyle found himself mocked and reproached by the most formidable array of Service chiefs who ever ganged up to put an insolently presumptuous civilian in his place. These admirals' opinions make interesting (and, since we are now on the verge of a suicidal World War, terrifying reading). "Stuff and nonsense...sort of thing you get in Jules Verne," said Admiral Sir Compton Domville; "We can rely completely on our warships' powers of resistance", was how Admiral Henderson expressed himself. As Conan Doyle had done, most of his critics had expressed *their* views in the newspapers. "Having already expressed my opinion in *The Times*,," said Admiral Sir William Kennedy, "I can only repeat what I then said, that as 'God made us an island, by all means let us remain so"—the Admiral here putting paid to *two* of Conan Doyle's urgings: that Britain arm herself against the German submarine menace and that Britain should join with France in building, as soon as possible, the often-postponed Channel Tunnel. Admiral Fitzgerald's opinion was confined to his examining Conan Doyle's fear that the Germans might (for that, read 'would') attempt to starve Britain out with submarine attacks on food-ships. As the Admiral's opinion was, by a long shot, the most fatuous of all, it deserves to be quoted last. Asked if *he* thought that the Germans (not yet, though soon to be, 'Huns') would torpedo our food-ships, the bluff old sea-dog declared roundly: "No, I don't. I have," said Admiral Fitzgerald emphatically, "*every* confidence in the Germans' sense of 'fair play'."

So that Conan Doyle's views were left with, in Britain, only two supporters of any social weight: one, a civilian: Sir Douglas Owen, of the London School of Economics, an institution founded by a German academic, and itself already beginning to be suspect of 'pro-German sentiments'; the other, the afore-mentioned Sir Percy

Scott, an admiral truly enough, but with an image slightly tarnished by his having a popular transvestite comedian as a brother. Not much support there.... But, as Pierre Nordon points out in his excellent *Conan Doyle*, the British Government was too much concerned with the violent activities of the Suffragettes and the struggle between the Commons and the Lords (Monsieur Nordon might have added 'and the threat of armed rebellion in Ulster') to pay all *that* attention to a *possible* Submarine Menace.

In all this, what was Churchill, now already three years in political authority over all those anti-Doyle admirals, doing in the face of what he, at least, recognized as the possibility of war with Germany?

In respect of the German submarine fleet...we shall see. In respect of the German surface fleet, Churchill, as the record plainly shews, did quite a lot. With the war-clouds gathering over Europe, he ordered the Grand Fleet, which had assembled for the annual Review at Spithead in July, not to disperse, and, further, had ordered a test mobilization of the entire Royal Navy. That war was imminent, Churchill, at least, began to fear. Now we must see what he did to prepare defences against a possible deployment of the impressively powerful German *Unterseeboot* flotillas.

In view of the immediate and tragic confirmation of Conan Doyle's fears—in the month following the outbreak of war on 4th August, 1914, Captain Weddigen, commanding the German submarine U9, sank no fewer than three British battle-cruisers, *Aboukir*, *Cressy*, and *Hogue*, all on the same day—it must not be thought that Churchill had prepared no counter-measures against the threat of enemy submarines.

He had. But he had not turned to his friend, Conan Doyle, for advice. He had, on the contrary, enthusiastically welcomed the plan brought to him by a naval officer on the retired list: Admiral Sir Frederick Inglefield, whose wife was one of Queen Alexandra's ladies-in-waiting, but who was otherwise in no way distinguishable from any of the many other peace-time admirals who were fretting out the boredom of their enforced retirement and wondering whether or not this new war might give them a chance of re-employment.

It was in such a hope that Admiral Inglefield took his 'brain-child' to the First Lord of the Admiralty. It is well known that

Churchill, like the Mountbatten of the second World War, was always attracted to bold—indeed, what are now colloquially called 'way-out'—ideas; the bolder, the more way-out, the more attractive did Churchill find them. And certainly, in Admiral Inglefield's plan, those eminently desirable qualities of boldness and way-outness were evident as never before in any plan submitted to a First Lord of the Admiralty. What the historian finds hard to reconcile is the apparent (to put it mildly) near-lunatic proposition of Sir Frederick's with the (I am sure, correct) image of the Admiral: a conventional Naval officer, reared in the old tradition of the Service, and conducting himself in every aspect of his private and public life, with the most gentlemanly decorum. Yet, to read the details of what he proposed to Churchill—and, more incredibly, what Churchill enthusiastically accepted—is like seeing, converted into print, the wilder imaginings of what, in Britain, is called 'a Heath Robinson contraption', and, in America, 'a Rube Goldberg gizmo'. But before I go on to describe the Inglefield Plan—actually, it combined two separate means of combatting the Submarine Menace; each 'guaranteed totally effective'—I must explain British Admiralty 'thinking' on the German naval arm: surface ships and underwater craft. Axiom No. One: the Germans *must* come through the English Channel. Like the rules of Fair Play that, in Admiral Fitzgerald's 'confident opinion', we might confidently expect the Germans to observe, the Admiralty might confidently expect the Germans to choose and to stick to the Channel Route—the 'normal, natural route'. So that all effort was put into the strengthening of the Channel Defences—which, of course, didn't prevent the Germans' sinking HMS *Formidable* off Plymouth. The route to the Atlantic across the north of Scotland, and from there, into the Irish Sea and St George's Channel, up which, on their way to Bristol and Liverpool, the majority of the supply-ships might be expected to come, was quite undefended as Britain entered into the war. Only after the vulnerability of the waters dividing Ireland from England had been dimly recognized by the Laputan strategists of Admiralty House were measures taken for blocking the vital sea- route to the German submarines. Among the more curious of the curiosities of our national history are the measures which were hastily taken, when, at long last, the possibilities of the submarine Menace—not so much the possibilities, as *certainties*, that Conan Doyle had been thundering into wilfully deaf ears for the past three years—penetrated the dense minds of our Naval High Command.

Obviously a matter of calling for volunteers!—and so the call went out for any who had some sort of sea-going craft to report in, and mount watch over the Western Approaches. The call brought in some seven thousand boat-owners: craft ranging in type from rowing-boats (by far the most numerous) to sailing craft and motorboats—though only seven of these last. Where the owners had firearms—revolvers, rifles, or shotguns—they were asked to take them on sea-patrol—though not all the boats had armed owners. And one craft in eighty-five carried wireless. Such was the ramshckle 'fleet' organized to deal with any German submarines that might seek to penetrate the Western Approaches.

Certain aspects of the Inglefield Plan remain so far secret. Where, for instance, did the retired Admiral meet Churchill? I like to think that it must have been in the Grill Room of the Carlton Hotel (then only twenty years old), one of the most enchanting restaurants that I have ever seen. It was a favourite with the senior staff of the Admiralty, the offices of which, across Pall Mall and around the corner to Whitehall, were a mere five minutes' walk distant. And I should like to know whether or not Conan Doyle had been invited to the luncheon. And, if not, at which point in this Gilbertian episode—during or afterwards—the Prophet of the Submarine Menace *was* told....

For this, in all its (and to Churchill, most persuasive) lunacy, was the double-faceted Inglefield Plan.

First Part: to remedy the shortage of weapons in the 7,000-strong rowing-sailing-motor-boat armada, each owner was to be provided with:

1 A black cloth hood, fitted with a draw-string;
2 A heavy hammer. And a trained swimmer.

To use:

1 On sighting the periscope of a submarine, as it is surfacing, let the swimmer make for the periscope as quickly as oars, sail, or motor will permit. The swimmer will then:

2 Slip the black hood over the eye-piece of the periscope, and pull the draw-string tight.

3 Using the heavy hammer, he will then SMASH the lens of the periscope.

4 The submarine, blinded, will now be powerless, and will continue to surface, to be easily captured by the two men.

The intelligent commander always provides himself with the insurance of an alternative strategy, even when the first is, as here, 'absolutely fool-proof'. So here, Admiral Inglefield was ready with his alternative; though the preparations for launching this half of the Plan would be more complex than in the swimmer, hood-and-hammer attack. The details of the second-half were as follows:

1 Over a suitable stretch of muddy shore, near Poole Harbour, put out-of-bounds to all but 'authorized personnel', and so richly provided with armed guards—all of course, under the undisputed authority of Admiral Inglefield, happily back in the Navy after all—dummy periscopes would be set up in the mud. This would be vital Stage One.

2 Stage One completed, and a good half-mile of British muddy foreshore now bristling with specially manufactured dummy periscopes, Stage Two was ready to be introduced into this anti-German Master Plan.

3 Stage Two involved the training of Patriotic sea-gulls to:
a. recognize a submarine's periscope, on the surfacing of the vessel;
b. learn to distinguish between British and German periscopes;
c. learn immediately to defecate on the latter, so blinding the vessel, and forcing it to surface and be 'easily' captured.

It is unnecessary to point out that the British gulls needed no training in defecation: Nature had made all adequate arrangement in that respect. All that the birds required was a crash-tutorial in the twin arts of recognizing specifically German subs, and letting fly at their periscopes, the birds' training-school being the half-mile of dummy periscopes planted by Admiral Inglefield's men in the muddy foreshore.

———

Among the most despised of clichés is the statement that 'the mind boggles'; but what could any mind, considering that Mad Hatter's luncheon-party in the Carlton Grill, do but 'boggle'? At which point in the Admiral's unfolding of his Double-plan did the euphoria of taxpayer-provided Champagne merge inevitably into the euphoria of the dream of Total Victory...?

Why...how...we may never know; but it is the fact that Churchill did pass the Admiral's double-plan; that the periscopes were ordered and planted in the mud, and that the task of educating the defecating seagulls was undertaken.

Of course, it is not to be thought that Churchill, even taking the Champagne into account, gave the 'go ahead!' to Sir Frederick without having made some reasonable enquiries, to clarify certain obscurities; to set the First Lord's mind completely at rest.

Assuming (as, indeed, I must assume) that the Ornithological Plan was presented and passed in the fantasy-encouraging luxury of the Carlton Grill,[5] it is not difficult to imagine the sort of questions with which Churchill, cigar in mouth, got the sort of answers that set his mind at rest.

"One thing, Admiral, I'm not *quite* happy about...."

"Oh yes, sir? And what's that...?"

"These seagulls of yours.... You say that they really can be trained to...well...let fly at a real periscope, after initial recruit-training on your dummy ones...?"

"Not a doubt of it, sir. We have the trainer all ready to start the training. Yes, sir: you may have heard of him.... Seen his act? Professor Colombino, he calls himself. That's his stage-name, of course. In real life, he's a Cecil Mapgood, from...er...Brixton, I

———

[5]No author, out of his own delighted experience, has drawn so nostalgically enchanting a picture of the Carlton Grill (1897–1941) as the late E. Phillips Oppenheim has done in *The Great Impersonation*. (A wonderful book in its own right, by the way, even had the London scenes not opened in the Carlton Grill.)

think. But my men have vetted him properly. He's British, and very partiotic...."

"What makes him an expert in training seagulls to...well: training seagulls...?"

"His Music-hall act, sir. He has a dozen trained doves; trained to pick out fortune-telling cards on the word of command. If he can train doves (very difficult creatures to train, I'm told)...."

"Precisely. But, Admiral, here's what I'd like to know. How may we be *sure* that...well...that these trained gulls will let fly only at *Their* periscopes, and not at *ours*...?"

Firm, clear, utterly confident, must have come the convincing answer: "Sir...these are *British* gulls...!"

———

There is no record, in the German naval records of the first World War, that any of the Imperial submarines ever echoed to the panic-cry of a sailor on watch at the periscope: "Achtung! Achtung, Herr Kapitän! Der verflugte engländer Kriegsvogel auf unser *Periskop* gescheissen hat!", nor that the commander of any German submarine was ever forced to say, in accents of despair: "The devilish cunning of this damned English admiral has rendered our periscope useless. I regret that there is but one course open to me: to surface and surrender to the British!" There is nothing at all like that, and did Admiral Inglefield and Winston Churchill, one wonders, think that there might ever be...?

But Churchill *did* give official approval to both parts of the Admiral's scheme, particularly that part that related to the patriotically controlled defecation of the sea-birds. (And after all, with all those trained doves, telling fortunes as popular Music-hall 'turns', was it beyond reason that seagulls might be trained to fight for Britain...?)

———

At which stage of this bizarre historical episode, Conan Doyle was made aware that Admiral Inglefield's ideas had been preferred to his own, we do not know. But the significance of the choice would not have been lost on Conan Doyle.

Winston Churchill had not been among those who, in the correspondence-columns of the newspapers or in Parliamentary utterances, had denounced the 'amateur's interference' of Conan
Doyle, but in this matter of The Politician, the Periscope, and the
Trained Seagulls, made it clear to the one man who would understand, first, that Churchill had resented, even more than any
of his admirals, Conan Doyle's impudent attempt to 'teach his
grandmother to suck eggs', and, second, that, in this 'officially'
preferring Inglefield's obviously insane scheme, Churchill wished
Conan Doyle to know how intentional was the master-snub that
Winston was administering. To use a modern colloquial phrase,
Conan Doyle, Arch-patriot, certainly 'got the message'—a message
which was still rankling when, in early 1927, Churchill, 'in retirement', was giving (and leaving out the seagulls) a more than col-
ourful version of recent history in *The World Crisis*, and reminded
Conan Doyle of what he had done in 1914.

As a student of Poe (see *The Cask of Amontillado*) Conan Doyle
had never let Churchill know how much 'Winnie' had hurt and
offended him. The men still exchanged courteous, even 'friendly',
letters—Conan Doyle, in 1916, was giving Churchill 'ideas' on the
Tank—but what Conan Doyle really felt about Churchill's 'monumental' snub has been buried, so far, in that cryptic reference to
'The Politician, the Lighthouse, and the Trained Cormorant' here
decyphered and explained for the first time.

Postscript

To take any account of the feelings of others is seriously to jeop-
ardize any promising political career, and no politician worth his
salt will ever make the mistake of caring tuppence about another's
feelings. Certainly Churchill never made that grave political mistake.

General Sir Alan Brooke had been promised by Churchill that
he would command the Invasion force planned to re-enter Occupied Europe. Roosevelt asked that an American be appointed instead—and Churchill immediately acquiesced.

Here is how Brooke remembers it:

I remember it as if it was yesterday as we walked up and down on the terrace...looking down on that wonderful view of the St Lawrence River and the fateful scene of Wolfe's battle for the Heights of Quebec. As Winston spoke, all that scenery was swamped by a dark cloud of despair....

Not for one moment did he realize what this meant to me. He offered no sympathy, no regrets at having had to change his mind, and dealt with the matter as if it were one of minor importance.

As, indeed, it was...to Churchill.

All things considered, I think that we may well take the view that Conan Doyle was lucky in that he suffered no more than as the victim of a calculated, well-planned snub.

MANY-SUITED SHERLOCK

But where did he stow that extensive wardrobe...?

I have known many people with extensive—some with *very* extensive—wardrobes; not all of them rich or even more than moderately well-to-do. These latter are the accumulators; those who never get rid of any article of clothing; those who 'hang on' to an old suit out of which they have grown ('You'll never see quality like this again.... You couldn't even *get* quality like this any more.'), but hesitate to throw it out, and decide to retain it in the hope—not *always* unjustified—that their body-weight will slim down to more youthful dimensions and that they will once again be able to wear the old but still 'presentable' garment.

I began this chapter with the intention of considering the extensive wardrobe of Mr Sherlock Holmes: its origin, its purpose, its cost—but I find, to my astonishment, that I have, quite unconsciously, been developing a talent for the assessing of a wardrobe's meaning; and this talent, of course, implies that I have succeeded in 'breaking down', in analysing and classifying, the various causes that generate the extensive, as distinguished from the normally adequate, wardrobe. Naturally, the classes into which the wardrobe-extensifying (if the reader will excuse the neologism) may be divided, are, like all other classes, almost infinitely divisible and sub-divisible. But the main, the master, classes—the heads under which all over-large wardrobes may be classified—are surprisingly few, and there is no need to split hairs (or woollen fibres) in subdividing those classes. The main classes—that is to say, the reasons, the causes, behind an abnormal accumulation of clothing—are these:

1 Plain *need*;
2 Vanity;
3 Belief that clothes will 'come in useful';
4 The 'Miser'—or 'Jackdaw'—complex: reluctance to part with anything once acquired, useful or not.

Of course, it will be instantly obvious to the reader that this classification is amenable to sub-division; for instance, clothes acquired under Head 1—'Plain need'—may, classifiably, 'stray' into other classifications. Even where clothes are acquired from plain necessity, their choice may reflect the vanity of the chooser, and the clothes may well be kept from motives neither of need nor of vanity.

Twenty years or so after World War II, I saw much of the late Lord Mountbatten, who had been Chief of Combined Operations in that war, and was now, when I was in frequent consultation with him, still directing the Ministry of Defence. One morning, when he was ill with influenza, I had occasion to talk with him in his bedroom, when he was still living in the Wilton-place house.

Now here was a man who—professionally—needed the largest of wardrobes, and I had a hint of the extensive range of that wardrobe from that single visit to his bedroom.

Always a practical man, Mountbatten had solved the small but irritating problem of achieving the quickest and easiest access to his necessary clothing. A very heavy arm of wood, at least three inches square by a good yard long, had been set securely in the wall by the wide clothes-cupboard, and from this heavy wooden arm, on an ingenious system of hooks, hung the heavy, gold-encrusted uniforms to which he was entitled, and that it was often his duty to wear: the full-dress uniforms of Admiral of the Fleet, General and Air-marshal—they made a brave show, and perhaps not so brave a show as did the scarlet uniform—its gleaming breast- and back-plates hung separately—of his recent appointment as

Honorary Colonel (the Queen being Colonel-in-Chief) of the Royal Horse Guards. These, and all the other clothes—the 'undress' uniforms, and all the formal and informal clothing needs of a more-than-ordinarily-busy social life—had been, no matter their superior and expensive character, assembled under Head 1 ('Plain need'), but it would have been a very short-sighted observer who, after only a few minutes of Mountbatten's delightful company, would have failed to give his extensive wardrobe a secondary classification under Head 2. It may, indeed, be more realistic to concede that even where Plain Need is the prime-mover in garnering up any superfluity (superfluous, that is, to normality, but not, of course, to Plain Need) of costumes, Vanity so often does enter into the choices imposed by inescapable Need that one might be tempted to bracket Heads 1 and 2 as a single classification, save that experience shews us that, however rarely, some with the need for an extensive wardrobe do, in fact, choose all without Vanity's having the slightest influence in the selection.

I think that I may venture to affirm, from all that I have seen and read of Mr Holmes, that his wardrobe grew, piece by essential piece from the scantily indispensable kit of an impecunious paramedical student to the super-extensive wardrobe of his established Baker-street practice always by deliberate Need-imposed choice— and that Vanity entered into that continuous wardrobe-expansion not at all.

And now let us see of what that extensive wardrobe *must* have been composed; where Mr Holmes acquired all his most necessary garments; *why* he had to acquire them; and what he paid for them in an age when clothes were inexpensive as never before or never since, and where the utmost value was given for every penny spent.

———

The point in time when one should examine Mr Holmes's wardrobe is obviously that to which nearly twenty years of dedication to his unique craft had brought him; when he had achieved a social position of unchallenged distinction; and when his wardrobe may be assumed to have attained its maximum variety and extent—the year, 1895.

By this year, Mr Holmes, if he had not already acquired all that he would need in the way of formal and informal dress—and note that both had to include clothing in widely differing states of 'presentability'—remember the 'seedy frock-coat' of the pretended old bookseller in *The Final Problem*? Certainly not the garment that Mr Holmes would ordinarily wear to, for instance, call on Lord Holdhurst at the Foreign Office. And do not forget that, in that *very* formal age, when Mr Holmes was shocked in noticing that his lordship's boots *had been repaired*, Mr Holmes and his companion would not have thought of walking down Whitehall, let alone entering the doors of the 'F.O.' in any costume but that ordained by unwritten law for the socially-educated male. A certain latitude might be—and, indeed, was—permitted in the matter of neckwear: a collar might be of the 'stand-up' or 'drainpipe', 'wing' or 'Eton' (turned down) variety, and the necktie be a 'four-in-hand', 'sailor's knot', 'Ascot' or 'butterfly'—but the linen visible had to be of unadorned white, starched and spotless (coloured shirts were for low-life cads only)—the breast or 'plastron' of the shirt being always stiffly starched. A waistcoat ('vest', only in the trade-jargon of tailors) was *de rigueur*, as was the gold albert that, slung between the lower two waistcoat pockets, joined the gold pocket-watch at one end of the chain to (usually) a gold vesta-box at the other. Gloves, of tan, canary, or lavender kid, were indispensable, and no man would be seen without a (generally silver- or gold-topped ebony) walking-stick and a well-brushed silk hat ('topper'). Either a frock-coat of 'superfine' black broadcloth or grey worsted—the former worn with worsted striped or 'sponge-bag' trousers; the latter with trousers of the same material as the frock-coat; either that or a morning-coat, of the same materials—and both frock-coat and morning-coat had black or grey satin revers. By 1895, the frock-coat was giving place, with the younger man, to the morning-coat, which, being 'cut away' (in America, it is called a 'Prince Albert'), gave more ease of movement to the legs. Spats, of drab hopsack or melton- cloth, or of white piqué linen, were 'optional', though most men wore them. Many are the thousands who, over nearly a century, have observed that Mr Holmes and Dr Watson, as they walk through the Regent-street Quadrant, furtively observed from his hansom by the disguised Stapleton, are not wearing spats.

Formality was not exclusive to the 'toff' or to those who dressed in a toffish manner; there were formalities, no less, in a working-man's 'clobber', as Mr Holmes would have known when he had to adopt the character, with the clothes, of a member of the la-bouring-classes. Take, for instance, the well-known illustration of Mr Holmes in the assumed *persona* of 'a drunken-looking groom' with tilted grey billycock hat, shabby jacket and waistcoat, and creased corduroy trousers. The costume is perfectly correct for the part chosen; but replace the billycock with a shabby cloth cap, tie the muffler (at the throat) in a distinctively different fashion, and put two thin leather straps around the trouser-legs just under the knees—a *sine qua non* of all men who worked among rats—and Mr Holmes would have looked, not like a groom, but like a common labouring-man who gained his few shillings a-week digging up the roads—that strip of leather belted under the knee would indicate, in the rigid sartorial code governing *all* classes in that most formal of all times, how the man gained his bread. That strip of leather made it clear that he was a 'navvy'; the additional marks of iden-tification: the heavy leather belt around his waist; the 'belcher' handkerchief of polka-dotted cotton in either red or blue encircling his neck—all these were superfluous in marking the man as a 'navvy': the under-knee strip of leather was sufficient. All these (to us, subtle; to the Victorians, so obvious as not needing mention) differences in the *details* of dress, would have been known to Mr Holmes; some as the result of his keen powers of observation; others—and these, almost certainly the major part—as known merely from that habit of taking the ordinary for granted that comes with the simple act of living and mixing with our contemporaries.

Certain styles of dress, then as now, might 'overlap'. We have the picture of Mr Holmes in the character of 'a common loafer'—that is, a man of accepted unemployment or unemployability, in the days before 'the dole' took him off the streets and into the pubs. Such men were accepted in Victorian society as members of a vast pool of available casual labour; men always 'there' and always willing to do some small job, such as 'helping' with the luggage or some such task, for the few pence that the momentary assistance would bring. Note, too, that the 'loafer' was regarded by neither the Public nor the Police, as a member of the criminal class; not even—and this is socially of the very greatest importance—of a class meriting pity. The loafer's wife was usually the breadwinner—earning twopence to threepence an hour as 'charwoman' ('scrub-woman' in America), washerwoman or whitener-of-steps, an essential in houses of *all* social classes in those self-consciously house-proud days. Days, if the reader will recall, when the struggling young physician, Dr Conan Doyle, waited until full night, to creep out—because he could not afford even the few pence for a char-woman—to polish the brass-plate (or 'shingle') identifying his modest 'villa' as the residence-surgery of a doctor. It was essential that his brass-plate be brightly polished, and though the many biographies of Conan Doyle do not specify this, the front-door step must have been whitened with holystone as well: such careful guarding the domestic decencies was not a mere (perhaps too often grudged) concession to 'what was done'; I have heard the sincere expression of opinion on Victorian lips that such rigid obediences to the strict canons of social behaviour were thought of as 'what we owed ourselves'—and the often minute differences in dress or the arrangement of dress are referable to this consciousness, never more acute than in Victorian times, of 'doing what was the laid-down rule'. Dress and manners, clothes and deportment, were indivisible. My Father carried a joking remark over from his late-Victorian youth; a remark that, though couched in flippant terms, yet strikingly deomonstrates the firm conviction of our grandfathers that the inward and outward man were inseparable: "Attitude," my Father repeated, "is the Art of Artillery; and whiskers make the Man."

How much, in the hands of a master of disguise (which also implies a mastery of deportment, of physico-psychic attitude) may be achieved by the slightest adjustments of clothes and body ('stance', the Victorians called it generally—a term now restricted to Golf). I call the reader's attention to the two pictures of Mr Holmes, the first as a 'drunken-looking groom'; the second as 'a common loafer', asking the reader to pay particular attention, not to the significantly contrasted 'stance' of each, but, here, to the clothing of each assumed *persona*. What did Mr Holmes's 'other wardrobe' contribute to each which was common to both? The answer is : Very little. But there is one garment, essential to all Victorian males of *every* class, that both share: the waistcoat—in their cases, well-worn and unpressed. A casual observer might also claim the common use of the neckcloth—but Mr Holmes's keen eye, which could mark the many variations of tobacco-ash, tattoo-marks, and the impressions of bicycle-tyres (to name but three objects of his special study), would not have failed to note the occupation-indicating, social-standing-indicating, choice and arrangement of necktie or neckcloth. Observe the differences! The 'groom' is wearing his white neckcloth in an 'Ascot turn-over', secured by a scarf-pin; the Cockney 'loafer' (I shall explain why he is a Cockney) is wearing his coloured—probably in a many-tinted 'Paisley' pattern—in a manner invariably adopted by the Cockney, whether loafer or costermonger (the difference between employed and unemployed Cockneydom). The neckcloth, always a large one, was rolled up into a long, narrow 'snake', and tied with care into a reef-knot, the two 'trailing edges' of the neckcloth being pulled tightly across the wearer's chest, and tucked firmly into the man's braces (American 'suspenders').

It is, to one who remembers these distinctive social types, easy to see that 'the common loafer' is a Cockney, albeit an unemployed and unsuccessful one. As with the man in the music-hall song of just after the first World War, who 'wears a dustman's trahziz (trousers)…and wears a dustman's 'at; an' 'e speaks a dustman's language…so wot do yer fink o' *that*!' Mr Holmes's 'common loafer' certainly 'wears a Cockney's trousers, and wears a Cockney's hat', though it is, to those who remember such things, as much the bodily posture of the 'loafer' as his clothing stamps him as a veritable Cockney, from London's eastern parts. Then, too, there is his habit of fastening the top-button of his jacket, together with his habit of putting (keeping, rather) his hands in his trouser-pockets to pull the two halves of his short jacket tightly away from that top button. He certainly wears a Cockney's hat: a cloth cap, with a small peak, and adorned with a top-knot, or 'pom-pom'. That this cleverly fabricated (in Mr Holmes's workshop) character 'spoke a Cockney's language', we may take for granted: in matters of disguise, it was perfection or nothing with Mr Holmes.

And still on the subject of the groom, note how carefully Mr Holmes has given him a character instantly recognizable—and given it in a manner that combines both clothing *and* the character-revealing mode of wearing it: the loose riding-jacket carelessly (almost arrogantly) open; the carelessly (or insolently?) tilted grey billycock; the defiant clay pipe (price: two for three-halfpence—two for three US cents); above all, the be-damned-to-you self-buttonholing of the far too self-confident pothouse know-all; ready, indeed, eager, to give an opinion on anything, from what went wrong at Khartoum to the chances of Nunthorpe, Colonel North's horse, to win the Jubilee Stakes. What masterpieces, not merely of disguise, but of characterization, these personifications of Mr Holmes's truly were!

The Victorian significance of neckwear is again noticeable in Mr Holmes's choice of impersonations—I refer to his 'taking- off' (as the old colloquial phrase went) 'a simple-minded clergyman'. Now, the text gives us no indication of the 'clergyman's' religious affiliation—but his neckwear; the (fortunate for us!) illustration has much to tell us. In the first place, he is not a beneficed clergyman of the Church of England ('clerk in Holy Orders', as the formal description has it): a clergyman of the Established Church would have worn a white starched linen collar that fastened at the back of the neck (a 'dog-collar'), obtainable—though I am not yet ready to discuss prices—at, for instance, Harrod's Stores, in the Brompton-road, at ten shillings ($2.40) the dozen. The 'simple-minded clergyman' wears no such definitive mark of the Church of England parson; instead, he wears a turned-down ('Come to Jesus') collar—'The New Shakespeare', in the Harrod's catalogue of 1895, at 5/6 ($1.32) a dozen. The wearer of this type of collar, with the white linen bow-tie and the shabby black 'wideawake' hat, mark him as a Nonconformist minister, one of that vast alternative-to-Establishment religion of Victorian England generically known as 'Chapel'. Observe the skill—and the simplicity—with which Mr Holmes gets his effects. In this case, the turned-down collar would not have been sufficient to identify the character as that of a Nonconformist clergyman—after all, Mr Holmes himself had a liking for turned-down starched white-linen collars, as may be seen from the illustrations to such cases as *The Norwood Builder, The Solitary Cyclist, The Man with the Twisted Lip, A Scandal in Bohemia, The Hound of the*

Baskervilles, and many another case; in this last-named case, he even wears a 'New Shakespeare' and tucked-under black bow-tie with the *de rigueur* Town costume of satin-faced frock-coat and gleaming silk hat as he walks down Regent-street with a morning-coated Dr Watson. No: a turned-down collar would have been insufficient for the impersonation of a 'simple-minded' Nonconformist clergyman, and even turned-down collar *and* white tie would not have settled the matter definitely, since Professor Huxley and some other eminent Victorians preferred their cravats white, during the day as well as at night. But to bring together turned-down collar, white cravat *and* shabby black wideawake—with these three simple elements, Mr Holmes has achieved yet another of his miracles of characterization. (The steel spectacles, not absolutely essential to the perfect representation of the clergyman, but welcome as 'the nice finishing touch', cost no more than one shilling—24 cents.)

The contrast between the carefree simple-mindedness of the Nonconformist clergyman and the 'decrepit' Italian Roman Catholic priest is one far beyond any consideration of doctrinal differences. Here the contrast between the happy-go-lucky Protestant and the careworn old Romanist *seems* to have been achieved by methods less subtle than those by which Mr Holmes's normal *persona* was so convincingly transformed into that of the Nonconformist minister. I can hear many a reader agreeing that the impersonation of the priest called for no great subtlety of disguise; that, with a 'Roman' collar ('The London', No. 16 in the Harrod catalogue; price ten shillings or $2.40 the dozen), a dusty soutane, and the wideawake of the Nonconformist given a slight but most significant alteration from Free Church insouciance...Who, the underestimators of Mr Holmes's skill may well ask, would mistake the old gentleman for anything other than a Roman priest of foreign extraction? (In this essay, I shall not deal with the masterly disguise-essential of facial change independent of false whiskers, skin-dye, and the rest—a supreme talent that he shared with his famous French predecessor, François Vidocq, nor—though I should greatly enjoy doing so—reflect on the dozens of different accents and turns of speech that all these disguises made mandatory. Here I am concerned only with the variety, many purposes, and cost of Mr Holmes's most extensive wardrobe.)

———

We come now, not to the *cost* (which will be examined later), but to the probable *extent* of a wardrobe comprising not only all the garments for indoor and outdoor wear normally needed by any middle-class professional man, but also the very many changes of new, newish, worn, and simply downright ragged; rendered indispensable by the need to disguise himself as anything and everything from the 'unshaven French *ouvrier*' of *Lady Frances Carfax,* to the 'old sea-captain' of *The Sign of Four*; from the 'living-rough' Dartmoor hut-dweller of *The Hound of the Baskervilles* to the 'old man...very thin, very wrinkled, bent with age', whose presence in *The Bar of Gold* opium-den so startled poor Watson.

The second-hand, worn-shabby, and some necessarily worn-out clothing, Mr Holmes could easily have bought, for sums to be counted in shillings (US 'quarters'), rather than pounds, in such places hidden away within the West End of London as Monmouth-street, St Giles—one of the streets of 'Seven Dials'—or any of the back-streets of Clare Market; or in the second-hand-clothing shops of Newport-passage, Charing-cross-road (one or two still open for business, but now dealing in pounds, rather than shillings!); or in Leather-lane, then at the back of Furnival's-inn, where Dickens started his married life, and now, in 1895, due to be replaced by the huge and monstrously ugly head-office of the Prudential Assurance Company, a still-standing offence against even the most basic aesthetics, carried out in unweatherable red brick of a horribly unfriendly shade, and designed in public-toilet Gothic. But for the really out-and-out shabby (and even ragged) clothes that he needed, Mr Holmes, in all probability, would have sought them in Aldgate High-street, just beyond the eastern limits of the City of London (trains direct from Baker-street to Aldgate, by underground District Railway: fare 2*d*.—4 cents) or in what was then and still is, the East End's most famous and well-patronized street-market: 'Petticoat-lane' (officially, 'Middlesex-street'). To say of this famous open-air market that 'Custom cannot stale it' is to invite the facetious question: 'Could it *possibly*...?', but certain it is that Age hasn't withered it, and that the grandsons and great-grandsons of the kerb-side hucksters of Mr Holmes's day are still doing a roaring, land-office business—but now for pounds, of course, and no longer for shillings or pence.

One word about this malodorous clothing; even more malodorous in an age when the bath was still something of a rarity even with the middle-class and accessible to the working-class and below only in the municipal bath-houses. The washing of linen was universally accessible, and, to our view, ridiculously inexpensive—most of the wives of the permanently unemployed earned the family's money either as charwomen or washerwomen. No man, even of the working-class, needed to go, save by his own wish, with a dirty shirt.

But with clothing—or, rather, the keeping of it fresh and sweet—that was a different matter. As far back as the late 1850s, the still flourishing firm of Carless, Capel & Leonard, Oil Refiners (they invented the trade-term, 'Petrol', in the Nineties, but omitted to register as a trade-mark), of Stratford, county of Essex, had put a benzine clothes-cleaner named *Apokarthartikon* (Commerce loved Greek and Latin names in those days; but only a few, such as *Lux*, have survived). Some tailors would 'dry clean' a suit by the process of unpicking all the seams, brushing out the lint, 'dry-cleaning' the separated pieces of cloth with the dangerously inflammable benzine, then sew the suit back again—a long and necessarily costly job, which had replaced the smell of sweat by that of benzine, a powerful odour that hung about the cloth for weeks.

Matters, however, had greatly improved by 1895, the year that I have selected as being most 'typical' in the career of Mr Holmes. The efficiency and cheapness of the British postal-system of those far-off days encouraged the development of firms far distant from London, conducting all of their business by post. The most successful of these, offering both cleaning and dyeing of clothes, were Clarks' of Retford (in Nottinghamshire, halfway between London and Edinburgh—say about two hundred miles from the English capital) and Pullars of Perth, a town adjacent to the Scots capital—some four hundred miles from London. With plenty of servants to fill and mail the special Clarks' and Pullars' boxes, the Victorians saw no disadvantage in the fact that these efficient firms were not 'just around the corner'—though, for Londoners there was a firm of (originally French) dyers and cleaners: Achille Serre. Did Mr Holmes make use of this handy convenience...?

All men's suits, in those days, were what the modern cleaners call 'three-piece'—that is, in addition to coat and trousers, the customer was always supplied with a waistcoat to match, though this, quite commonly, was replaced in actual wear by a waistcoat of 'check Tattersal cloth', or, more generally for 'the City' and formal engagements, a waistcoat of white linen, washable and with removable buttons, was worn.

Harrod's Stores were offering what reads as (and certainly was) a full service of Dyeing and Cleaning, all Gentlemen's Clothing being returned 'Tailor-pressed'. The prices offer not the slightest excuse for those who continued to go about in dirty or malodorous clothes. Here are the prices for the essential items in a gentleman's wardrobe:

	Cleaned	Dyed
Coats, Morning and Walking	From 2/3	3/0
Frock and Dress Coats	3/0	3/6
Overcoats, light	3/0	3/6
Overcoats, heavy	4/0	5/6
Trousers	1/0	1/6
White Waistcoats	0/9	—
Tweed suits	3/9	5/0
Flannel trousers	1/0	—

...and so on. Gloves—an essential for the Victorian, man or woman, were cleaned at 3*d.* a pair. Prices did not change for twenty years (2/3 = 54 cents; 3/0 = 72 cents; 4/0 = 96 cents; 5/0 = $1.20; 1/0 = 24 cents and 3*d.* 6 cents).

Yet, with this 'dry-cleaning' available, it is possible that Mr Holmes, in his passion for verisimilitude in the matter of disguise, may have felt that it was not enough to *look* like a tramp; to make the disguise acceptable, convincing beyond the faintest trace of suspicion, one ought to *smell* like one.

Could Mr Holmes have carried his self-sacrificing dedication to his art so far above and so much beyond the call of duty...? At first consideration of that question, I doubted that even that man of iron resolution could endure, for hours on end, the fearful miasma exhaled from those never-cleaned Monmouth-street rags. Impossible!, I instinctively cried—though a hundred images of the classically insensitive—all crowding in on me from my life-long, vast, and totally unregulated reading—disturbed me with the conviction that history does record hundreds of men (history courteously leaves the ladies undescribed) who...well, I rememered the eleventh Duke of Norfolk, 'Dirty Jockey of Norfolk', who died, aged sixty-nine, in the year of Waterloo. 'Dirty Jockey', so strange a friend for the fastidious Prince Regent to have had, could be bathed by his servants only when lying in bed, 'paralytically' drunk. I recalled that eccentric Irishman, John Barrett, Vice-provost of Trinity College, Dublin, who, to try to warm himself in a bitter Irish winter, used to go down to the kitchen—only to be turned out (as *The Dictionary of National Biography* tells us) by his own servants, 'on account of his dirty and ragged condition'. Nathaniel Bentley was nicknamed 'Dirty Dick' from his refusal to permit his home to be dusted or cleaned for forty years; His personal hygiene having received no more cleansing attention. (The famous pub, 'Dirty Dick's', in Bishopsgate, City of London, honours his mysophil memory.)

The list is very long indeed of these hydrophobes—but all these, I reflected, are the more exceptional cases of insensitivity.... But then...well, well! I remembered a nightmare journey one damp winter's morning, on the every-window-closed top of a tram (or trolley-bus) from Catford, dingiest of all London's suburbs, to the Thames Embankment at Westminster—a memory really relevant to the subject that I am discussing.

———

It is now a little more than fifty years ago that I made that unique journey—just about the time when Penguin Books had published Apsley Cherry Garrard's *The Worst Journey in the World,* a trek over the Antarctic ice. My nightmare journey was shorter—hardly more than an hour; but what I suffered in that hour-long hell has never left my memory.

For the tram-top was an 'early'—a 'workmen's'—one, timed to arrive in London to get the men to their jobs by eight. The top was filled; every hard wooden seat occupied—and every man there, save only me, was smoking. Shag. Clouds of noxious smoke within the tight-closed windows blotted out the dull winter's light, suffocated one in a miniature foretaste of Hell—'No light, but rather Darkness visible'. It would have been useless to ask these honest working-folk to open at least one window, and, knowing the prejudices of my countrymen, of almost all social classes, in favour of 'fug', I did not make the attempt. But as, stinking of shag-fumes—clothes, hair, hands, mouth—I stumbled, half-dazed, from the tram at Westminster, I saw, for the first time, the implications of a passage that I had known from childhood:

"I have my eye on a suite in Baker-street which would suit us down to
the ground. *You don't mind the smell of strong tobacco, I hope?"*
  "I always smoke 'ship's' myself...."

*Remembering—and now understanding—those remarks, it seemed to me
unnecessary to add to that remembrance the paragraph immediately following:*

"That's good enough. I generally have chemicals about, and occasionally
do experiments. Would that annoy you?"

I found myself concluding that Mr Holmes was either suffering from
anosmia, or that his nose had a hardihood denied to inferior organs of
smell. And then again, I remembered something that confirmed
the...well, goodness me!...all that I had been suspecting. I remembered
the 'dottles'—the revolting masses of smoked tobacco leaf and distilled
nicotine and 'tar', and stale, dried saliva—tapped out of an empty pipe
left to dry on the hearth, and then—God save the mark!—to be re-used
in one of those famous pipes of Mr Holmes's triple-pipe 'ratiocinations'.

Anyone who, having acquired a 'dottle' by tapping out the pipe—
bowl inverted—on any hard surface, and did not do what anyone else
would have done: just throw it away with a nose wrinkled for its re
pellant aspect and smell, but (the dottle dried out on the hearth-stone
replaced it in the pipe for a further 'smoke', must be held insensitive
to an abnormal degree.

So—not forgetting the nidor of those 'occasional' chemical experi
ments, nor what Dr Watson must have puffed out of a pipe loaded with
'ship's'—it really does look as though the occasional fragrance of a tramp's
rags bought of a Monmouth-street old-clo' shop or a Petticoat-lane street
stall must surely have passed unnoticed in the permanently smoke-rich
atmosphere of Mr Holmes's consulting-room. (It may also explain, it
occurs to me, the curiously brief stay of the various clients—long enough
and never more, to 'state their case'. It has been suggested that the
obviously repressed impatience of Mr Holmes made all those clients
willing, and even eager, to 'get on with it'—but the atmosphere may
well have made them all disinclined to extend their visit in idle social
chit-chat....)

Well...let us leave these olfactory musings; these theories concerning
Mr Holmes's possible acquisitions in Monmouth-street or Petticoat lane
these wonderings whether or not he availed himself of Harrod's Stores
dry-cleaning services. Let us now leave Mr Holmes's 'other wardrobe'

and examine that requisite for his appearing, normally dressed, in a society that took clothes very seriously indeed....

———

By 1895, Mr Holmes's wardrobe, of the 'respectable' sort, must have attained its maximum, and have included those costumes of ultra-normal-formality rendered essential by the necessities of his now numerous Imperial and Royal connections. In the more broad-minded days at the beginning of the 19th Century, when warfare was restricted to the military, scientists particularly were held to be immune from the hostilities practised by warring nations. The Imperial Academy of Sciences of Napoleonic France—France then being at war with Great Britain—awarded a prize of fifty thousand gold francs (then £2,000 or $10,000) to the eminent *English* physicist, Sir Humphry Davy, who decided, since he was so invited, that he would go to Paris with Lady Davy, to collect his prize. Great Britain, save for a short breathing-space interval in 1802, had been fighting France for more than ten years. No obstacle was placed by the British government in the way of Sir Humphry's visiting Paris, and he and his lady duly arrived there, to be greeted as an eminent scientist, albeit 'an enemy', deserved to be. However, when an emissary of the Imperial Court called on Sir Humphry, to cause him to be measured for the gold-encrusted uniform in which it was laid down that all men should appear when being received by the Emperor, Sir Humphry refused to wear anything other than his usual British evening wear of blue cut-away dress-coat, white knee-breeches, black silk stockings (from Thresher & Glenny, hosiers at *The Sign of the Peacock*, in the Strand), steel-buckled black 'pumps', white waistcoat with gold buttons, frilled white cambric short, high starched white linen collar and black satin stock. Sir Humphry, in explaining to the affronted Court functionary that, Emperor or not; Court-regulations or not; Sir Humphry was not prepared to wear French Court-dress, the Englishman offered no excuse, no apology—only a thoroughly British comment: "You tell your master, Mounseer, that if what I wear at Carlton House is good enough for His Royal Highness the Prince of Wales, it ought to be quite good enough for your Emperor—and you can tell him that, with my compliments." What happened then is not really relevant at all to Sherlock Holmes, but is included here for the sake of completing the tale.

Sir Humphry's intransigence was reported to the Grand Marshal o the Court, and he, in turn, reported it to the Emperor, whom it amused "Tell the old John Bull," said Napoleon, "that he may come as he li kes...naked, if that's what he'd prefer...."

———

It was an American ambassador to the Court of St James's who, not s< many years ago, refused to wear the traditional costume of an ambas sador when presenting his credentials to His Late Majesty, King George the Fifth. Correctly, I think, for the ambassador had in mind those voter who believed that King George the Third was still on the throne, and still plotting the downfall of the Thirteen States. The Soviet, curiously did not refuse to wear a Court-dress, but unwisely left the design t< one of their own, who made their gold-trimmed diplomats look like the elevator-attendants at a Miami hotel of the more expensive kind. There have been many reasons for the refusal to wear the customary outfit— but Mr Holmes (autonomous as he was) offered none of these. He wa perfectly willing to ask Davies & Son, of Hanover-square, one of the Prince of Wales's two 'preferred' tailors (Poole, of Savile-row, was the other), to make him a civilian Court-suit of the new, 'revised', design dark-blue velvet open coat, with matching waistcoat, both with cut-stee buttons; black satin knee-breeches; black silk stockings; black patent leather 'pumps' with cut-steel buckles. A jabot and stock—the jabot o lace—encircled the neck, and a black cocked hat, always closed; neve worn on the head but carried under the left arm, and a sword with cut steel handguard and quillons, completed the outfit. This Court-dress with a black, white-satin-lined cloak, was regarded by Mr Holmes, ir his palmy days, as not the least important of all the items in his wardrobe

———

What, then, might we expect to find in the wardrobe of Mr Holmes ir the year, 1895, when he was in the prime of his life at age forty-one We shall be safe if we list the essentials only; for any man's fancy ma take him into elaborations of self-indulgence impossible for another t< follow. Essentials, then; and essentials *only*. (Clothes and accessories shall list separately.)

Clothes

	£	s.	d.
2 Frock-coats, waistcoats and trousers	12	12	0
2 Pairs extra trousers @ 35/– each	3	10	0
2 Morning coats @ £3 3s. each	6	6	0
2 Tweed suits @ £3 10s. each	7	0	0
1 Navy-blue serge suit ('Lounge')	3	10	0
4 Pairs, white flannel trousers @ 7s. 6d.	1	10	0
1 'Macfarlane' caped-coat, Union tweed (erroneously called an 'Inverness'—a caped coat with	1	7	6
1 'Inverness' waterproof shooting suit	3	3	0
1 Black waterproof cape	—	9	3
1 Dress-coat, black waistcoat, trousers	6	6	0
1 Dinner-coat, black waistcoat, trousers	5	5	0
1 Black face-cloth Town overcoat (day)	3	3	0
1 Black, satin-faced overcoat (night)	4	4	0
4 Dressing-gowns, various cloths	10	0	0
6 Pairs Pajama sleeping-suits @ 8/11	2	13	6
1 Smoking-jacket	2	10	0
12 Dress shirts @ 5/6 (at discount)	3	3	0
12 White day-shirts @ 4/6 (at discount)	2	12	0
12 Coloured cotton shirts @ 3/6	2	2	0
12 Flannel shirts, plain and fancy @ 4/11	2	19	0
12 White linen collars ('Guards')	—	8	0
12 White linen collars ('New Shakespeare')	—	5	6
6 White linen collars ('Clerical'—'London')	—	10	0
12 India gauze underpants (for summer)	1	10	0
12 White merino undervests (for summer)	2	2	0
12 Shetland lambswool underpants (winter)	3	6	0
12 Shetland lambswool undervests (winter)	2	7	0
12 Wool 'half-hose' (socks) @ 1/6	—	18	0
2 Wool cardigan jackets @ 10/6	1	1	0
36 Hemstitched Cambric handkerchiefs	—	19	6
2 White silk mufflers (day and evening)	—	13	0

Clothes	£	s.	d.
4 Pairs tan calf gloves, 2-button (day)	—	13	0
6 Pairs lavender kid (dress-wear)	1	10	0
4 Pairs tan driving, one-button	—	14	0
8 Ribbed wool cholera-belts	1	0	0
	£100	2	3

...or, in United States currency, at par: $480.54. And now, a wor
of explanation before I go on to mention all (or most) of the other in
portant—though not absolutely *essential*—items of a gentleman's warc
robe of 1895, along with the accessories associated with them, as, fc
example, the 'Gent's silk hat, the finest quality made' (one guinea–
twenty-one shillings; $5.04), for which the owner surely 'needed' a leathe
hat-box, both to preserve and (when not in use) transport it—preferabl
the one advertised as 'best solid leather, for three hats, satin-lined', a
Two Guineas—$10.08. All of us know what the paradoxically-name
'inessential necessity' is—something that, theoretically, we do not ac
tually *need*—that is, and still theoretically, something that we may d
without. But that, practically, we can't see our way to get along withou
it.

The list of essentials given above appears to be something in th
nature of a trousseau, or a 'complete outfitting' such as is required (an
bought) by the parents of a boy going for the first time to his boarding
school, or a subaltern taking off for India, or an Arctic explorer equippin,
himself for a long and shop-less Polar stay.... And this, I confess, give
a false impression: at forty-one (Mr Holmes's age in 1895) many—indeed
perhaps most—of the items on that list will already have been acquired–
and long before 1895. By that year, he had already travelled extensively
both in Britain and abroad, so that there must have been, of both M
Holmes's and Dr Watson's property, more than one Railway Portman
teau ('Stout solid leather, turnover edges and corners, brass lever loc
and 2 keys, hand-sewn throughout; 30 inches, 66/–'—$15.84); more that
one Cabin Imperial Trunk ('Solid leather, with tray, for lady or gentle
man, best make, hand-sewn, and riveted; 33 inches, 79/6'—$19.08) an
Mr Holmes must have had one of those travelling-cases— 'Gentleman'
Fitted Gladstone Bags'—that were considered indispensable for the Vic
torian traveller, whether by rail or by ship.

In making out that list of the *essentials* of Mr Holmes's wardrobe,
had no intention of persuading the reader that, at some point in 1895

e had suddenly found himself in need of an entirely new set of clothing.
r from it! All the items listed were, without doubt, already in his
ossession and use. Of course, certain small articles—handkerchiefs,
irts, collars, undervests, socks, and so on—need constantly to be re-
aced (hand-washing, in those days, was even harder on garments
an anything mechanically modern). What I intended to do—and no
ore—was to indicate what Mr Holmes's essential wardrobe might have
en expected to contain, with an indication of the *average* cost of each
em. As it is, there are still certain items that seem to be classifiable, if
ot under the strictest essentiality, then at least under the head of 'ines-
ntial necessities'—and here are the main items:

ats	£	s.	d.
Silk hats, 1st and 2nd quality, @ 1 inea and 18/6	1	9	6
Opera-hat, extra quality		12	6
Tweed helmet (now called eerstalker')		7	6
Hard felt hats, 'Extra quality (the st made)'	1	8	6
Soft felt hats, in Drab and Lock own	—	18	0
Clerical hats; soft felt, round crown 4/6	—	9	0
Straw hats ('boaters') @ 2/– each	—	4	0
Leghorn (straw) hats @ 3/6	—	7	0

OOTS AND SHOES ('Inessential' in respect only of the quality)

Pair Levant slippers (low heels), best ality	—	13	0
Pair Grain Derby, brown shooting ots, @ 15/– pair	2	10	0
Pair Real Porpoise shooting-boots, nd-sewn	1	9	6
Pair Calf goloshed lace boots, 'equal bespoke'	2	11	0
Pair Russia-calf hand-welted walking oes	1	17	0
Pair Patent Calf Court shoes @ 10/6	1	1	0
Pair Canvas spats @ 2/6	—	10	0
Pair Drab Melton cloth spats (best ality) @ 4/9	—	19	9
	£17	7	3

Hats	£	s.	d.
INDULGENCES (Just a few of them....)			
1 Flush-frame cigarette case, lizard	—	8	11
1 Amber cigarette-tube, 14 carat Hall-marked gold rim	3	5	0
1 'Smokers' Companion Patent Automatic Lighter; will light a pipe, cigar, or cigarette in any weather. Extra quality, silver-plated	—	2	11
1 Bronzed brass match-stand, with porcelain ash-tray	—	5	6
4 White porcelain match-pots; silver-mounted, hall-marked @ 4/3 each	—	17	0
12 Pipes at varying prices (and of varying shapes, @ an average price of 15/–)	9	0	0
2 Silver-plated Vesta-boxes, Extra Fine Quality	—	3	2
1 Pipe-rack, Best Quality, London-made. Carved oak, for 6 pipes, representing double horseshoes and whips	—	3	6
1 Pipe-rack, for 6 pipes, representing Double Pipe and Canister	—	3	3

...and so on. But let me not forget to mention and price that unus smoking-apparatus (unusual for England, that is to say) which ou properly to have gone with one of Mr Holmes's more unusual way making himself comfortable, and that is so described by Dr Watsor *The Man with the Twisted Lip*;

> He took off his coat and waistcoat, put on large blue dressing-gown, an then wandered about the room collecting pillows from his bed and cush ions from the sofa and armchairs. With these he constructed a sort c Eastern divan, upon which he perched himself cross-legged, with an ounc of shag and a box of matches laid out in front of him. In the dim light c the lamp, I saw him sitting there....

Surely that Oriental resting-place; that totally unEnglish crossed meditative position; deserved something more fitting than 'the old k pipe' ('Peterson's Patent, always Sweet, Cool and Dry Smoking;

quality, 10/6') that he was smoking. Here is something from the Harrod's Stores' Catalogue of 1895 more suitable:

Turkish "Hookah," 4/6, 7/6, 10/6

Mention of so indispensable an item as a tobacco-pouch seemed unnecessary to me, but here is a price for those readers who wonder how much it would have cost Mr Holmes to carry his shag around with him.

Crocodile Pouch, to hold 4 ozs.....1/2/1/2 (29 cents)

The friends' preferred tobaccos, by the way, cost:

(Holmes) 'Dark Virginia Old Matured Shag'...4/6 per lb
(Watson) 'Cavendish Navy Plug'..............6/0 per lb
(respectively, $1.08 and $1.44 per lb)

And, before I leave the consideration of the friends' 'indispensable dispensabilities', their 'inessential necessities', I must mention those two domestic conveniences that, to modern Sherlockdom, have come to symbolize the cozy domesticity of 221B Baker-street, even as the Deerstalker hat has come to symbolize every physical, mental, and moral aspect of Mr Holmes: 'our' Tantalus and 'our' Gazogene. (The latter, by the way, is usually, when illustrated, depicted as a 'Seltzogene', an apparatus constructed on the same chemical principle, but as different from the 'Gazogene', not as chalk is from cheese, but certainly as Edam is different from Brie.

Harrod's Stores' Catalogue has the following entry:

GAZOGENE

3 pint...each 12/6 [$3.00]
5 pint...each 18/0 [$4.32]

Five pints seems a little excessive, when it is borne in mind that whisky (They must have preferred the V.V.O., '14 years old guaranteed', at 54/——$12.96—the dozen bottles. Dearer than some, but well worth the superior age and quality!) needed, even in those lavish days, 'only a splash'. A three-pint Gazogene ought to have lasted a good week before a refill was needed.

As for that other symbol of Baker-street cozy domesticity, the Tantalus: it came, like all the other humanizing products of that Golden Age, in many qualities, and at many greatly differing prices. And, just as haberdashers name what we call 'socks', 'half-hose', and what we know a 'ties', 'cravats', so the Victorian retailer called this useful (indeed, indispensable) convenience, not 'Tantalus' but 'Liqueur Frame'. (He would!)

The 'Liqueur Frame' was made in two designs, of which only the one enclosing—literally locking-in—the three bottles (there were generally three) really justified the classical allusion to Tantalus—the man punished by the Gods by being given a never-to-be-quenched thirst—the 'Tantalic' allusion being sustained by the fact that the three bottles were fully visible, but could not be sampled because they were secured by a firmly locked bar. The booze was put out of the reach of both children and servants and uninvited guests....

Even for 1895, it is remarkable how inexpensively one might embark on Tantalus-ownership. A 'Lock-up Liqueur Frame' of oak, with electroplated mounts, containing two *plain* bottles, cost only 24/6 ($5.88); with three bottles, a mere five shillings ($1.20) extra. In view of the fully justified respect in which the two friends (as the Canon records) held wines and spirits of all types—beer, too, when necessary, I think that the Baker-street sitting-room was graced with a rather more costly tantalus—something, I suggest, on these lines:

LIQUEUR FRAME...3 Best cut Glass Bottles, Polished Oak and Plated Mounted Frame, Patent Spring Lock Top................... 100/0 ($26.40)

(Very much *en passant*...and *almost*—considering that we are now dealing with the year 1895—irrelevant. But the pages of the Harrod's Stores catalogue did have one item listed that surprised me—surprised me very much indeed. The entry is on page 1070 of the Catalogue, under the heading, 'DRUGS. No. 20 DEPARTMENT—*FIRST FLOOR*', and in the section titled LOZENGES—here (astonishingly) it is:

Cocaine Pastilles...................................... per box, 0/9 ($.18)

Handier to take than the Seven Per Cent Solution...?

---

can hear several of my readers, not so much complaining (they are too well-mannered for that) as expressing surprise that, having promised them an accounting of Mr Holmes's wardrobe, together with the answer to the question: Where on earth did he put it all?, I should have strayed so far into irrelevancy as to list such non-sartorial, such non-wearable, articles as a leather flush-frame cigarette-case, a bronzed-brass match-stand, a silver vesta-box, a Gazogene and a 'Liqueur Frame'—better known to the Sherlockian by its more familiar Canonical name of 'Tan-alus'...to name only a few of the seeming 'irrelevancies'. So that I had better (not defend, but) explain my dragging in these 'irrelevancies', before getting on with the next promise: to look into the business of storing all those clothes that Mr Holmes's needs did not immediately call for.

As to the 'irrelevancy' or otherwise of his material possessions, it may be useful here to stress that not all of our 'clothing' is comprised in articles of knitted or woven fabric or of leather or canvas. In those days of much more rigid sartorial formality, any man above the labouring class (and, note, very many within that class) was not fully, correctly, 'properly', dressed until he had tricked-out the 'basics' of suit, tie, socks, boots, and hat with a multitude of what were then truly essential ac-cessories—the variety of which used to astonish me every time I was permitted to watch my Father's dressing himself to catch the early-morning train for the City.

To be correctly dressed in those days of morning-and frock-coats, silk hats and spats, one had also to wear a tie-pin (my Father's was of a diamond in a claw-setting, but Harrod's, I see, were offering several, all in 15-carat gold, with or without diamonds or pearls, at prices ranging from 7/3 ($1.74) to 30/– ($7.20); for the expensive tie-pins and other male jewelry, one went to Streeter's, of Bond-street or, if a City-man, as my Father was, to Sir John Bennett's, of Cheapside)—and an albert and gold-watch were positively *de rigueur* in 1895 and for a full quarter-century after. 'Gentlemen's gold albert chains' of 18-carat were sold only by weight, at £3 16s. 6d. ($18.36) the Troy oz.; but there were plenty of 15-carat alberts available at prices ranging from Five to Seven Guineas ($26 to $36.08). It was the custom then—though whether Mr Holmes followed it, I cannot say—to wear a gold 'charm' suspended from the centre of the albert: an inexpensive decoration, costing, in 18-carat gold, something between two guineas and 54 shillings ($10.08 and $12.96). As I have explained, at one end of the albert hung the gold watch; at the other some useful object such as a cigar-cutter or vesta-box (or, often both).

Watches, then, as to-day, varied enormously in price, though (unlike those of to-day, very little in quality—that is, performance). A good silver open-face watch could cost as little as a guinea-and-a-half ($7.58) but I think that, in the matter of a watch—so necessary for a man of precise habits, with many a train to catch—I feel that Mr Holmes would have made no false economies in the matter of his acquiring a watch both for accurate time-keeping and, quite as important, for keeping-up appearances. I think that his purchase might well have been in this class

English lever, very superior finish half-hunter, fully jewelled, compensated balance, all latest improvements, extra-heavy 18-carat gold case. Handsome presentation watch.......£28 10 0

...or $116.80.

Every gentleman wore a signet-ring, usually engraved with monogram or (if he was entitled to one) crest. Rings, even of Hall-marked 18 carat gold, were remarkably cheap; a heavy signet with plain, 'engravable' bezel, cost but 51/6 ($12.36). An 18-carat gold ring with a bloodstone bezel cost even less: 42/0 ($10.08). Gold propelling pencils; gold-mounted wallets, etc., were, as they say, 'optional'. Let us go back to Baker street....

———

The Liqueur Frame, the Tantalus, and all the other 'indulgences' that I have mentioned, were no less a part of Mr Holmes's outward appearance than his ring, his albert, his gold hunter, his 18-carat cuff-links (32/6—$7.80), or his 18-carat gold collar-studs (*three* for half-a-guinea—$2.52). A gentleman's 'appearance' depended on far more things than what he used for clothing or personal adornment. The conventions of contemporary social usage demanded of him that he not only entertained modestly, if necessary, but fully; either in his own house, flat, or chambers, or, if that were not possible, at his club. (The way, in fact, that Mycroft Holmes both lived and did his infrequent entertaining, whilst his more famous brother, it is clear, did *his* never-very-frequent entertaining at home.) It should be too obvious to need stating that entertaining cannot be done without the requisite apparatus and ingestibles; 'gracious' hospitality called for, in entertaining the guest, as many accessories as made a man correctly dressed for the street— tantalus and

Gazogene were as much essentials of hospitality as the Worcester por-
celain tea-service, the silver sugar-bowl, the silver cake-dish, or the da-
mask table-napkins (6/11—$1.66 a dozen). In short, a gentleman's house-
hold-furnishings, especially those designed to make the reception of a
guest conform to the rigid standards of Victorian hospitality.

———

And now for what we have been taught to call the 'logistics' of what
must have been a collection of clothing capable of filling many a wardrobe (or clothes-closet) of even Victorian vastness. Where were the many
suits hung up; where were the chests-of-drawers into which went the
shirts, day and evening; the underwear, the socks, the cholera-belts, the
neckties and cravats? Where were hung those overcoats, day and evening; that opera-cloak, those two weatherproof coats—the 'Macfarlane'
and the 'Inverness'? Where were stored—suitably segregated, they must
have been—all those disguises, from the merely shabby frock-coat of
the pseudo-bookseller to the odorous rags of the pretended opium-
addict? I have no doubt that the blue velvet Court-dress was given a
slim closet of its own. And, though Dr Watson's was surely modest
indeed compared with Mr Holmes's rich overplus, yet Dr Watson's clothes
had to be put away somewhere. The point is...where?

The several 'Reproductions of the Interior of 221B Baker-street',
which span a quarter of the Earth's circumference, from London to San
Francisco; copying or adapting the 'reproduction' made for the dingily
unsuccessful 'Festival of Britain' in 1951; and further adapted for numerous Sherlock Holmes films; have done, it is clear, a gross disservice
to the facts of life at 221B, Baker-street, in making it seem that the friends
shared a cluttered but cozy, yet abominably cramped little one-room
'pad', with few of the ordinary comforts of existence—least of all,
'breathing-space'. That this seemingly carefully-cultivated view is wrong
needs no erudite historical research: No. 109, Baker-street, though the
sole surviving house in the street which has not been altered since its
erection, is enough to shew us the impressive dimensions of a Georgian
Town-house, and to understand how much space would be available to
the two men, even in a Baker-street house of which the ground-floor
had been converted into a shop.

I have known the interior of three of these houses well, and the first
time that I stayed in the 'top half'—the General Strike of 1926 having
stranded me in London—I was amazed at the number and size of the

rooms. They certainly 'thought big' in the 18th Century—and these wer houses designed for the big Georgian families with their impressiv retinue of servants. To see the mean little room in a Sherlock Holme film, in which, as the saying goes, there is hardly room to swing a cat is, for the average viewer, to be quite unaware of the vastness of th house in which this little room seems, as it were, to cringe in its shabb humility.

The houses, even with the ground-floors removed, are vast: thre large storeys above the ground-floor shops, with attic-space inside th hipped roofs.

Even on their first sharing 'diggings' in the Baker-street house, th friends had ample room: 'a couple of comfortable bedrooms and a singl large airy sitting-room' is a description that conveys little to a generatio unfamiliar with the interior arrangements of these old London house but hadn't to be explained to the first readers of *A Study in Scarlet*, al of whom, rich, middling, or poor, would have been familiar with th lay-out of one of these houses, for they were multiplied, not merely ir their hundreds, but in their thousands as the Capital grew.

That, as Mr Holmes's fame and fortune increased, he took over mor and more of the house from Mrs Hudson is clear—in *The Beryl Coronet* we are told, not only that he went upstairs to change into his disguis of 'a common loafer', but that (by inference) it was in a room upstair that his more malodorous changes-of-costume were stored—so that the Holmes tenancy extended at least to two floors of the house.

But what did the friends have at the beginning....?

As, when they took the Baker-street 'diggings', the ground-floo had already been given over to shop-premises, this floor need not con cern us, save to observe that, originally, it had contained four rooms, of which the 'parlour' and the 'morning-room' were both the principal and the largest. That Mr Holmes and Dr Watson had the first (American, second) floor, means that they enjoyed the use of the 'drawing-room' floor; that their 'large airy sitting-room' was, in fact, the principal room (both in size and in importance) of the whole house. They had, it is clear, not only the drawing room, which extended across the entire width of the house, but the room behind, which (as originally planned) opened into the drawing-room by means of large folding-doors. The room thus opened-up into one (by modern standards) vast room, in which Geor-gian and Regency and Victorian hostesses had entertained anything up to a hundred guests without undue 'crowding'. This back half had been

Winston Churchill as First Lord of the Admiralty, as war with Germany broke out—sketch by the late Sir David, who has caught Churchill's "impish" look always at his most dangerous.

The "Metroland" steam-engine, **Sherlock Holmes,** *leaves Baker Street Station, 1953, seen off by some dedicated Sherlockians, all members of the Sherlock Holmes Society. Examining the engine's name-plate, the late Sir Sydney Roberts.*

Windlesham, the Conan Doyle country-house, as it is to-day; an unpretentious, confortable residence suited to the modest tastes of the owner. Considerably altered internally, to transform it into a residential hotel, the exterior is quite unchanged. The window on the extreme left marks "ACD's" den.

The "Conan Doyle" corner in the old Doyle House, Windlesham, near Crowborough, as photographed when I visited the house in the company of Dame Jean Conan Doyle. Now a private hotel for the elderly, the house has changed greatly, though this small corner is reverently preserved as it was when the Coyles lived there.

Major William Murray, late of the crack Tenth Hussars, of which Albert Edward, Prince of Wales, was Colonel-in-Chief. The victim of a murderous attack by a jealousy-maddened "rival," the Major, despite appalling wounds, succeeded in escaping with his life.

"I left London Bridge by the 'penny boat'," said the Major, giving evidence. In spite of numerous accidents—mostly the exploding of the boats' boilers—travel on the Thames was the early- and mid-Victorians' favourite mode of intercity travel.

On his way to his being attacked, the Major had passed through Hungerford Market, seen here just before its demolition in 1862, to make way for the Charing Cross railway-station and the famous Hotel—both surviving, hardly changed, to this day.

Roberts, alias "Grey," the murderous attacker of Major Murray. A heartless usurer, Roberts's offices in Northumberland-street were filled to overflowing with goods seized from debtors unable to pay him off. Here he is bringing back loot.

Like Conan Doyle, Arthur Sarsfield Ward ("Sax Rohmer") was greatly taken with the house-name, The Gables, and, like Doyle, used it in a story—in Ward's case, a story of his villainous Chinese, Fu Manchu.

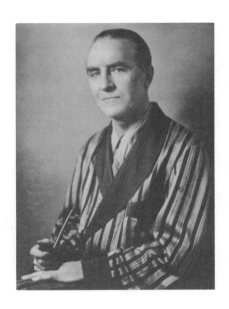

Maiwand, Afghanistan, 27 July 1880. This painting, now in the Museum of the Berkshire Regiment at Salisbury, England, shews "The Stand of the Last Eleven"—two officers and men facing certain death, from which only Bobbie, the regiment's pet mongrel, escaped—to be awarded the Afghan Medal by Queen Victoria.

Revenge for the disastrous defeat of Maiwand was soon sought. Here, under the command of General Sir (later Field-marshal Lord) Frederick Roberts, the British Army's Ghurka allies are storming the defended Afghan stronghold of Peiwar Khotal.

Revenge for Maiwand—the final stage. Face-to-face with the ''murderous Ghazis,'' the kilted Highlanders attack with ''cold steel''—their irresistible bayonet-charge against the Afghans at Baba Wali in 1880.

The coat-of-arms of the Churchill barony, shewing the double use of the heraldic device called a **frette**, which seem to resemble the plan of a cross-roads or "carfax." This may have been one of the reasons for giving the fictitious (but based on fact) Lady Frances the surname of "Carfax."

Oscar Wilde, as he was when he met Conan Doyle at the dinner-party given by Stoddart, the London manager of Lippincott's Magazine, who succeeded in getting a novel out of both Doyle and Wilde. Conan Doyle was greatly impressed by Wilde's brilliance and charm and remained loyal to Wilde's memory when so may turned against Wilde in his downfall.

In 1905, Robert Ross, Wilde's friend and literary executor, opened his Carfax Gallery in Ryder-street, St James's, choosing a well-thought-out position opposite the fashionable Dieudonné Restaurant, where King Edward the Seventh had often dined when Prince of Wales. The names, both "Carfax" and "Ryder" occur in Conan Doyle's Sherlockian writings, shewing that each had great significance for him.

Ὁ μαστήρ

The Greek letters of the hand-drawn title above spell out the words Ho Mastèr, Greek for "The official Tax dodger chaser of Athens." It is curious that, by sheer coincidence, this old Greek word for "detective" should so closely resemble what so many dedicated Sherlockians call Holmes: "The Master."

Ancient Greek culture was a most literate one, and shorthand was an accomplishment of most of the clerks on official duty. Here the Architelónes and his staff work out the arrested man's indebtedness in the matter of his tax-evasion.

This scene, from an ancient Greek vase, looks remarkably as though an Athenian tax-dodger has been apprehended by the Mastèr and is being hauled off for examination before the Architelónes, the City-state's "Chief Collector of Tolls."

Invariably (and incorrectly) referred to as an "Inverness," this particular type of caped weatherproof overcoat is displayed here in all its catalogued—by Harrod's—lifelessness. The stiff drawing gives little idea of what it must have looked like in vigorous use.

However, the lively penmanship of this Du Maurier drawing from a **Punch** of 1888—*the year of* A Scandal in Bohemia—*shews that the garment could be both* practical *and* elegant . . . *and by no means confined to the railway-traveller, as a well-known illustration to* Silver Blaze *has led so many to believe.*

A talent of Sherlock Holmes's which mightily impressed all who knew him intimately was his ability to adopt the most effective disguise—talent on which Mr Holmes was complimented by "old Baron Dowson," the murderous Judge, on the night before he was hanged. Here is Mr Holmes in one of his more striking transformations, as a dyed-in-the-wool Victorian "rough."

TAILORS, &c.

A. Atkinson,

33, Brook Street,

Grosvenor Square,

W.

Speciality—**Dress Suits.**

That all the three names to be found in this late 19th Century tailor's advertisement have been used in the Canon—Atkinson (SCAN), Brook-street (RESI), and Grosvenor-square (NOBL)—make it certain that this was the principal London tailor to whom, in Conan Doyle's opinion, the socially-settled Sherlock Holmes gave his orders.

ich in late 17th Century
rchitectural fantasy, Winstanley's
rick-and-timber structure of 1698
as the very first of the Eddystone
ghthouses. Completely destroyed in
e great storm of 1703, its baroque
arm still lingers in the minature
reproduction that the Victorian
rchitect placed on the roof of a
lapham board-school—and there
as recognized by Sherlock Holmes
s he passed.

The Eddystone lighthouse of
to-day—in very heavy, but not
abnormal, winter weather. Built
entirely of granite, to the designs of
Sir James Douglas, between 1879
and 1882, it is the fourth Eddystone
Light, replacing the third, also of
granite, erected by Smeaton in 1759.

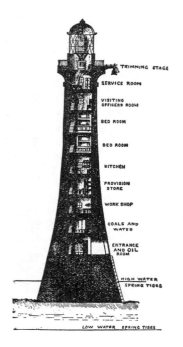

Sectional view of the fourth—and present-day—Eddystone Light, as it was when first brought into use in 1882, when recruits to the staff were allowed three weeks in bed to overcome the "screaming" claustrophobia! It is now no longer illuminated by oil and is completely automatic.

TRIMMING STAGE
SERVICE ROOM
VISITING OFFICERS ROOM
BED ROOM
BED ROOM
KITCHEN
PROVISION STORE
WORK SHOP
COALS AND WATER
ENTRANCE AND OIL ROOM
HIGH WATER SPRING TIDES
LOW WATER SPRING TIDES

NO use for Board-schools—"Lighthouses" or not! Here two guardians of the Education Act—Schools-inspector, correctly top-hatted, and a typically Victorian "bobby" find and rout out wilful school-dodgers, for compulsory education, by depriving children of the ability to start earning money at a tender age, was hated by parents, even more than by their children.

The first Education Act, of 1870, provided national and compulsory teaching for all children unable to attend private schools. The national schools were administered by Boards—hence "Board-schools." Originally, children were admitted at seven years of age and could leave (to work, usually) at ten, an age which was progressively raised. An army of zealous inspectors was enrolled to see that all children were receiving their proper schooling. Here is one at a child-employing factory.

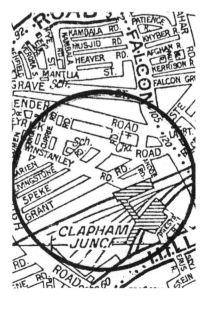

The 'Lighthouse' Board-school at Clapham Junction. The school, at Winstanley-road, lies just to the left of the Junction; London is to the north of the map.

ARGENTI NITRAS

[Argent. Nit.]
Silver Nitrate

$AgNO_3$ . . . . . Mol. Wt. 169·9

Silver Nitrate may be obtained by the action of nitric acid on silver. It contains not less than 99·8 per cent. of $AgNO_3$.

Characters. Colourless, tabular crystals ; odourless ; taste, bitter and metallic.

Soluble in about 0·5 part of *water*, and in 25 parts of *alcohol* (*90 per cent.*) ; slightly soluble in *ether*, and in *glycerin*.

Tests for Identity. Yields the *reactions* characteristic of silver, and of nitrates.

Test for Purity. Dissolve 1 gramme in 5 millilitres of *water*, and add a slight excess of *dilute solution of ammonia* ; the mixture remains clear and colourless (limit of copper, of bismuth, and of lead).

Assay. Dissolve about 0·5 gramme, accurately weighed, in 50 millilitres of *water*, add 2 millilitres of *nitric acid*, and titrate with *N/10 ammonium thiocyanate*, using *solution of ferric ammonium sulphate* as indicator. Each millilitre of *N/10 ammonium thiocyanate* is equivalent to 0·01699 gramme of $AgNO_3$.

Storage. Silver Nitrate should be protected from light.

Preparation. Argenti Nitras Induratus.

DOSES

Metric.	Imperial.
0·008 to 0·016 gramme.	$1/8$ to $1/4$ grain.

The formula for Silver Nitrate, as officially given in The British Pharmacopoeia, *the "Bible" of British pharmacology. Known to have been in use as a prophylactic against ophthalmia by the Arabs as early as the 9th Century AD, the administration of silver nitrate is now routine at all births.*

H.R.H. the Prince of Wales, Victoria's pleasure-loving Heir, as he was at the time of the unpleasant Mordaunt divorce-trial, in which he entered the witness-box to perjure himself in the approved Victorian fashion, to defend the good name— unsuccessfully, alas!—of Lady Mordaunt.

"St Blaise," property of Sir Frederick Johnstone, baronet; one of history's most famous racehorses; winner of three British classic races (including the Derby) in one year. The racehorse of Conan Doyle's classic **Silver Blaze** *was only the slightly altered "St Blaise" of Sir Frederick's—Society roué very much in Conan Doyle's morally disapproving mind when he wrote the story in late 1892.*

Times change, as do all Advertising presentations. Here in a modern ad for a depilatory, Captain Hudson has retired to his well-earned rest, and the Ever-grateful Sepoy is no more than a dim memory—if even that. No more is the Secret of Total Depilation a matter of Oriental secrets—Wisdom had moved West, to Europe. But the promise is the same. . . .

Even with much rebuilding and the addition of up-to-date surgical and medical departments, "Bargs"—the ancient London hospital of St Bartholomew, founded in the 12th Century by the King's jester, Rahere—still presents, almost unchanged, the look that it had when Holmes and Watson first knew it in the late 1870s.

The Charing Cross Hotel, Strand, London, built 1863, but still flourishing. It was here that the Sherlock Holmes Society of London held the banquet to commemorate the Centenary of Conan Doyle's birth in 1859, and it was here that I was rebuked for shewing insufficient respect for The Master!

onverted into a large bedroom; the original double-doors having been
eplaced by a door of ordinary proportions. This was Mr Holmes's bedroom; a chamber which served, as the Canon clearly indicates, for a
epository of records as well. Dr Watson's own bedroom had, from the
eginning of the friends' tenancy, been on the floor above, and again,
om my own knowledge of these Baker-street houses, I may affirm that
is bedroom was a large one indeed.

The floors above that of the drawing-room had, on the average, four
rge rooms and one much smaller; it is certain that, long before 1895,
Ir Holmes's needs and ability to pay would have led him to acquire
ie use of at least the whole of the second (American, third) floor, and
ossibly the whole or the greater part of the floor above. He may have
otained permission from Mrs Hudson to store certain not-often-to-
eed-consulting records in the attic. Mrs Hudson herself was amply
rovided with living-space: she had the former butler's pantry and hou-
ekeeper's room and servants' hall, besides the kitchen and scullery and
ie extensive wine-cellers, not all of which were used at this late day
ir the storing of her lodgers' wines. The long-overdue plans of a Baker-
reet's house's interior arrangements will, I hope, make it clear how
uch living-and storing-space (for records, no less than for clothing)
as at Mr Holmes's disposal even from the very beginning of his Baker-
reet tenancy. By 1895, he might almost have doubled his material
ossessions—and still have had room in which to put them neatly away....

THE HOUSE OF SEVERAL GABLES

Continuing a personal mystery...

In the very first of all my Holmesian books, published as long ago as 1958, I gave the beginnings of what is still an unfinished account of how Conan Doyle's story of the unlucky Maberleys, *The Three Gables*, seemed to echo, in a fashion hardly to be dismissed as pure coincidence, some extremely curious circumstances centring about a large Victorian house that my Father had rented, on a long lease, at Harrow Weald, where the Maberleys' house had been situated in the Doyle story. Our house was also, as was theirs, secluded among a lot of trees, and set well back from a secondary road that meandered through the still heavily wooded, still more than half-rustic, residential district some ten miles north-west of London. Our house was named, *The Gables*—but that similarity of name was only one of the several points linking the *Three Gables* of 'fiction' with *The Gables* of verifiable fact—points which, after long consideration of both Harrow houses, now convince me that, in examining the points of resemblance that bring the two 'Gabled' houses so persuasively together, we may—indeed, we *must*—exclude coincidence completely.

It is astonishing how much *more* one may instruct oneself in even the most deeply researched subject in the discussing it aloud; particularly when, as has been happening to me over the past three years, that open discussion takes the form of the public lecture; in my case, the subject usually having been Sherlock Holmes as we study him through the pages of the sixty 'Canonical' (or 'Conanical') stories.

Looking back over those many Sherlockian talks, given mostly, though not exclusively, in the United States of America, I am now aware that a profound change of emphasis, of direction; a change which, so it seems to me, occurred almost without my being aware of it; certainly without my conscious volition. The change consisted in my switching the character of my talks from an examination of Sherlock Holmes *per se* (I always consider Dr Watson as part of the Sherlockian *persona*) to a close examination of Holmes's creator, to be minutely studied as he reveals himself through the patterns, and particularly through the nomenclature of people and places, in the various stories.

I have already mentioned Dame Jean's indignant repudiation of the existence of those 'private papers' of her Father's, that too many of his modern biographers have assumed as a matter of fact. And I have mentioned, too, my realization that the 'private papers' that the biographers say will eventually clear up all misunderstandings, brightly illuminate all shadowy places, tie-up all loose-ends, really do have no material existence (at least, in my opinion), but I did add, in mentioning this, that the private *records* of Conan Doyle did as surely exist—within a seeming collection of casually-named persons and places, with plots sometimes apparently echoing real-life happenings; at other times apparently 'just made up'—but all the stories in reality carrying the honest record of all the hopes, the fears, the prejudices, the regrets, the sentimental and never-to-be-realized longings of an ordinary man, hidden though not concealed within a 'code' as simple as the simple soul who devised it.

Many years ago, I detected the evidence of a similar 'code' in the writings—especially the earlier writings—of Edgar Allan Poe, and, to a large extent, 'broke' that code, revealing, among other importances, the true feelings that young Poe entertained for all those intimately concerned with his childhood and adolescence, and, most importantly, his opinion of John Allan, conventionally-historically assessed as 'the wealthy, kindly Scots merchant who adopted the orphan Eddy Poe'. That Poe, though certainly, with the death of his Mother (his Father having, for reasons as yet unascertained, disappeared) a veritable orphan, had, both in America and in England, a numerous family, and had no need to be 'adopted' by Allan, save that Allan, on the verge of bankruptcy (so much for the 'wealthy' Scots merchant!) needed to plunder, if only for the time being, Poe's truly wealthy London relatives—the existence of whom Allan had learnt through his studying the papers left by the dying Mrs David Poe. But it is with what I have discovered of the 'sub-surface' records of Conan Doyle that I am concerned in this (what, as I shall explain, must necessarily be an incomplete) monograph.

———

Let me give an example of what I mean by the 'interpretation' of what, so far, have seemed even to scholars, Conan Doyle's apparently fortuitous selection of names, places, and 'situations'. Take, for instance, the jacket of Neville St Clair's, seemingly a mere 'prop' in the story of *The Man with the Twisted Lip*. Neville St Clair, in a tale not merely 'borrowed', but shamelessly lifted, from Thackeray, is ostensibly a 'City man', living in the most respectable bourgeois comfort with his wife in a detached 'villa' in Lee, on the outskirts of South-east London. He certainly goes each day to the City of London, but not to a desk in bank, insurance-office, or stockbroking firm—still the principal activities of 'The City'. Instead, after changing from his City-going uniform of black morning-coat, striped pepper-and-salt trousers, white linen waistcoat, yellow wash-leather gloves, drab-olive spats of hopsack or Melton, and a shiny 'topper' in a room above a Thames-side opium-den, *The Bar of Gold*, young Mr St Clair assumes the character of 'Hugh Boone', whose "hideous face," Holmes explains, "is familiar to every man who goes much to the City. He is a professional beggar, though, in order to avoid police regulations, he pretends to a small trade in wax vestas." (In the Thackeray original, the quick-change artist becomes a crossing-sweeper, with a lucrative practice outside the Bank of England.)

On a visit to the City, Mrs St Clair loses her way, and finds herself by chance passing by *The Bar of Gold*. Glancing up, she is startled to see, in an upper window, the face of her husband; even more scared to see him 'terribly agitated'. She noted that though he was wearing the coat with which he had set out for the City that morning, he was wearing neither collar nor tie. She darts through the open doorway, to rush upstairs (as she believes) to her husband's assistance, but is rudely pushed back into the street by a Lascar and (how did she know this?) 'a Dane'. But she meets an Inspector of City Police, and all mount up to the room from which Mrs St Clair saw her husband look out. He has vanished. The only occupant of the frowsy upstairs-room is 'the sinister cripple' Hugh Boone, who has managed to rid himself only of his coat; his wife's return, with the Inspector, has been too sudden for his ridding himself of the rest of the City duds, which are found stuffed behind a curtain.

The coat, that St Clair has managed to throw from the window, is easily spotted as it lies on a mud-bank; and presents some pretty problems:

> "...It was Neville St Clair's coat...which lay uncovered as the tide receded. And what do you think they found in the pockets?"
>
> "I cannot imagine."
>
> "No, I don't think you would guess. Every pocket stuffed with pennies and half-pennies—421 pennies and 270 half-pennies. [Then worth £2 6s. or $11.12.] It was no wonder that it had not been swept away by the tide. But a human body is a different matter.... It seemed likely enough that the weighted coat had remained when the stripped body had been sucked away into the river."

Here we shall leave Mr Sherlock Holmes to solve the problem of Neville St Clair's disappearance, that he does, as we know, successfully. (Though he fails to solve the quite insoluble problem of finding Mr St Clair a new source of income, now that his 'Hugh Boone' racket has been blown....)

Instead, we shall note that, less than three years before Doyle wrote *Twisted Lip*, a coat, weighted down with coins, was fished out of the icy Thames in January, 1889. But, different from Mr St Clair's coat, there was a body within: that of a failed barrister turned small-time schoolmaster—thirty-two-year-old Montague John Druitt, who has since acquired a most dubious *post mortem* fame in having been most improbably cast as a likely Jack the Ripper.

However, though I find the arguments in support of Druitt's Ripper-guilt entirely unconvincing, there does seem to be evidence that poor Druitt 'came under suspicion' as, in their despair of finding 'The Ripper' by any normal, rational method of detection, the police resorted to the old, traditional methods of mass-arrest and mass-questioning that has never yet uncovered the real criminal, though it has, regrettably, provided many a convenient substitute victim. The Coroner, 'sitting on the body' of Montague John Druitt, found that he had taken his own life while 'the balance of his mind was disturbed'. What had rendered Druitt an object of suspicion to the police, not even the most tireless of the 'Druitt-theorists', the American Tom Cullen and the English Daniel Farson, have ever told us. Nor, at present, can I tell what it was about the report of the Druitt suicide which so caught Conan Doyle's interest that he used the coin-weighted coat in *Twisted Lip*—Druitt's suicide had stayed with Doyle for more than two years. Doyle's allusions to the Ripper are not, as so many have remarked, non-existent: they are to be found, as is to be expected in a writer who read the newspapers so assiduously that he could even pick up and remember the details of a relatively unimportant suicide. I shall 'reveal' the Ripper-allusions in another place; here I may simply ask the question—since Doyle must have been at least as interested in the Ripper murders as was everybody else in England, from Queen Victoria downwards: Had Doyle taken some *special* interest in the Ripper so as to have gained access to the confidings of the police—even to the extent of learning the names of the suspects? But these are matters for another monograph; and I have strayed far enough from the Gables already. It is time to return there....

———

First, let me compare my true-life experiences in *The Gables* in 1911 with the supposedly fictional treatment that Conan Doyle gives of Mrs Maberley's experiences in what appears to be, despite the slight change of name, *The Gables/The Three Gables*, not merely a house similar to ours, but, to be sure, the very same house. Here is the description of Mrs Maberley's house, set in the then wooded Harrow Weald, as was ours:

> ...a brick and timber villa, standing in its own acre of undeveloped grassland. Three small projections above the upper windows [i.e., gables] made a feeble attempt to justify its name. Behind was a grove of melancholy, half-grown pines, and the whole aspect of the place was...depressing.

It was indeed, as I remember it. The mock half-timbering of the principal gable at the house's front (there were other gables, at the sides and back) had originally been painted a 'Tudor' dark-brown, but wind and rain and sun had bleached this colour to a sort of pinky-mauve. And even in the sparkling sunshine of that Spring day on which I first walked up to *The Gables* along the bold sweep of its yellow-gravelled carriage-drive, that house, with its fading paint and general air of neglect and abandonment looked like something out of the Poe that I was yet to read.

But if the exterior of the house was darkly forbidding—"We won't recognize it after the painters have done their job," said my Father, resolutely cheery, but we had left *The Gables* long before the decorators had done their best to brighten-up that dismal Harrow villa.

In the first place, there was 'something wrong' about the house's interior, no less than with its exterior. The 'public rooms' were not too bad, but the vast and cavernous kitchens, with their over-long, dark and gloomy passages, were 'off-putting' (as we used to say) in the extreme—the gloomy impression being emphasized by the fact that all the woodwork had been painted—'grained'—a striped-ginger-cat colour. In memory, this grim place seems to recall a passage in a book that I once read: 'It was the sort of house where anything could happen...and usually did'.

In our case, it certainly did....

———

As regards my brother and myself, who used to sleep together in a bedroom of which the woodwork was of the same ginger-cat shade as was that of the basement, we were terrified from the very beginning of our stay at *The Gables*—our night-fears apparently originating in, and centring about, the right-hand cupboard of two built-in closets that flanked the huge, old-fashioned fireplace. I have a memory of a flight of stairs descending from this cupboard into unimaginable depths, and of *Something* that ascended and descended that stairway—but whether this be a true memory or (which is, I think, more likely) a fear-bred fantasy, I cannot now say. But it is a wonder to me that my brother and I—children though we were—could ever have managed to sleep in a room engendering so much of terror....

My Mother was no less affected by the house's general feeling of *wrongness*, but in her case, though equally inexplicable, this wrongness was specific as well as general: she declared, with a positiveness that there was no shaking, that, at night, she could hear, coming from a point far beneath the house, a steady, regular *thumping*, as of some rhythmically-operating machinery. "Do you think," my Mother wondered fearfully, "there are *coiners* at work down there...?"

My Father's laughingly contemptuous dismissal—at first—of my Mother's 'imagination' merits, I think, some defence. It was *not* the traditional, then customary derision of any and all of 'the Little Woman's' (though my Mother was hardly to be called *that*) 'fancies'.

At that time, we already had two other houses, both in Kent; the further distant some seventy-five miles from London; the nearer, something less. The house at Harrow Weald had been taken as, a mere seven or eight miles from London, it provided a much more convenient dwelling for my Father, who, unlike Mr Neville St Clair, had his own well-staffed office as one of 'the City's' established Insurance-brokers.

The furniture had made its laborious journey up from Kent— nearly a hundred miles—in a couple of Pantechnicon's huge, horse drawn vans, and was soon put into place in the newly-acquired house. The contemplation of his having to 'go through all this rigmarole again', after having only just settled into *The Gables,* made my Father, understandably enough, most reluctant to uproot himself again so soon. No wonder that my Father sought to pooh-pooh the house's menacing atmosphere out of court.

He did not succeed, and whether or not he heard the regular thumping from, as my Mother expressed it, 'the bowels of the earth', which had so disturbed her, he came, in no great time, to agree that the house had better be given up. At first, his argument had been that the thumping, whatever its cause, could not have come from a coining or printing-press: "The last thing that coiners or forgers would want," he reasonably protested, "would be that witnesses should be allowed to rent the house above! Surely they'd ensure their privacy by taking over the house themselves"—all of which made good sense...but didn't stop the thumping, nor the disquiet (to give it no stronger name) that that insistent noise evoked.

My Father decided to give up *The Gables*.

———

Mysteries are like the stones in a farmer's field: clean up one crop, and the next morning there's a whole new crop to be dispersed. This principle—and *The Gables* was still generating its mysteries seventy years later, as I shall tell—was notably evident in *The Gables* affair: for if there was (still unsolved) mystery behind our family's forced departure from the 'haunted' house, another, and quite as inexplicable, mystery came with my Father's negotiations for his giving up the long (normal seven, fourteen, twenty-one year) lease. He sent a formal letter to the estate-agent through whom the lease had been arranged, asking him on what financial terms my Father would be permitted to break the lease—for in those more highly-traditionalized days, an agreement, as they said, was an agreement, and it was normal to be charged heavily for the privilege of breaking it.

So that no-one could have been more astonished than was my Father, when he received the estate-agent's answer.

It simply acknowledged my Father's letter, and, without further comment, asked when it would be convenient for my Father to return the keys. Nothing was said of a fine for the breaking of the lease—nor could my Father, try as he certainly did, extract from the estate-agent the reason for his client's unusual—indeed, then surely unprecedented?—generosity in the matter of the terminated lease. Our speculations continued for years, as we discussed a *Gables* mystery even more puzzling than that of the nocturnal, subterranean thumping which had driven us out.

Had there really been a thumping, of criminal explanation, that we, as occupants of the crime-concealing house, had been supposed not to hear, or, if hearing, to dismiss the noise as just 'one of those odd sounds you always hear in the country'? Did the immediate and unquestioned acceptance of my Father's wish to break the lease mean that others—and for the same good reasons— had wished to break their leases also? Did the owner *expect* his tenants to request termination of their leases, sooner or later? And who was the owner of *The Gables*...? A search of the local Rate-books (records of local taxation), which are open to public scrutiny, failed to reveal to my Father the houseowner's name, for the 'ratepayer' was recorded as none other than the estate-agent who had 'negotiated' the lease. Was *he* the owner? No: merely the owner's nominee, and so long as he paid the rates, the Rating Authority cared nothing *who* paid. We shall see later with what carelessness and neglect the rate-records were being kept in that distant year of 1911—it was no wonder that my Father's search of the books yielded no useful information.

———

"Dear Mr Sherlock Holmes," Mrs Maberley wrote, "I have had a succession of strange incidents occur to me in connection with this house...."

Had my Father been writing to Mr Sherlock Holmes about *The Gables* (rather than about *The Three Gables*), he must have expressed himself in precisely similar terms.

And now let us see, as Conan Doyle describes them, the 'strange incidents' about which Mrs Maberley complained....

———

By any standard, *The Three Gables,* is not only not one of the best of the sixty tales in the Sherlockian Canon, it is hardly to be reckoned a good story at all, and the Holmes that we meet in it has, at irritating times, much of the nauseating coy heartiness of Bulldog Drummond, especially in those scenes where he is insulting the black, Steve Dixie, 'the bruiser', or—even more embarrassing for admirers of The Master—when he is 'humorously' chiding the maid, Susan, the eavesdropping agent of the crook, Barney Stockdale. This Sherlock Holmes 'Adventure' was written in the latter part of 1926, the year of the British General Strike, when, even to Conan Doyle, Holmes may have seemed an irrelevance; and in explanation—or even excuse—for its poor quality, the story was written when Doyle was in his sixty-eighth year, and to most of us, advancing years bring only deterioration of our physical and mental powers; for the writer, especially, the weakening of his creative talent. The kindest way in which we should view *The Three Gables* is to accept it as the work of a respected artist in the twilight of his imaginative capacity. Why I deal with this third-rate Sherlockian 'Adventure' here is because of its so strangely echoing the facts of my true-life *The Gables*. In one other way—that is, apart from its mediocre plot and inferior story-telling—*The Three Gables* has been hotly criticized on grounds which had no relevance at the time that this 'Adventure' was written in the latter part of 1926. As far as England is concerned, retrospective legislation, though infrequent, has still been planted firmly into the Statutes; but the ordinance—carrying savage penalties—which forbids the spoken or written expression of certain prejudices: this has still no retrospective application, and to fault Mr Holmes for using certain derogatory expressions to Steve Dixie a half-century before the passing of the hypocritical (but, to the vote-catcher, essential) 'Pretend to Love thy Neighbour—or Take the Consequences' legislation is as ridiculous as unjust. Sensible people will deplore the pejorative and contemptuous tone of Mr Holmes's words to the Negro, not on the preposterous grounds that Mr Holmes was committing an illegality under the Race Relations Act (which, in 1926, lay in the quite unimaginable future), but on the much more rational grounds of those words' regrettable childishness. They were quite unworthy, not only of Mr Holmes, but af any adult of ordinary education.

———

Now for Mrs Maberley's 'strange incidents'.

A widow, and now—through the death of her only son—without immediate family, Mrs Maberley lives alone in that gloomy fastness in Harrow Weald. In an age when to employ only *one* servant marked the strict social edge between mere-survival and certain loss-of-caste, Mrs Maberley must strike the sociologist-historian as living perilously near destitution—a fact obviously (though Mr Holmes makes no comment on it) not lost upon those who were about to offer Mrs Maberley money.

This excessively *outré* (as Poe would call it) 'Adventure', has *two* beginnings: the first when the Negro bruiser, Steve Dixie, calls on Mr Holmes at Baker-street to warn the Great Detective that 'his life ain't safe if he go down Harrow way'—and this, before Mrs Maberley—surely by sheer coincidence—calls on Mr Holmes, who had been of service to the late Mr Maberley 'in some trivial matter', for his advice.

A man, 'who said that he was a house agent', had approached Mrs Maberley to buy her house, with all the furniture, for a sum that was well above market-price, seeing that Mrs Maberley—on the 'Why not?' principle—had upped by a 'cool' five hundred pounds. That was for the house alone; on the estate agent's expressing a wish to buy the house's contents on behalf of his client, Mrs Maberley again named a sum, which was accepted without objection. But now a curious difficulty arose.

"Yesterday the man arrived with the agreement all drawn out. Luckily I shewed it to Mr Sutro, my lawyer, who lives in Harrow. He said to me, 'This is a very strange document. Are you aware that, if you sign it, you could not legally take *anything* out of the house—not even your own private possessions?' When the man came again in the evening, I pointed this out, and I said that I meant to sell only the furniture.

"'No, no, everything,' said he.

"'But my clothes? My jewels?'

"Well, well, some concession might be made for your personal effects. But nothing shall go out of this house unchecked. My client is a very liberal man, but he has his fads and his own way of doing things. It is everything or nothing with him.'

"'Then it must be nothing,' said I. And there," said Mrs Maberley to Mr Holmes, "the matter was left, but the whole thing seemed to me so very unusual, that I thought—"

...To call on the advice of Mr Holmes.

And that is the second of this 'Adventure's' two beginnings.

———

Mr Holmes does not, in this case, produce one of his usual classic rabbit-out-of-the-hat solutions—at least, not immediately, though he does leave Mrs Maberley's house with an important piece of information that he has acquired there: a servant, detected in eavesdropping, has revealed that the 'all-or-nothing' client of the self-styled estate-agent is not a man, but a woman. Leaving the house, 'Holmes's eyes, which missed nothing', lighted upon several trunks and cases which were piled in a corner. The labels shone out upon them.

"'Milano'. 'Lucerne'. These are from Italy."

"They are poor Douglas's things."

"You have not unpacked them? How long have you had them?"

"They arrived last week."

Mr Holmes, hearing of the generous offer to buy the house and its contents, and of the restriction on Mrs Maberley's taking anything away—added to the warning that Steve Dixie has given Mr Holmes to lay off the Harrow business—has already deduced that something of value, is, unknown to Mrs Maberley, concealed within the house.

It was, then, inexcusable that he did not ask her then and there to go through the cases and trunks, and to ascertain that the object of value which was *possibly* that coveted by the estate-agent's lady client. How Mr Holmes came to overlook the possibilities—nay, more: the almost certain probabilities—of that luggage's contents is quite inexplicable. These were the late Douglas Maberley's 'things'. Yet only an hour before—possibly even less—Mr Holmes had heard, from the lips of Douglas's mother, the brief account of a son's most promising career ended by premature death: "Dear me! Are you the mother of Douglas Maberley? I knew him slightly. But, of course, all London knew him. What a magnificent creature he was. Where is he now?"

"Dead, Mr Holmes, dead! He was attaché at Rome, and he died there of pneumonia last month."

"I am sorry. One could not connect death with such a man. I have never," said Mr Holmes, tactlessly rubbing it in for the bereaved mother, "known anyone so vitally alive. He lived intensely—every fibre of him!"

"Too intensely, Mr Holmes. That was the ruin of him. You remember him as he was—debonair and splendid. You did not see the moody, morose, brooding creature into which he developed. His heart was broken. In a single month, I seemed to see my gallant boy turn into a worn-out cynical man."

"A love affair—a woman?"

"Or a fiend...."

———

The identity of the fiend was revealed after the house had been burgled and Mrs Maberley chloroformed to permit the leisurely and full search that the burglars required. Summoned to *The Three Gables* by a telegram from Mrs Maberley's lawyer, Mr Sutro, Mr Holmes, with Dr Watson, arrived to find that the thieves had indeed secured what they had been seeking: a manuscript which had been in one of the trunks; a page of which was left behind when Mrs Maberley, recovered from her anaesthetizing, had grappled with one of the intruders.

The rest is easily told.

The manuscript—its tenor was plainly recoverable from the fragment left behind—told the story of the unhappy affair between the late Douglas Maberley and the 'fiend': Isadora Klein, widow of 'the aged German sugar-king, Klein'—and now hoping to marry the young Duke of Lomond. The publication of Maberley's autobiographical love-betrayal—even though that publication was no more than Mrs Maberley's sending the manuscript (better, a photograph of it) to the Duke—would have been good-bye to Isadora's dream of strawberry-leaves. (The leaves on a ducal coronet.)

Holmes tracks her down to her West End mansion, and—not for the first time in his history—puts the bite on her in the name of his highly individual concept of Justice: a cheque for five thousand pounds, to send Mrs Maberley 'round the world in first-class style'.

———

So much, the reader may comment, on the *differences* between the Gabled house of the Harrisons and that of the Conan Doyle 'Adventure'—and, on first consideration, the differences do seem more important than the admitted resemblances.

On *first* consideration...perhaps. But it is hard to resist the strong impression that the Conan Doyle house echoes, is firmly and consciously based upon, the real-life house at Harrow Weald that we occupied for so short a time in 1911, and that the differences, involving Steve Dixie, Mrs Maberley and her son, the estate-agent and Isadora Klein, have been introduced by Doyle for the express purpose of diminishing the overt resemblances between the two houses in Harrow Weald.

Accepting this hypothesis, the reader may well agree with me that it is the basic situation that is important—the lonely house in the Harrow Weald, isolated amongst its trees, with something unusual about the tenancy, and, above all, a strong suspicion that *something unusual* (the thumping coiners' or banknote-forger' press of my Mother's fancy; the unknown object of value coveted by the estate-agent's client) was concealed within the house. These resemblances, which lay down the essential foundations of *both* the 'Gables' stories, make it impossible, despite the Conan Doyle 'variations on the original theme', that the two stories, one true, one 'fictionalized', have other than a common origin. But what happened at the original 'Gables', which impressed itself so forcible on Conan Doyle's mind, and caused him to use the name, not in one story merely, but in two, I cannot, alas!, find out.

That 'Gables'—as trebly 'The Three Gables', and singly as 'The Gables'—appears twice, in stories written in 1926, within a couple of months of each other: in *The Lion's Mane*, where 'The Gables', 'quite a large place...is Harold Stackhurst's well-known coaching[1] establishment', and, as we have seen, in 'The Adventure of the Three Gables', published in, respectively, (first publication) *Liberty Magazine*, November, 1926, and (first publication) *Liberty Magazine*, September, 1926, where the first deals with apparent murder (later revealed as pure mischance), the second with what was, in effect, murder, though no legal system would treat it as such.

---

[1]'Coaching' here does not mean the art of handling the ribbons of *The Highflyer* on the London-Brighton run, but special tuition designed to get students through (usually Army and Civil Service) examinations. An alternative phrase for 'coaching' is 'cramming'; both the tutors and the place of their work being known as 'The Crammers'.

The elusive—and, so far, untraced—event, or series of events, that stamped the memory of 'The Gables' on the mind of Conan Doyle imposed what seems to be an equally enduring recollection in that in another writer of adventure-detection tales: Sax Rohmer.[2] In *Daughter of Fu Manchu*, 'The Gables' appears, too—this time as one of the very temporary headquarters of 'The Devil Doctor'; endlessly pursued, but never brought to full account, by Special Commissioner Nayland Smith.

Sax Rohmer sites *his* 'Gables' at Streatham, still a fairly 'scattered' suburb of south-east London, but in 1914, when Rohmer wrote his follow-up on the wildly successful *Dr Fu Manchu* (helped to best-sellerdom by the best-selling E. Phillips Oppenheim's even more successful *The Great Prince Shan*), Streatham was a quiet, highly 'respectable' district of large private houses, each within its acre-or-so of land, and each plot of land with a handsome provision of privacy-guarding trees. So quiet was the district, though within only a few miles of London, that some hospitals had been sited there: The Hospital for Incurables being the best-known. It was, in 1914, an ideal temporary headquarters for the evil Fu Manchu, but the name of his temporarily rented house, 'The Gables', shews that Sax Rohmer must have looked back in time and elsewhere in place, so confidently to find the name of 'The Gables' ideally suitable as a centre of fictional malfeasance, as (or so I firmly believe) it was once a centre for only too real real-life misdoing, in the 'Gables' that we occupied in 1911.

———

There is a curious pointer to the fact that, for what reason we cannot at present say, the house named 'Gables'—one or three of them—was very much in the forefront of Conan Doyle's interest in 1926. We have already seen that he used the 'Gables' name twice in the course of two months; a 'chosen' name occurs, also, twice, in that same year: the name, 'Ferguson'.

---

[2]So named because Arthur Ward, 'Sax Rohmer', had a house at Stoke-by-Nayland, in the county of Essex.

'Ferguson', like 'Johnson' (or 'Johnstone'—the same pronunciation in British usage) is a favourite name with Conan Doyle. When Mr Holmes asks Mrs Maberley who tenanted the house before she took over, she replies: "A retired sea-captain called Ferguson." Now, the name had already been used by Conan Doyle as far back as 1892, in one of his earliest stories, 'The Engineer's Thumb', but between 1922 and 1926, the year in which, in two stories, the house-name, 'Gables' was used, the personal name, 'Ferguson', was used again in no fewer than *three* 'Adventures': *Thor Bridge, The Sussex Vampire,* and, as I have said, *The Three Gables.* The name, 'Ferguson', then, must have had, like that of 'The Gables', a special significance for Conan Doyle, though, at present, I cannot tell what that significance was. However, in the hunt for the significance of both these well-used names—the house-name and the personal-name—we ought to make a note of each.

Two other names—one, a single name; the other a hyphenated double name—come into the 'Adventure of The Three Gables': Mr Sutro, Mrs Maberley's lawyer, and Haines-Johnson, the estate-agent who is acting for the lovely and fiendish Isadora Klein in trying to get possession of 'The Gables'.

'Sutro' was the name of one of a pair of most successful playwrights of Italian-Jewish extraction, the other being the renowned Arthur Pinero, best remembered now for his *Gay Lord Quex* and *The Second Mrs Tanqueray.*

I have pointed out elsewhere the strange—the seemingly perverse—impulse by which Conan Doyle bestowed the names of those whom he had cause to admire on either the unimportant or the worthless in his writings, and so the use of the manufactured name, 'Haines-Johnson', presents us with a small puzzle. Does this allocation of the names, 'Haines' and 'Johnson', indicate Conan Doyle's usual habit of giving to a criminal (or, at least, an accomplice in dirty work) the name of a person deserving of admiration? Or, since every rule must have its exception, is there a *real* 'Haines', a *real* 'Johnson', *really* bad, recalled here by remembered name?

For the name, 'Haines' was indeed well-known (as 'Haynes') to Conan Doyle: E.S.P. Haynes, a London solicitor with a valuable 'social' practice, and later-to-be-handsomely-realized literary ambitions. E.S.P. Haynes—as he always preferred to be known—was a fellow-agitator of Doyle's for Divorce Reform. So that, if Conan

Doyle had any admiration—even any mild liking— for his fellow-fighter, we should not be astonished that Doyle gave his name to that of the agent for the plotting Isadora Klein. (Remember that Doyle gave the Christian-name of the 'revered' Dr Bell—Joseph—to the mean betrayer, Joseph Harrison, of *The Naval Treaty*—and examples of this 'inverse name-giving' could be multiplied fifty times from The Canon alone.)

But E.S.P. Haynes was a man of curious sexual impulses—an addict of what, in an earlier century, the French called *le vice anglais*; a Swinburnian masochism that he paraded rather than attempted to conceal. This perversion would not have sat easily with Conan Doyle, who had all the prejudices of the sexually-normal man—and Haynes's facetious references to the syphilis that he had contracted at a bawdy-house in Boulogne, during one Long Vacation,[3] would have sat even less easy with that Conan Doyle who had gained his M.D. from Edinburgh with a thesis on Venereal Disease. I think, then, that, in naming the 'estate-agent' 'Haines', Conan Doyle was reversing his usual rule, and—here, at least—naming a villain after a villain. As for the 'Johnson', the reader is referred to the chapter on 'Silver Blaze and Silver Nitrate'.

———

As I have described in my book, *In the Footsteps of Sherlock Holmes*, my Wife and I took the car up to Harrow Weald, to try to find 'Our' house—'The Gables' of 1911; and, as I have written, we found a Harrow Weald in the process of its being cleared, not only of the detached houses—ranging in size from 'villas' to mansions—but of that extensive woodland within which, for a century and more, the well-to-do and rich had lived their comfortable, isolated and exclusive life. We did not, as I have reported, find 'The Gables'.

———

[3] I heard those facetious references from his own lips at a luncheon-party in Hampstead in 1935. The chill comments of a Harley-street doctor—a guest—not only 'considerably dampened Haynes's ardour' as we used to say, but provoked an explosion of hysterical rage on Haynes's part that deserves to be recorded for (what one hopes will be) a more balanced posterity—but not here.

I said earlier that one mystery breeds another, and that, seventy years after the events of 1911, 'The Gables' yet had a further mystery in store.

Well, seventy years after we had left 'The Gables', I decided that I should like to know exactly when we were all living in hearing-distance of the coiners' (or banknote-forgers') nocturnal thumpings at 'The Gables'. I wrote to the appropriate department of the Harrow & Wealdstone municipality, asking the dates between which my Father had been a tenant of 'The Gables'. I suggested that reference to the Rate Books for 1911 should give me the information that I required.

The courteous answer astonished me. It still astonishes me.

The Rate Books for 1911, I was informed, had no record of the name of my Father, for that, or any other year. Nor, since 'extensive demolition in the Harrow Weald district', as I was informed in a later telephone-call, could the location of 'The Gables' be given to me. The non-appearance of my Father's name in the Rate Books might be explained in his tenancy's having been over-and-done-with so rapidly that his name had never come to be registered with the local Rating Office as the tenant of a Harrow Weald property.

But...the non-existent name of the tenant of a non-existent house...? Is there, hidden within this Chinese-box of one-inside-another *ad infinitum* mysteries, perhaps the greatest mystery of all...?

FRIGHTFUL ENCOUNTER IN NORTHUMBERLAND STREET

How Sir Henry came to stay there....

The 'Frightful Encounter', as *The Annual Register* described it, took place when Arthur Conan Doyle was a child of no more than two, but the circumstances of the murderous waylaying of the Major by the Moneylender were so unusual; so very shocking; that the crime gave Northumberland-street, Strand, a notoriety that had certainly not been forgotten even as late as August, 1901, the month in which *The Hound of the Baskervilles* began its serialization in *The Strand Magazine*—exactly forty years after Roberts, the solicitor-turned-usurer, had tried to murder Major Murray, and, in the desperate struggle that had followed the attempt, had lost his own life.

Thackeray was not the only one to have been fascinated by the affair; nor, indeed, the only writer. But his essay on the Northumberland-street crime, written for *The Cornhill Magazine*—'On Two Roundabout Papers Which I Intended to Write'—has survived, not only because of its literary superiority, but also because of the assured fame of its distinguished author. The ephemeral journalistic comments of lesser authors have long been forgotten.

However, the fullest—the most detailed—account is to be found in *The Annual Register,* for July, 1861 (pages 119–127), where the narrative fills nearly seventeen columns of type.

━━━━━━━

I had known the outline of the Northumberland-street affair for many years, but it was not until I was pondering the reasons why Sir Henry Baskerville had landed up in what, when Conan Doyle wrote *The Hound of the Baskervilles* in 1901, was no more than a 'bed-and-breakfast' tavern of decidedly low repute, that I made the connection between the notoriety of Northumberland-street itself and Conan Doyle's evident fascination with that still dark and narrow little street, spared when the broad new Northumberland-avenue cut across the grounds of Northumberland House and many small alleys, to join Trafalgar-square with the new Thames Embankment in 1878.

I have pointed out often enough the proof of Conan Doyle's interest in any particular crime or scandal is to be found in his use of the names involved, and, perhaps, some unusual detail revealed in the newspaper description of the affair. The 'echoes', in Doyle's writings of the Northumberland-street Affair cover a period of at least forty years—more like a half-century, in fact; for the name, 'Murray', occurs as early as 1885, when *A Study in Scarlet* was almost certainly written (it was published at Christmas, 1887); and several 'echoes' of Northumberland-street may be noted in the long interval between *A Study in Scarlet* and *The Hound of the Baskervilles*; 'echoes' which prove how deeply the memory of the Roberts-Murray affray had marked itself on Conan Doyle's consciousness. For instance, *The Adventure of the Speckled Band* (February, 1892) recalls, in Dr Grimesby Roylott's bending of the poker, the murderous use of the fire-irons (including the poker) in Major Murray's self-defensive attack on Roberts; whilst Roberts's habit of discharging his pistol at his own walls is 'echoed' in *The Musgrave Ritual* (May, 1893) where we find Holmes 'patriotically' doing the same thing. Holmes merely made his bullet-pocks form the letters, 'V.R.'. for 'Victoria Regina'—Latin for 'Queen Victoria'—whereas, as we shall see, Roberts had quite another aim in mind when he let off his pistol indoors—to get the neighbours accustomed to the noise of the shots, and to ignore them.

There are other 'echoes' of this strange case, to prove how tenacious was its hold on Conan Doyle's memory; and we shall note them as we come to them.

And now let us see exactly what happened in that 'Frightful Encounter in Northumberland-street' in July, 1861—an affair that drove even the looming American Civil War tragedy off the front pages of the British newspapers.

———

"On the east side of [Northumberland-street], near the river, is an old-fashioned, dingy-looking house (No. 16), with narrow windows, which, being unsuited to the modern taste of dwelling-houses, has been converted into 'chambers'; which are let in various divisions as 'offices' and are entitled 'Northumberland Chambers'." Thus *The Annual Register's* description of what was to prove the scene of quite unusual crime.

> On Friday, the 12th inst., about 11.45 A.M., some workmen, at the back of this and the next house, heard two pistol-shots, apparently fired on the first-floor of No. 16. This excited no surprise, as the same sounds had frequently been heard before. But, about five minutes afterwards, one of the windows was thrown open, and a man, apparently in the greatest excitement, and whose face was covered with blood, appeared at the window, and put one leg out, as though about to jump down—he appeared to have some kind of weapon in his hand. The witnesses called out, "For God's sake, what's the matter?" The man answered to the effect, "That murder had been done."

The workmen shouted to the man to stay where he was, and they would come upstairs to help him. But when they reached the first floor, they found the doors locked, and so returned to the back-yard, to find that the man, in his terror, had managed to make his way, out of the window, and along a very narrow ledge, to 'the wooden casing of a water-pipe, by the aid of which he had reached the ground without injury'.

> In his blind terror, the man now attempted to climb the wall dividing the back-yards of Nos. 15 and 16, but while so doing was pulled back, by the coat-tails, by one of the workmen. He instantly turned, and ran through the passage into the street, where he was stopped by some of the persons who had given the alarm. It was found that he was desperately wounded in the back of the neck, and that his

hair and whiskers were singed and burnt. He seemed almost un-conscious of his injuries, and only to be desirous of getting away. On being told that he was wounded, he said, "Am I?", and on being again told that he was fearfully wounded, he said, "It's that damned fellow upstairs, Grey." His informant said that there was no person in that house named Grey, and that if he meant the person with whom he had been seen to enter the house some time before, his name was not Grey, but Roberts. To which he answered, "He told me his name was Grey." As a head police-station [*Scotland Yard*] is near at hand, numerous constables were by this time on the spot; and the injured man was taken to the Charing Cross Hospital, where with much difficulty, it was ascertained from him that he was 'Major Murray,' and the officers then proceeded to investigate this strange occurrence, and made startling discoveries.

———

And startling those discoveries were: the presence of a desperately wounded, but still living man, in a two-roomed apartment that had been, so far as the furniture was concerned, almost literally destroyed.

> The back room presented a hideous spectacle. A large pool of blood was under the mantel-piece, another large pool in the corner near the furthest window; in the centre of the room was a broken table; broken wine-bottles and pistols were on the floor; the carpet was much disordered, the drawers were pulled out from the furniture, and the papers scattered about; and every part of this disordered area was smeared and splashed with blood.

Both rooms of the apartment, the outer doors of which had been so securely fastened that the police had had to enter through the window overlooking the back-yard, presented the same 'dis-ordered' appearance. As for the wounded man:

> Amid the obscurity and dirt, the object that fixed the attention of the police was a man sitting or crouching on the floor near the door, with his hand on the handle. He was evidently frightfully injured. On the police-sergeant asking him, "How did this happen?", he answered distinctly, "It was done by that man who has just gone down stairs." [The injured man] was Mr Roberts. He, also, was conveyed to the Charing Cross Hospital. His condition is best de-scribed by the popular phrase—he was "battered to pieces."

He was, indeed!

His head shewed 13 distinct wounds, one of which was 8 1/2 inches, others 5 and 6 inches in length: by these the skull was beaten to pieces, one cheek-bone crushed, the temporal artery divided, the eyes closed, the flesh ruptured, and the whole face, especially the left side, beaten to a jelly: the left shoulder was found to be frightfully bruised; the right hand was much beaten, the index finger broken, and a deep cleft made between the thumb and that finger; the left hand and arm greatly beaten.

That anyone should have survived such terrible injuries, the doctors of Charing Cross Hospital (among them a very young intern named Mortimer?) found little short of miraculous, as well they might; and even more miraculous that Roberts was able to reply to some of Inspector Mackenzie's questions, though not, to the Inspector's disappointment, to explain how the injured man had come to be in his present condition.

> ...the Inspector asked [Roberts] if he knew him, and he said he did. Witness then asked him, "How did this affair occur?", and he replied, "Murray did it." [The Inspector] asked him to tell him how, but [Roberts] replied, "My head is too bad. I cannot tell you now." On the next night, [the Inspector] again saw [Roberts], and asked him once more if he could tell how it had all occurred, and how he had received such dreadful injuries about the head. [Roberts] replied, "Murray did it all." But [the Inspector] said, "You must tell me how he did it, Mr Roberts"; and [Roberts] answered, "Murray attacked me with the tongs, and also hit me over the head with a glass bottle." Witness said to him, "You must tell me more particularly than that. Did you know Murray before?", and [Roberts] replied, "I have seen him before, but not spoken to him." Witness asked, had they met by accident or appointment, to which Mr Roberts answered, "By accident, in Hungerford Market,[1] and he came to my office with me about a loan." [The Inspector] then asked him what was the amount of the loan, and Roberts replied, "50,000 pounds." He then added, "Murray shot himself in the neck, and then attacked me like a demon, and hit me with a glass bottle." Witness asked him if he wished to make any depositions before a magistrate, and [Roberts] replied, "No, I have nothing more to say."

Roberts died on the evening of 19th July, 1861, without adding anything to what Inspector Mackenzie had already decided was hardly the truth. It had been Roberts who had begun the affray, and not Major Murray. It now remained for the Inspector to dis-

---

[1] On the site of which, Charing Cross Station has stood since 1863.

cover why the solicitor-moneylender, Roberts, had planned to murder the retired Army-officer.

> Major Murray was very communicative as to the events of the frightful affray in which he had been a party; but he professed utter ignorance of the person and motives of his assailant, and inferred that he had been led into a trap for some mysterious purpose of violence. Mr Roberts was too fearfully injured to make any statement; and though, notwithstanding his dreadful condition, he rallied sufficiently to make known his wants, he never attempted the slightest reference to [*i.e.,* explanation of] the affray.

———

To *The Times*, the scene of the 'affray' was of almost as much interest—fascination, even—as the murderous combat itself; for murderous it had surely been, with the Major, pistolled at close quarters, recovering sufficiently to take his assailant's life. But the strangeness of those offices of Roberts, in which, practising daily with his potshots at the walls, he had waited, like some spider of a malignancy unknown in the entomological world, for the victim of his criminal planning.

As for what *The Times* called 'these ensaunguined apartments', 'a description of these rooms would read almost like a chapter from a French novel', though what they most sound like to us now is that room of Miss Havisham's in Dickens's *Great Expectations,* where the abandoned wedding-feast has been mouldering under the dust of thirty years and more. After describing 'the most costly and luxurious style' in which Roberts had furnished his offices, *The Times's* account goes on to describe, in awed tones, into what unimaginable squalor this luxury and costliness had been permitted to degenerate.

> It is not, however, until one has been in the room some time that the richness of the furniture attracts notice, for glasses, pictures, statuettes, and vases—even the very cabinets themselves—are almost concealed under the accumulated dust of years. The shades and ornaments are enveloped in this, as if coated with a positive fur, and even the slightly relieved figures that on a copy of the Portland vase that stands on a sideboard in the corner, are barely distinguishable under their fine black coating. In spite of the costliness of its furniture, and the taste that has been bestowed upon its

arrangement in the room, it is evident that it has never been cleaned or dusted since the things were first placed there many years ago.

In the centre of the room is the table at which Mr Roberts used to work, with the fireplace on the right hand, having an exceedingly handsome white marble mantel-piece, which is marked with bullets. Yet, almost immediately under the mantel-piece, making a great mound that stretches out into the centre of the floor, are the waste papers that have been crumpled up and thrown aside, and allowed, like the dust, to accumulate undisturbed. The back drawing-room was as righly furnished and as dirty as the front....

But the fascination of the dust of decades could not distract *The Times*'s reporter from his almost morbid interest in the 'ensanguined' condition of the apartment.

If two wild beasts had been turned loose to kill each other in this apartment, it could not have presented traces of a more prolonged or deadly contest than it does. The furniture is broken and over-turned in hideous confusion; the walls, the gilded tables, backs of chairs, and sides of dirty inlaid cabinets are streaked and smeared about with bloody fingers. One may almost trace where blows were struck by the star-shaped splashes of blood along the walls, while over the glass shades of the ornaments and doors of the cabinets it has fallen like rain, as if a bloody mop had been trundled round and round there....

And very much more: all the 'ensanguined' traces of 'the most desperate of all contests—a contest where strong and angry men struggle to tear and beat each other down with whatever weapon they can seize in their frenzy'.

———

That Roberts survived even to make what the police already knew to be a false accusation was miraculous; that Major Murray, with two bullet holes in his head, should not only have survived, but have recovered almost completely, is an even greater miracle.

By an irony of Fate (and the old cliché is permissible here) some pencilled notes left by Roberts on a blotter, not only completely exonerated Major Murray of all murderous intent, but explained how and why Roberts had tricked the Major into what was planned to be his death.

At the Coroner's inquest on Roberts, Major Murray gave his account of the affair. His name, he said, was William Murray, and he lived at 32, Harley-street and at Tottenham. "I was a major in the 10th Hussars, but I have sold out"—the Tenth, as all the well-informed in the Court would have known, being *the* crack cavalry regiment of the British Army, having the Prince of Wales as its Colonel-in-Chief. The Major then went on to explain how he had come to be in the first-floor office at No. 16, Northumberland-street.

The police had already confirmed, to their complete satisfaction, that Roberts, and not the Major, had been the aggressor; no contradiction, then, was offered when, at the invitation of the Coroner, Murray entered the witness-box to tell his story.

He told the Court that, on Friday morning, 12th July, he had left London Bridge, by 'the penny boat', for Hungerford.

> As I was going down the right side of the market, a man came up to me from behind, on my left, and said, "I believe I am speaking to Major Murray?" I said, "Yes, that's my name"; and he then said, "I believe you are a director of the Grosvenor Hotel Company?" I said, "Yes, I am; and pray, who are you?" He said, "My name is Grey." I had never seen him before in my life. I said, "How do you know me?", and Grey replied, "I have seen you at meetings of the company." ...He then went on to say that he had a client who had 60,000 pounds, and that he understood the Company wanted to borrow money, and his client was anxious to get the investment....

Though, the Major told the Court, he explained to 'Grey' that he had no power to commit the Company to a decision in the matter of raising capital, and that he could but convey a message to the other shareholders, 'Grey' persuaded him to come up to his office, and 'answer a few questions'. When the Major had entered the office, and had been seated at 'Grey's' desk:

> [Grey] then said, "You will excuse me for one moment", and left the room.... I took a look around, and thought it was the most extraordinary place I had ever seen; torn papers, bottles and pictures lying about a most disreputable-looking place....

Then 'Grey' came back, still discussing the proposed loan to the Grosvenor Hotel Company, and agreeing to the Major's insistence that the Company would not agree to pay more than five percent on the loan. Murray asked 'Grey' for a business-card and 'Grey' said, "Immediately." Then, said the Major, 'Grey' got up from the table, walked around him, and began 'rummaging' among some papers on a desk. Now well behind the seated Major, 'Grey' drew his pistol:

> Presently, I felt a touch at the back of my neck. There was a report of a pistol, and I dropped off the chair on the ground. I was perfectly paralyzed. I could not move any part of my body. My head, however, was quite clear...when he fired, I believe he left the room. After some little time, I felt returning life in my leg and arm, and I was just raising myself on my elbow when I heard a door open, and he came in again. He immediately walked up behind me, and fired a pistol into my right temple. I dropped back on the carpet, and the blood gushed all over my face, and eyes, and mouth. He either stooped or knelt down close behind me, for I could feel his breath, and he watched close to see if I was dead. I then made up my mind to pretend to be so. I felt that the bleeding was bringing life back to me fast all over my body...I knew if I could get on my feet, I should be able to make a fight of it.

And fight he did! 'Grey' had walked over to the window, when this extraordinarily tough Major seized a pair of tongs, and rushed at Grey-Roberts just as the murderous usurer turned from the window.

The Major made no secret of the ferocity of his attack, with both tongs and bottle—nor, he admitted, did he have it all his own way. The usurer fought back, and though the other returned again and again to the fray, as did the Major ("After a long struggle, I got the tongs. As they came into my hand, I lost my balance, but was up again in an instant...."), he managed, at last, to get a 'full, fair blow at his head with the tongs', and, the Major added, "I gave it him with all my might and main." Roberts (which was his real name) tried to escape the Major's blows by hiding under the table, but this did not save him, and, in full detail, the Major told the Court with what savagery he had rained blow after blow on the man who had tried to murder him. He ended thus:

> That is all I have to say. There was no word passed between us but what I have mentioned. I have not the slightest notion in the world why the man should have attacked me. I have never had any communication with the man, good, bad, or indifferent. I did not know, even, that such a man was in existence.

That fight must have been between two of the toughest men outside the improbable pages of Superman tough-guy fiction. The injuries to Roberts have already been enumerated and described; and it must be remembered that, despite the earlier of these dreadful woundings by Major Murray, Roberts, by the Major's account, had fought on with a tenacity and ferocity that, at times, threatened to make him the winner in what was literally the bloodiest of conflicts. ('These tongs,' *The Times* observed, 'broken, bent and covered with blood and hair, Major Murray had in his hand when first seen escaping from the window'.)

But how did the Major fight, after what had happened to *him*?

> The wounds of Major Murray were few, but one of them was so placed that it is a marvel how he escaped instant death. In front of the right ear was a long but superficial wound, and his legs were much contused [doubtless from the fight with Roberts]; but on the back of his head, between the right jaw and the cervical vertebrae, was a circular mark, surrounded by burnt and scorched hair, in the centre of which was a jagged opening which would scarcely admit the top of the little finger. This jagged aperture was the commencement of a wound which led by a long track downwards to the spine. On sounding this, the probe struck against a metalic substance—a pistol-bullet—rather large, which was extracted with difficulty, and which was found to have struck against the spine with such force as to have been indented to the shape of the part against which it struck.

And still the Major managed to overcome the murderous Roberts!

———

Major Murray told the Coroner, truthfully, that he could not explain Roberts's attempted murder—but, by this time, the police had found the reason in some notes that Roberts had made on a sheet of blotting-paper, in which the name, 'Mrs Murray' occurred. Further search of the blood-soaked office-apartment, brought to light several letters 'in a female hand', some signed 'Annie', others, 'A.M. Murray'—and when the police went to make enquiries of the lady, they found that she was not the Major's wife, but his young mistress—and here, in the handling of the lady by police, Press, and Coroner, we have yet another of those pleasant inconsistencies not so very rare in the expression of conventional Victorian morality; for nothing could exceed in tenderness the treatment accorded to this 'soiled dove', to use one of the many contemporary euphemisms for a 'fallen woman'. 'Unfortunate' was yet another.

> The unfortunate young woman was able to make a statement which gave an object and motive to the murderous proceedings of Mr Roberts.

He desired the Major's mistress for himself.

> She had, it appeared, been living for several years under Major Murray's protection, and had had one child, a daughter, by him. He had behaved to her with uniform kindness, and had been sufficiently liberal; but the expenses attending her confinement had brought her into debt, and unwilling to apply to the Major for money, she unhappily applied to Mr Roberts, the usurer, who gave her fifteen pounds for her bill at three months. This seems to have been renewed several times, for the poor young woman was seldom able to save from her allowance more than the quarter's interest—£5.
>
> She was naturally terrified lest Major Murray should know of these transactions, and the usurer was well aware of her anxiety for secrecy.

The Annual Register rarely permitted its columns to exhibit an emotional comment in its straight reporting of the year's most interesting events. But indignation fairly bubbled out of the generally sedate column at this point.

> The low, coarse-minded brute—who was a married man with a family, and keeping every appearance of staid respectability [*a description that could, in all fairness, have applied equally well to the Major*]— began to lust after his unhappy client, and sought to turn her necessities to his advantage. Nor did he use any delicacy about the gratification of his passions; for on one occasion when she went to deprecate [*sic*] his forbearance, and offer the quarter's interest for renewal, he plainly told her not to make herself uneasy about it, for that if she would be his, he would forgive her the whole of it.

The Annual Register makes no attempt to hide its sympathy for the lady, nor its disgust for the usurious lecher who sought to buy her.

> The poor creature (whose appearance and conduct while under examination were most becoming) indignantly repudiated his disgusting proposals. But the idea seemed to have got complete pos-

session of the man, and ruled him as with an absolute passion; he pursued her in every direction, watched her in her outgoings with Major Murray, knew where she had been, could tell where she had sat, and with whom; he passed her in cabs in her walks [*as Stapleton, in a hansom, followed Holmes and Watson down Regent-street, in* The Hound of the Baskervilles!] and even sought to introduce her to his wife and family, for which she again had moral sense to rebuke him.

She did, however, in her anxiety to keep Roberts's pursuit of her from her protector, permit Roberts to send her 'presents and ardent letters', and to reply to the letters 'in a too corresponding style, fearing that he would betray her if she did not'.

Either with an eye to business, or urged by a morbid curiosity, Mr Roberts also kept a watch upon Major Murray, and by his continued knowledge of [the Major's] proceedings, kept the young woman in continual alarm; and from her forced a knowledge of the Grosvenor Hotel Company, and of Major Murray's circumstance. About a month before the fatal affray, [Roberts] ascertained from Mrs Murray that the Company was desirous of borrowing a large sum—£40,000 to £50,000. He professed to have a client who was willing to lend it....

—and the rest followed, almost, one might say, inevitably.

The Annual Register ended its account of 'The Frightful Encounter' with some speculations on the attempted murder of Major Murray:

Under what circumstances the idea of destroying the Major in order to get possession of his mistress first entered the wretched man's mind cannot be known—whether the one overpowering frenzy so blinded him to the futility of the scheme that he had dwelt upon it until it took shape and consistency, or whether it was a momentary impulse, so sudden and so thrilling as to allow no time for pause or reflection. From the brute's pursuit [of the Major] it seems rather more probable that he desired to entangle the Major in an usurer's toils, and then to force or purchase from his necessities the object of his desires.

As for the pistol-practice:

Nothing was stated which would suggest that the long-continued pistol practice had any other purpose than amusement; yet it is very possible that the presence of these weapons and habit of using them may have suggested the frenzied idea. Shakespeare truly says:
"Oft-times, the sight of means to do ill-deeds
Makes ill-deeds done."

A conclusion that may or may not be tenable. At least, Conan Doyle preferred the theory that, originally, Roberts had fired off his pistols for 'amusement' only; for, when, in *The Musgrave Ritual* (1893), Sherlock Holmes is made to copy Roberts's odd habit, it is for 'amusement' only that Holmes shoots his gracious Sovereign's initials in bullet-pocks on the wall of the Baker-street apartment.

As for Major Murray:

> After a very protracted enquiry, the general concurrence of circum-stances corroborated the main points of Major Murray's statement, and the jury returned a verdict of "justifiable homicide, and that Major Murray slew the deceased to save his own life."

Fully recovered from his appalling injuries, this remarkably tough ex-cavalry officer was free to return to the 'becoming Mrs Murray', now free for ever from the blackmail and importunities of the lust-crazed Roberts.

The 'echoes' of this case, which so fascinated Conan Doyle, are of two kinds: the obvious—the use of names from the press-accounts: Northumberland, Murray, Charing Cross Hospital, Harley-street, London Bridge, Charing Cross (Hotel), Grosvenor Hotel, Totten-ham (Court-road—three times used), Annie (Murray)—three times—and the not-so-obvious: the 'pistol practice' within a room; Roberts's trailing Annie Murray in a cab; the Turkish Bath at the very end of Northumberland-street: across the narrow alley from *The Northumberland Hotel*; Conan Doyle's putting the American, Moulton, in one of the then grand hotels of Northumberland-avenue, into which dingy little Northumberland-street emerges.

But by far the most striking 'echo' is to be found in *Shoscombe Old Place*, which, written in 1927, is the last Sherlock Holmes story that Doyle wrote—and that it is so late testifies to the grip on Sir Arthur's imagination that the 'Frightful Encounter' in old Nor-thumberland-street had continued to have on him over so many decades.

For *Shoscombe Old Place* not only concerns a money-lender of a Roberts-type, but so closely 'echoes' the Northumberland-street affair, that the usurer's victim, Sir Robert Norberton, the racehorse-owner and 'daredevil rider', is actually made by Conan Doyle to launch a murderous attack on the money-lender—'...when he horse-whipped Sam Brewer, the well-known Curzon-street moneylender, on Newmarket Heath, and nearly killed him'. (Note the Christian name of the baronet, and note, too, a casual, almost irrelevant, inclusion of the street in which Major Murray lived: "First of all, Mr Holmes, I think that my employer, Sir Robert, has gone mad." Holmes raised his eyebrows. "This is Baker-street, not Harley-street," said he).

Of course, we must expect, and so we have here, all Conan Doyle's perverse love of the 'back-to-front'; his constant inclina-tion—that he never resisted—of presenting remembered facts in a sort of Leonardoan 'mirror-image'. Here, too, we have that old Doylean trick of altering the social class: Major Murray, an officer of field-rank in Britain's most prestigious cavalry-regiment, is 'echoed' as 'Murray', that prudent *orderly* who saved Dr Watson (and, of course, himself) in the battle of Maiwand. Yet note that, as the 'Major Murray' of the murderous attack on the usurer, Brewer, the 'echoed' original of the killer of the usurer, Roberts, is elevated to the rank of a baronet. And, too, the reverse-action is here: in Northumberland-street, it was the usurer who was the assailant; it was the proposed victim of the usurer's plans who was attacked. In *Shoscombe Old Place*, it is the resentful victim of usury who is the aggressor. But, shadowy as the resemblance may be in detail, the overall picture is clearly enough the loudest 'echo' of the Nor-thumberland-street affair of 1861. It is interesting, too, to see that Holmes's well-known tolerant disregard for the Law is here clearly on view, as he permits some illegality on the part of Sir Robert, so that his horse may win the Derby, and get the owner free from a moneylender's clutches.

———

Conan Doyle's treatment of another of his fictitious baronets calls for attention: what made Conan Doyle put Sir Henry Baskerville into so humble an hotel as *The Northumberland*—to give it no worse adjective? Conan Doyle obviously knew Northumberland-street well, and so must have known its condition and social-standing at the time (the Sherlockian chronologists have fixed on the year, 1888) at which the action of *The Hound of the Baskervilles* is set. Three years after 1888, the murderous Dr Neill Cream, whose pleasure it was to induce the lowest type of street-woman to take a capsule of strychnine, and enjoy the thought of her dying in excruciating pain, had picked up, and given, another of these women, Lou Harvey (whose surname Conan Doyle gave to an innocent 'lad' in Sir Robert Norberton's racing-stables), a capsule, 'to eradicate a few spots on her forehead'. Dr Cream had met Louisa in a London music-hall; they had spent the night together in a Berwick-street, Soho, hotel; and now, on the following night, Dr Cream was preparing to send her to join the other harlots whom he had killed. But Louisa was the lucky one who got away. As she explained in her evidence at Dr Cream's Old Bailey trial (which convicted and hanged him):

> Met him same night opposite Charing Cross Underground Railway-station. Walked with him *to the Northumberland public-house [My italics— and it never occurred to the lady to call that 'public-house' an 'hotel'...so why did Conan Doyle?]*, had a glass of wine, and then walked back to the Embankment, where he gave me two capsules. But not liking the look of the thing, I pretended to put them in my mouth, but kept them in my hand. And when he happened to look away, I threw them over the Embankment.

From which strumpet's evidence, it will be gathered *exactly* what the social status of *The Northumberland* was....

So, once again, comes the question: Why did Conan Doyle, who certainly had had time (he was forty-two when he wrote *The Hound*) to know his way about London, put Sir Henry in such a frowzy pot-house as *The Northumberland,* a tavern frequented, as Doyle well knew, if merely from reading the reports of the Cream trial, by common prostitutes and their bullies, and by the smaller criminal element of the West-end? Was it to emphasize that a Canadian—any Canadian; even one who had inherited a baronetcy—was so ignorant of polite usage; so lacking in social *savoir-faire*; that, arrived in London, he could do no better in the way of finding hotel-room than in blindly ending up at the pot-house in narrow, dingy (and then, as to-day, faintly sinister) Northumberland-street?

And how, when we consider the fact, *did* Sir Henry come to go there? Dr Mortimer had met him at Waterloo Station (so that Sir Henry had arrived in Southampton from Canada). The two men would then have taken—as Sir Henry had his baggage with him—a 'growler'; a four-wheeler; at the station, and crossed over to the Strand by way of Waterloo Bridge. Even before reaching the seatings of the Bridge, they would have passed several small hotels—the well-known *York* among them; and, turning out of the Bridge left, into the Strand, they would have come to the newly-built *Savoy*, or, if something cheaper were preferred, several smaller hotels on both sides of the street: *Haxell's*, on the right, and the *Adelphi* on the left; but they could hardly have missed the still fairly-new (built 1863) *Charing Cross Hotel*, eight stories towering above the Station yard. At the corner of that yard, at the Strand end of Craven-street was the old-fashioned but still comfortable and respectable *Craven Hotel*, and, at the nearer corners of Trafalgar-square, a small block further on, where the now somewhat old-fashioned *Morley's Hotel*, dating from the Regency, and, on the other side of the Strand, the modern *Grand Hotel*, less than ten years old; first of the splendid hotels that had sprung up along the newly-planned Northumberland-avenue.

Why all these—and so many other—hotels had been rejected (or Conan Doyle had made Sir Henry reject)—in favour of the seedy, harlot-frequented *Northumberland Hotel* will never be explained. The explanation—alas!, no longer available—is to be found only in the peculiar and highly idiopathic psychology of Arthur Conan Doyle, who so often saw life reversed and through a diminishing-glass, and whose idea of the straightest length of cord joining two points was a cat's-cradle.

───────

What was the element in the Northumberland-street Affair that held such fascination for Conan Doyle? I think that we may say that there were two attention-rivetting elements, one minor, the other major. The minor element was the clinically detailed and vivid descriptions of the antagonists' injuries; attractive to both the medical man in Doyle, and also to that streak of cruelty to which (as I have mentioned elsewhere) the English novelist, Pamela Hansford Johnson drew my attention some years ago; that interest in the horrible that is so keen, so all-consuming, that it is almost of the nature of love. Go back for a moment to that description of the vitriol's eating away, not merely the beauty of the Baron's features, but the very features themselves; and the horror described, as I say, with a care that has something of tenderness in it—not tenderness for the ruined man ("The wages of sin, Watson....") but for the chemical changes that are dissolving the flesh; and (one must admit it) that intense interest in the physical and mental agony that that grim change is causing. (And, by the way, had Kitty Winter not intervened at that moment with her bottle of vitriol, a savage fight of the Northumberland-street order was about to take place.)

This cruelty, this savagery, is the minor element in the Roberts-Murray fight's attraction, and, really, minor it is—certainly in comparison with the major element in the affair's attraction.

I suggest that what really drew Conan Doyle to the Northumberland-street story; what truly held and retained his interest in it for so long a part of his life; was the unusual tenderness shewn to the Major's young mistress by every aspect of Authority and Officialdom, as well as by the Press. To read of this tenderness; the more so as demonstrated with every (and I think genuine) appearance of *respect*; of the sort usually reserved for ladies of undeniable respectability, as the Victorians understood that social quality; must have seemed so strikingly unusual to Conan Doyle as to stamp the memory of 'Mrs' Murray's last-minute rescue from blackmail and lust indelibly on his over-romantic mind.

For, as Police and Court and Press behaved towards this 'becoming' young woman in distress—and so strangely, by Victorian conventional standards—so Conan Doyle knew that he himself would have behaved; and his heart went out, not only to the young girl who, so surprisingly, had met with nothing but sympathy and kindness—but went out, too, to all who had shewn her that strange tenderness.

If for Conan Doyle, Woman—and so, all women—had been placed, not *by* him, but *for* him, on a pedestal since his earliest awareness of Her and Them as a different sex, so, inevitably, for him, Woman, being perfect, might do no wrong. The true story of how he swiped young Adrian so savagely across the face as to send the boy sprawling, is well known—and completely in Conan Doyle's character. (The boy had incautiously said that a certain woman was 'ugly'.) And, Woman's relations with him in his Doyle-

Holmes *persona* can do no wrong: they can, in the most literal sense of the colloquial phrase, 'get away with murder'—the lady who shot 'The Worst Man in London' did actually do so.

That Holmes slipped from his usual standards, as regards Woman, in making love to Milverton's pretty housemaid cannot be denied; but, in his defence, it must be remembered that he was doing this in the strict line of duty—and, so far, it is the only instance on record where he treated Woman with anything less than understanding, sympathy, and respect—and, in one famous instance, Love....

———

No-one may be astonished that the Northumberland-street Affair should so greatly have fascinated Conan Doyle, so that 'echoes' of it—for instance, Grimesby Roylott and the poker-bending; the two Scots Inspectors' names, McDonald and McKinnon, 'echoing' that of Inspector Mackenzie; and so many other 'echoes'—are to be found throughout the Canon, from the very first Holmes story to (*Shoscombe Old Place*) the very last.

For, to Conan Doyle, this true-life affair had every element calculated to catch and to hold his perpetual interest: Lust (*cf.* his use of that word in *The Illustrious Client*) using blackmail of the defenceless to gain its own abominable ends; the prolonged and ruthless savagery of the Roberts-Murray fight; and—above all—the universal tenderness shewn to a young woman—with the 'happy ending' that, at last, freed her from the nightmare of Persecution.

DR WATSON GOES TO READING

Maiwand—A Poetic Tribute

In all the accounts of Dr John H. Watson's activities so far discovered and published, no mention has been made of one of the most important engagements of his life—his visit to the Berkshire town of Reading on Wednesday, 15th December, 1886. He travelled down from Baker Street on that bleak December day at the urgent solicitation of Lord Wantage, VC, the Lord Lieutenant of the County of Berkshire; and Dr Watson's companion on the 9:30 am "through" train to Reading—a 36-mile journey from London—was Mr (afterwards Sir) Richard Holmes, late of the 66th Berkshire Regiment, and thus, besides being a cousin of Mr Sherlock Holmes, a companion-in-arms of Dr Watson.

The Town of Biscuits and Jailbirds

For those to whom the name of Reading be unfamiliar, let me say briefly that, in 1886, its fame (or notoriety, if you wish) depended upon two things: its biscuit industry, centred about the firm of Huntley & Palmer, and its red-brick jail, afterwards world-famous as Oscar Wilde's place of detention. It was also known, though less famously, for a statue of Queen Victoria, that the loyal directors of Huntley & Palmer had caused to be erected in such a way that it was clearly visible from all the trains which pass along what is still one of England's busiest stretches of track. It is not an attractive piece of sculpture, and none was less appreciative of it than its Royal subject, who invariably ordered that the blinds of her compartment should be lowered as her train passed through Reading—thus sparing her the offensive sight of her own statue. It was to be a present at the unveiling of quite another sort of statue that Dr Watson and Mr Richard Holmes were travelling on this foggy December morning of over a century ago.

The Lion of Maiwand

The two men—respectively companion and cousin of the famous Mr Sherlock Holmes, soon to be appointed the first Private Consulting Detective-in-Ordinary of any British monarch—were travelling down to Reading on the 9:30 train (conveniently provided with a restaurant-car for any needed alcoholic refreshment) to be present, as honoured guests, at a ceremony so impressive that it is strange, indeed, that it has never been mentioned, even obliquely, in the chronicles of Dr Watson and Mr Sherlock Holmes. The ceremony was the imminent unveiling, by General Lord Wantage, of the memorial to the men who had fallen during the Afghan War of 1879–1880.

"In the beginning of August, 1880," runs a contemporary account of the facts behind the unveiling, "England was startled with the news that the British troops in Afghanistan had been defeated, and terrible slaughter inflicted on General Burrows's army at Maiwand. This would probably have meant annihilation *but for the bravery of the 66th Berkshire Regiment,*[1] who, when duty called, were ready to sacrifice their lives to cover the retreat of the fleeing troops. Two hundred and eighty-two of these brave fellows[2] were left dead on the field."

By modern standards—losses of over 25,000,000 incurred by the Russians alone in *both* World Wars; over six million German casualties before the Allies landed in Normandy in 1944—the whole

---

[1] My emphasis. M.H.

[2] Estimates of the Berkshires's losses vary considerably—we may ignore McGonagall's poetic hyperbole: 'massacred to the last man'. Doubtless the inscription on the Maiwand Lion may be taken as giving the correct figure of the losses in battle.

Afghan campaign was a trivial affair, even though Shere Ali opposed some 25,000 men against the British force of a mere 2,500. It was not one of the most glorious moments in the history of British arms, and though the men of Maiwand were to be completely avenged in the brilliant counter-stroke of General Sir Alfred Roberts (afterwards Field-Marshal Earl Roberts of Kandahar, K.G.), the circumstances of the defeat left an ineffaceable legacy of bitterness and shame to all who had survived that sad affair—to none more than the sensitive Dr Watson, who may have thought at times that it would have been better for him had he not survived that field of dishonour.

In the first part of Mr Sherlock Holmes's memoirs, that I have had the privilege of editing for their publication by Messrs Dutton, of New York, the deep and lasting effects of Maiwand on Dr Watson are dealt with in some detail by Mr Holmes; and we may assume that it was in a mood of sentimental regret, not merely for his lost comrades, but for a nation's lost opportunities, too, that Dr Watson with his companion—both veterans of Maiwand—alighted at Reading at 10:08 am (British trains were *always* on time in those pre-Welfare State days!) to unveil the Bronze Lion.

Six Years for a Memorial

It is clear, looking back, that the tardiness with which the British public subscribed the necessary funds to erect a Maiwand Memorial was not unrelated to an understandable desire to forget what then ranked as one of Britain's worst and most shameful defeats—not even at the hands of white enemies, equipped with modern weapons, but at those of a "horde of savages"—the "murderous Ghazis" of Dr Watson's bitter recollection. The wonder is that enough money was ever subscribed to erect a memorial that most English people thought, at the best, unnecessary; at the worst, in downright bad taste. As it was, it needed four full years of public-badgering before the trustees of the Maiwand Memorial Fund were in a position to commission the eminent sculptor, Mr E. Simmonds, to prepare designs for a monument in Forbury-gardens, Reading. The design passed, Mr Simmonds took two years to cast the bronze lion and erect the plinth of terra-cotta—the memorial was ready for unveiling in December, 1886, halfway through the first of those Jubilee Years in which the majority of the Queen's subjects evinced their loyalty towards Monarch and Crown.

Defeat into Victory

Whilst it may be doubted that the shame of a defeat may ever be wiped out by the victory of some other body of soldiers, there is no doubt that, in Sir Alfred Roberts's "licking" of the Afghan Shere Ali, the prestige of British arms and the authority of the Raj were restored as fully as though Maiwand had never happened. And certainly the spirit in which the bronze lion of the Reading memorial had been designed exhibited neither apology nor shame—the lion had been conceived, not in the spirit of regret for defeat, but in the almost cock-a-hoop pride in victory.

In the circumstances, we ought to have expected that the bronze lion would be no modest member of its memorial species—and in this we find we are not wrong. In the Services idiom of the day, the lion was—and is—a 'whopper': measuring 13 feet 4 inches from mane to paw, with a chest-girth of 14 feet, and with a "forearm" (so a contemporary description calls it) no less than 5 feet in circumference. "From this," exclaims an admiring Victorian journalist, "the huge size of the beast may be judged; it is the largest and undoubtedly the most magnificent representation of a lion in the world."

Each of the four faces of the terra-cotta oblong pedestal bears an inscription, of which that on the front face is the most important:

> This monument records the names and commemorates the valour and devotion of 11 officers and 317 noncommissioned officers and men of the 66th Berkshire Regiment, who gave their lives for their country at Girisk, Maiwand and Kandahar, and during the Afghan campaign of 1879–80. "History does not afford any grander or finer instance of gallantry and devotion to Queen and country than that displayed by the 66th Regiment at the battle of Maiwand on 27th July, 1880.
> —Dispatch of General Primrose

On the rear face of the pedestal it is recorded that the monument was "Erected in 1884 by residents in Berkshire and by comrades and friends of those whose names are here recorded." Among those who subscribed most generously were Dr Watson and Mr Richard Holmes, the Librarian of Windsor Castle; sometime Colonel Commanding the Volunteer Battalion of the 66th (Berkshire) Regiment. A handsome subscription was also received from Mr Sherlock Holmes.

A Neglected Sherlockian Shrine

Like the majority of other British towns, Reading has suffered terribly from the ravages of profit-obsessed and (mostly) exotic "planners". It was never the most beautiful of English towns, but it had a certain charm that not even the "mediaeval" Victorian prison quite spoiled, but which has been effectively swept away by the soulless, meaningless "architecture" of glass-and-concrete "progress".

Nevertheless, what remains of Reading's old charm is to be found in its ornamental gardens by the river; and here, against a screen of weeping willow, will be found, undamaged by the bombing of two World Wars, and the more destructive attentions of Progressive Authority, the Maiwand Lion.

Reading is not far from London—under forty miles, with one of the better train-services of a decaying railway system. I was told by a local bank-manager that it is a place of pilgrimage; that many, especially foreigners, come to Reading to see the prison in which Wilde wrote *The Ballad of Reading Gaol*. It seems strange that it is not also a place of pilgrimage for Sherlockians. I can think of no surer way in which to put the clock back to 1886— and, beyond that, to 1880—than in standing before the monument at whose unveiling Dr Watson assisted on that bleak December day of a century ago; to stand there to-day, and read, as he read, with tears in his eyes, of that brief, small and hopeless military action of which "history does not afford any grander or finer instance."

The next time that you are in London, do not give Baker Street all your attention; take a taxi to Paddington Station, catch the first of the very many trains always leaving for Reading, and—standing before "the most magnificent representation of a lion in the world"— see if you do not share with me some newer thoughts about the self-effacing Dr John H. Watson.

MAIWAND: POETICAL TRIBUTE

The Baskerville Banquet—each of the annual dinners of the Sherlock Holmes Society of London has its own title—was held on 6th January, 1959: Twelfth Night being the assumed birthday of Mr Sherlock Holmes.

There were two guest-speakers—the late Mr Hesketh Pearson, memorable biographer of Sir Arthur Conan Doyle, and myself, both of us being accompanied by our wives. The Chairman was that dedicated Sherlockian author and journalist, Edward Holroyd—and it is a melancholy fact that, of all of us who sat at the High Table that night, only Dame Jean Conan Doyle and I are left. (I know now, unhappily, what Sir Bedivere felt when he stood, 'revolving many memories', as the black barge took from him what he had most loved and cherished....)

I forget now what we said; but one jesting remark of Edward Holroyd's stays firmly in my memory, since, after the dinner, my Wife asked me who 'the great McGonagall' was whom Mr Holroyd had mentioned in his speech. Parodying the unique style of the Dundee rhymester, William McGonagall—and punning with it, too: 'The doggerel in the night-time,' was the parodist's description of his pastiche—the Chairman gave us this almost pure McGonagallese; he was referring, of course, to some verses just spoken:

> ...I fear that our Editor, Lord Donegall,
> Will bracket them with those of the great McGonagall;
> Or at least will say: "Good heavens, this fellow's brash;
> He never seems to have heard of a chap called Ogden Nash!"

"Who's McGonagall...?" my Wife asked me at the first opportunity. "*I've* never heard of him."

———

In the nearly three decades which have passed since that pleasant dinner in the even then century-old Charing Cross Hotel, William McGonagall has become, if not exactly internationally famous, at least well known to many more people than had known his name in 1959, for McGonagall, the greatest Poet of the Doggerel, has been, as they say, 'taken up', and his lamentable but emotionally sincere 'poems' have become quite a craze.

William McGonagall was the last, and certainly the most talented, in the great tradition of the 'broadsheet'—the 'poem' hastily composed to commemorate some stirring event, usually though not always, a hanging, with a 'poetic' description of the crime behind the punishment. Sold in the streets and in the meaner newsagents' shops for a penny, the broadsheets, mostly produced by the firm of Catnach, often reached astonishing sales. The tradition is not yet dead; I bought a 'poem' of quite incredible doggerelity that began (it celebrated the Coronation of our present Sovereign):

> In famous Westminster Abbey
> When they crown her Gracious Majesty
> There are wonderful robes and uniforms, nothing shabby
>
> The old walls of the Abbey are hung with costly tapestry
> And everything is just as it should be seen
> All of the very best as they crown our Lovely Queen...

This isn't as good as the worst of McGonagall, who, in his class, stands unrivalled, but it is good to know that the old tradition of the *ad hoc*, here-and-now rhymester ('Poems for all occasions, to order!'), in which he was so shining a light, is not yet dead. I should be sorry to think that Progress has 'educated' the populace out of its taste for the fugitive poetic commemoration of some memorable event, though, alas!, the 'True Confession and Last Word' of the hanged felon has vanished as completely as has hanging itself. (At least, in Britain....)

———

There were few events, in the latter part of the last century, that did not call forth an immediate response in the form of an effusion from McGonagall's ready pen, and even readier poetic imagination. Battles (even those where the Ever-victorious British *didn't* come off best), shipwrecks, the funerals of the Great, calamitous fires, tragedies involving great loss of life (the collapse of the Tay Bridge on 28th December, 1879, as a train was crossing, with the death of eighty persons, called forth one of McGonagall's most memorable poetic efforts), though he was not above commemorating in his own brand of verse events as tame as the laying of the foundation-stone of a hospital or Town Hall.

Like his fellow-poet, Alfred, Lord Tennyson, McGonagall was given to paying poetic tribute to Queen Victoria, though informed opinion denied McGonagall's superiority to the Poet Laureate.

In one important respect, the Scots doggerelist spoke for sound public opinion; the heroes of the day were his heroes, too—and with Dr Watson (and with tens of thousands of others, of course) McGonagall shared the hero-worship of General Charles Gordon, 'the Martyr of Khartoum'—and took a poem of many stanzas to proclaim his fervid admiration for Gordon.

But, though he was to compose a poem describing how General Roberts avenged the grisly defeat of Maiwand, McGongall's honest acceptance of Fact, however distasteful, impelled him to commemorate the defeat before he came to celebrate (to the Victorians) the inevitable victory. His collected poems fill three thick volumes—all of them having been spoken in public by the proud author in the 'dramatic recitals' that he gave in Dundee and Glasgow. His tribute to the gallant—and unlucky—men of Maiwand ranks, I feel, among his very best:

The Last Berkshire Eleven: The Heroes of Maiwand

'Twas at the disastrous battle of Maiwand, in Afghanistan,
Where the Berkshires were massacred to the last man;
On the morning of July the 27th, in the year eighteen eighty,
Which I'm sorry to relate was a pitiful sight to see.
Ayoub Khan's army amounted to twelve thousand in all,
And honestly speaking it wasn't very small,
And by such a great force the Berkshires were killed to the last man,
By a murderous rebel horde under the command of Ayoub Khan.
The brave Berkshires under Colonel Galbraith stood firm in the centre there,
While the shouts of the wild Ghazis rent the air;
But still the Berkshires held them at bay,
At the charge of the bayonet, without dismay.
Then the Ghazis, with increased numbers, made another desperate charge
On that red line of British bayonets, which wasn't very large
And the wild horsemen were met again with ringing volleys of musketry,

Which was most inspiring and frightful to see.
But the Berkshires stood firm, replying to the fire of the
musketry,
While they were surrounded on all sides by masses of cavalry;
Still that gallant band resolved to fight for their Queen and
country
Their motto being death before dishonour, rather than flee.
Oh, heaven! it was a fearful scene the horrors of that day,
When I think of so many innocent lives that were taken away;
Alas! the British force were massacred in cold blood,
And their blood ran like a little rivulet in full flood.
And the Ghazis were afraid to encounter that gallant little band
At the charge of the bayonet: Oh! the scene was most grand;
And the noble and heroic eleven fought on without dismay,
Until the last man in the arms of death stiff and stark lay.

The unique quality of McGonagall's verse puts it, I feel, outside
any criticism; but a note here for non-British (or, at least, non-
cricket-playing) readers may be useful. The title of the Maiwand
poem, *The Last Berkshire Eleven,* may not unreasonably be thought
to allude to the 'eleven'—the full number of any cricket 'side'—
playing for the county of Berkshire. The likening of a murderous
battle to a game of cricket is in the soundest of Victorian (and,
indeed, later) tradition, and to see the British Tommy, whether in
defeat or in victory, as a Sportsman, rather than as a Killer, had a
literally universal appeal for the 'far-flung' British of the Queen's
world-empire. 'The Last Berkshire Eleven....' The allusion would
not have been lost on any of McGonagall's audience, nor would
any have felt it as belittling the men of Maiwand to liken them to
the Berkshire County Cricket Club.

In one of the great marches of history, General Sir Frederick Roberts
('Bobs' to all his admiring troops), covering, through the heat and
dust of an hostile country, three hundred and twenty miles in
twenty-one days, brought his troops to battle with Ayoub Khan at
Kandahar, Afghanistan, and soundly thrashed the victor of
Maiwand.
    Sixteen stanzas McGonagall needed to pay his own poetic trib-
ute to the one-eyed, diminutive General who had become, with
that far-off victory, the Hero of the Empire. The poem, *General
Roberts in Afghanistan* is quite up to McGonagall's highest literary

standard: the ferocious (and completely successful) bayonet charge by the 92nd Highlanders particularly exciting McGonagall's admiration:

> Then the British with a wild cheer dashed at them,
> And on each side around they did them hem;
> And at the bayonet charge they drove them down the hill,
> And in hundreds they did them kill.

There is no need to quote the other fifteen stanzas; but, whatever the quality of McGonagall's verse, we had nothing from Tennyson on either Maiwand or Kandahar....

MORE ABOUT THAT CRYPTIC 'CARFAX'

One of the oldest and still most hotly debated questions concerning the ante-Canonical life of Mr Holmes concerns the identity of the University that he attended; loyalty to British tradition limiting the questioners' choice to a mere couple: Oxford or Cambridge? (Unthinkable that Mr Holmes could have attended any of the others—and quite venerable some of them; established long before he was born. No: it was either Oxford or Cambridge; nothing lower in the academical-social scale would satisfy the hero-worshippers....)

The question—still unsolved as I write this, on a blazing late-June day, only a few miles to the east of Mr Holmes's retirement-home at Fulmer, on the Channel coast—is simply: which university?, this Sherlockian exegetist arguing the merits of Oxford; this other warm for Cambridge. (To me, the balance of proof seems to dip slightly in favour of Oxford; but this essay is not about to add me to the list of this branch of Sherlockian puzzle-solvers: I am concerned here only with the significance of a single name.)

When the Holmes 'adventure', *The Disappearance of Lady Frances Carfax*, was published in both *The Strand* and *The*

American magazines for December, 1911, the Higher Criticism—the scholarly commentary on the Sherlockian narratives of Dr John H. Watson—had hardly got under way; but when, in the next two decades, the commentaries began to come thick and fast, Dr Watson's choice of that surname, 'Carfax', seemed to many to hint at the identity of Mr Holmes's university, since the principal crossroads in the ancient city of Oxford is called 'Carfax'.

To the late Lord Donegall, that Dr Watson's use of the name, 'Carfax', certified Mr Holmes's academic connection with Oxford, seemed, to my friend 'Don', 'confirmation strong as proofs of Holy Writ'. He was not to be budged from this almost emotionally-held conviction (that he himself was an Oxonian had, I think, much to do with the convincing), even though I pointed out to him that the main crossroads in Oxford weren't the only ones to bear the name, 'Carfax', and that, as one who, like me, had had a Classical education, he might recall that our word *carfax*, derives, through old French, from the Latin *quadrivium*—'where four roads meet'. But much more to the point, I added, was that there was another 'Carfax'—another important cross-roads—in a large market-town only a few miles from where Conan Doyle was living in 1911: the north-west Sussex town of Horsham. And that Doyle might well have had this 'Carfax' in mind in 1911, and not the more famous one in Oxford, may perhaps be suggested by the fact that every time he came down Horsham's principal shopping-street to turn into Carfax, the name over an old-fashioned men's outfitters, PHELPS, must have reminded him of a *Strand Magazine* story of almost twenty years before: *The Naval Treaty*...and this reminded him more of Holmes than of Oxford.

In short, there is nothing specifically of Oxford in the name, *Carfax*; and for proofs that Oxford was indeed, as Lord Donegall warmly argued, Holmes's university we shall need something more decisive than that use, in the Lady Frances story, of the—here it is a surname—'Carfax'.

———

To the 'Sherlockian Anthology', *Beyond Baker Street*, that I edited, I contributed (under a pen-name) an article, *Why did he call her 'Carfax'?*, in which I advanced an entirely novel explanation of the choice of that name; an explanation thar had nothing at all to do with Oxford, and only very tenuously with Horsham.

As I have repeatedly pointed out, in talks both in Britain and in the United States, as well as in my many Sherlockian writings, Conan Doyle, intensely interested—as he made Sherlock Holmes out to be—in the more wayward doings of the world as reported in the newspapers, of which, again like Holmes, he was a dedicated reader. But, I pointed out, Conan Doyle never did what so many other crime-fascinated authors have done; are doing; and will, I have no doubt, continue to do: that is, to tell the story of some scandal or tragedy, dress it up with 'fictitious' names, and offer it as fiction. What Conan Doyle did—as I have explained in the article, "Silver Blaze and Silver Nitrate," in this book—was to 'echo' what, with remarkable psychological insight into human motives, he perceived to be the essence of the case. And, in this present article, I shall point out yet another 'echo' to be found in the story of *Silver Blaze*. But first, let me briefly tell what the story of Lady Frances Carfax echoes: the true-life tragedy that Conan Doyle had read of in the newspapers in 1895, and which had so moved his compassion that, sixteen years later, he was still so moved by it that he had to 'echo' it in a story which, in his fiction, makes the point what the real-life tragedy made so clear (*in the words of Sherlock Holmes*): 'One of the most dangerous classes in the world is the drifting and friendless woman. She is the most harmless, and often the most useful of mortals, but she is the inevitable inciter of crime in others.... She is a stray chicken in a world of foxes....'

In 'echoing' fiction, these remarks applied perfectly to Lady Frances Carfax; in real life, they applied with no less force, to Frances, Lady Gunning, whose real-life Christian-name is thus patently reflected—'echoed'—in that of the fictional Lady Frances Carfax, another (in Holmes's words) 'rather pathetic figure...a beautiful woman, still in fresh middle-age'.

Lady Frances Carfax was a spinster; Frances, Lady Gunning, was a widow, and, in 1895, when she went on trial before the Common Serjeant (the senior judge of the City of London), on multiple charges of fraud, she had been so for ten ever-more-worrying years.

However, there are differences between real-life Frances Gunning and 'echoing' Frances Carfax; as I pointed out in my original *Beyond Baker Street* article, Frances Gunning, born Frances Spencer, was not (as was Frances Carfax) the innocent victim of a designing and conscienceless rogue, but of her own panic-generated impulses.

That she had been guilty of the several charges of fraud presented against her, there was no doubt: she had forged her father's name to documents to obtain money; she had forged a Bill of Exchange; forged the renewal of a Bill; forged a letter from her father; forged a Transfer of 500 shares...and so on. The list of offences, all involving that financial credit by which the money-conscious Victorians set such store, was long—and damning—indeed.

Yet it must have struck Conan Doyle, as, no doubt, it struck many others, both inside and outside the Court, that Frances, Lady Gunning, had got off remarkably lightly with a sentence of Twelve Months at Hard Labour; and pondering upon the relative triviality of the sentence, Doyle must have reflected that there was also something a little odd in the manner in which Counsel for the Crown—the redoubtable and generally far-from-sympathetic Horace Avory (later one of the harshest of judges)—presented, not Lady Gunning's offences, but rather Lady Gunning herself to the Court. It seemed to Conan Doyle that Avory had quickly—rather too quickly—run through a brief, a *very* brief, account of the prisoner's background: "The Prisoner is the widow of a baronet, a clergyman of the Church of England, and the daughter of another clergyman of the Church of England." That was all that he had to say of Frances Gunning before going on to detail the charges against her.

Why, Conan Doyle must have wondered, this kid-glove treatment, so completely out-of-character, contrasted with Avory's usual chill mercilessness? What was being hidden?—what being 'brushed under the table'...?

In that poverty-stricken (but, to Mrs Doyle's eternal credit, let it be said: never poverty-mastered) home in which Conan Doyle had been reared, pride of birth, passionately taught by his Mother, 'the Ma'am', had been one of the antidotes to the pain of barely-endurable want. It was not so much snobbishness that the Ma'am taught her son, as the means—self-deceptive though it might be—

of taking comfort in his thinking himself one of that noble company, rich and distinguished, that less arrogant minds would have thought of as their 'betters'. Those books that record the nobility of Britain— *Debrett, Burke, Dod, The Blue Book*, etc.—he learned well how to consult, and though the Doyle Family could not afford to buy such costly works, they were all easily accessible in Edinburgh's public-libraries and (after he had become a student there) in the University library.

By 1895, with his literary fame established, and his large income assured, so that he might build a house for himself, with stained-glass windows brilliant with the armorial bearings of his 'ancestors', *Debrett* and *Burke* were to be found in his library. He turned up 'Gunning' in the Baronetage....

Yes: *Debrett* confirmed what Avory had told the Court: the prisoner *was* the widow of a baronet: of the Reverend Henry John Gunning, 4th baronet of Eltham in the County of Kent, who died in 1885, and whom Frances Gunning had married in 1879, as his second wife.

But, almost indifferently, so it had seemed, Avory had mentioned that she was also the daughter of 'another Church of England clergyman'—and so, indeed, she was!

The entry under GUNNING, in *Debrett*, read thus:

> Widow living of 4th Baronet—FRANCES ROSE (*Lady Gunning*) da. of the Rev. the Hon. William Henry Spencer *see* B[aron] Churchill; *m.* 1879, as his second wife, the Rev. Sir Henry John Gunning, 4th baronet, who *d.* 1885.

So *that*, marvelled Conan Doyle closing, with seemly reverence, the pages of *Debrett*, is who she is! Not simply the impecunious (and thus driven-to-crime) widow of a baronet-clergyman, but a relative of the wealthy Barons Churchill, and so a member—albeit now the poorest of poor relations—of the powerful ducal House of Marlborough. Frances Spencer Gunning was the great-grand-daughter of the 4th Duke of Marlborough, whilst the present Lord Churchill was a Lord-in-Waiting to Queen Victoria. As I said in my original article: 'Here were powerful names indeed! No wonder that the prisoner's regrettable connection with these influential Toffs was glossed-over by Crown Counsel as 'she is the daughter of another Church of England clergyman'. The wonder of it all was,

Conan Doyle must have reflected, that the Spencer-Churchill family ever let the case come to Court.

————

The Court, one feels, might have entertained a similar opinion, for, in a day when offences involving money were not treated leniently, Frances Gunning was treated, when all is said and done, almost tenderly. Her troubles, said Avory, not at all unsympathetically, arose from the fact that she, a 'widow from 1885, without any previous experience, [had] embarked on the gigantic enterprise' of founding and running a Social Club.

Her financial malfeasances might all be accounted for by the fact that her lack of any business-sense had got her deeper and deeper into debt, and that, panicking, she had adopted improper means of fending off her creditors. We know that Conan Doyle sympathized with her: later, allegorically, he would make that sympathy clear in his tale of another lonely woman with the same name.

Once again he reached for *Debrett*, and turned, this time, to the entry for the Barony of Churchill, a title dating from 1779. One must bear in mind that Conan Doyle, through the influence of his Mother, had developed a deep interest, not only in titles, but in heraldry also—and, more, that interest had led him to become something of an authority on armorial bearings, as the (to me, deadly dull) listing of the knights' coats-of-arms in those historical novels by which he set such store makes clear. So that, when he saw the Churchill arms, as given in *Debrett*, he not only, to use his Mother's term—according to John Dickson Carr—could 'blazon' the arms, but could recognize the curious map-like design in the first and third quarters of the shield as a 'frette'—though, like most of us, he must have been struck by the *frette's* likeness to the street-plan of a cross-roads...or, in other words, to a *carfax*. Frances, Lady Gunning, the original of Lady Frances Carfax, had had a *carfax* in her family's coat-of-arms.

————

I produced the evidence of a third Carfax-source some eleven years ago. Now, within the last few weeks, a fourth possible source of the name has come to me, quite by chance. In 1905, Robert Baldwin Ross, intimate friend and, since his death, literary executor of Oscar Wilde, opened, in Ryder-street, St James's, a picture-dealer's shop. He called it 'The Carfax Gallery'.

━━━━━━

Conan Doyle, it must be said to his credit, was one of those who, conceiving a great admiration for Wilde, and falling (as Doyle tells us in his autobiographical *Memories and Adventures*) under the enchantment of his personality, never joined in condemning Wilde, when so many others were finding it fashionable or prudent to do so. As Doyle tells us, he never lost that admiration and liking for Wilde that he had acquired at that dinner-party which, in 1890, had brought them together. Of the sexual aberration that had brought Wilde (though neither his works nor his literary reputation) to ruin, Conan Doyle, the Doctor of Medicine, expressed the opinion—more to be expected in our day than in his—that Wilde should have been treated for mental instability rather than criminality.

The two men were about 'to arrive' when they were brought together—an Irish M.P. named Gill being the third guest—at a dinner-party arranged by Stoddart, the London representative of the American publishing-house of Lippincott—more specifically, of *Lippincott's Magazine*, the Editor of which had asked Stoddart to get, if possible, a novel out of each of the guests. Gill, as it happened, came up with nothing; but, within the following year, Oscar Wilde had produced *The Picture of Dorian Gray*; Conan Doyle, his second full-length Sherlock Holmes adventure, *The Sign of the Four*. It was *Dorian Gray* which, at the beginning, made the bigger stir—though its success was something of a *succès de scandale*—whilst Holmes had to wait for world-fame until the appearance of the first of the short-stories, *A Scandal in Bohemia*, in *The Strand Magazine* for July, 1891—that is, before Lord Alfred Douglas had yet come so disastrously into Wilde's life.

From that dinner-party, at which Wilde had captured Doyle's admiration by brilliant conversation and charm of manner—Doyle actually tells us, thirty years later, one of the stories with which Wilde entranced that small dinner-party—the two young men (Wilde, thirty-six; Conan Doyle, thirty-one) burst upon the world's consciousness; each imposing his own highly individual personality upon Man's awareness, in such a manner that, in neither case, is either likely to be forgotten. Wilde did not continue with his writing: he went on to be the greatest writer of light comedy since Sheridan—and, in the opinion of many, outtopped that other witty Irishman.

But Doyle, though he experimented with the Stage, sought and gained his most enduring success in writing—and of all his characters, none brought him such fame as did the one creation that he (though the world knew better from the start) regretted, even if, for all his protestations, he did not actually despise: Sherlock Holmes. Doyle, for all that he was brought up in that most Scottish of all Scottish cities, Edinburgh, was born, brought up, and remained all his life, as Irish as though he had never moved a mile from 'Dublin's fair city'—and all his sentiments were as Irish as the shamrock. To him, that invitation from Stoddart to 'bring me a book', united him, sentimentally—superstitiously, if you like; would have bound him for ever in a tie of shared-experience; to the fellow-writer who had 'divided his luck with him'.

It is reported that Doyle, asked to comment on Oscar Wilde's ever more flamboyant behaviour, and all that it implied, dismissed Oscar's eccentricities with no more harsh a judgment than to murmur, "He's quite mad...."

But, though Doyle's own sexual normality may never be doubted; save that he seems to be under-, rather than even normally-, sexed, Wilde was not the only sexual pervert for whom Doyle shewed what, for those times, was an astonishing and socially-dangerous tolerance and sympathy, even though it might be argued that the tolerance was extended because the men were Irish, and not that Doyle sympathized with their sexual tastes. In the case of Wilde, old friendship and not-to-be-denied admiration prevented Doyle's condemning Wilde when all around him were doing nothing else—and pretty indignantly, too. But, in refusing to condemn Roger Casement, accused of High Treason and (through Casement's widely-circulated so-called 'Black Diaries') convicted of that vice that had brought Wilde to prison, Conan Doyle was risking very much indeed: his reputation as a loyal subject of the Crown in petitioning on behalf of a pro-German 'traitor'; even heading the Casement Defence Fund with a subscription bigger than all the other subscriptions put together; and asking for mercy for a man whose diaries proved him to have been a tireless and no-holds-barred 'corrupter of male youth'. (The subscription of £700 should be borne in mind here.)

———

Robert Baldwin Ross was the son of a former Attorney-general of Canada, and was only seventeen, preparing to go up to Cambridge University, when he was introduced to Wilde. He was thus an established member of Wilde's band of disciples even before that productive Lippincott dinner-party, and Doyle must have heard of Ross's irregular devotion to 'dear Oscar', even had Doyle never seen them together at the Café Royal.

Ross has been condemned, but only by those of his own sexual tastes who have been jealous of the 'influence' that he had upon Wilde, and also because of his skill in edging the other Wilde-lovers out of the picture, so as to keep Oscar to himself. But Ross, of all those who were attached to the Wilde circle, was the most loyal—loyal throughout Wilde's trials; loyal to the end, not merely of Wilde's life, but of his own. He is reported, by jealous friends of Wilde, of having manoeuvered himself into his becoming Wilde's literary executor; but who else could have put Wilde's books back into circulation; restored his literary standing, and marketed Wilde's works so skillfully that, despite the fact that the Wilde copyrights were still in the administration of his Trustees in Bankruptcy, Ross managed to get £800 (then $3,200) from the Estate to give to Wilde on his release from Reading Gaol? He really did 'put Wilde back on the map'—the literary and dramatic map, at any rate. No-one else did it—and no-one else could have done it.

Ross never made any secret, either of his emotional feeling for Wilde, or of the sexual aberration upon which that feeling was based; from which that feeling sprang. Many a normal man or woman might well thank God for a friend as disinterestedly loyal as Ross proved himself to be to Wilde.

———

Ross spent only a year at Cambridge, having been forced to leave, not by reason of any sexual irregularity, but because of a nearly-fatal pneumonia. However, even a year as a 'Cantab' gave him the *cachet* of a 'Varsity man' in Wilde's entourage, which was pretty sharply divided between Varsity men and errand-boys. On coming down from the University, Ross began to build up a modest reputation and earn a proportionately modest income as a literary journalist and art-historian, and, four years after Wilde's death in Paris in 1901, Ross opened, as I have said, his Carfax Gallery in Ryder-street, a typically practical move that seemed to justify his appointment as the Assessor of Picture Valuation to the Board of Trade.

By 1909, all the debts of the Wilde Estate had been paid off, thanks to the energy that Ross had put into the restoration of Wilde as a selling, money-making author—*The Importance of Being Ernest*, 'removed' on Wilde's condemnation in 1895, was back on the London stage as early as 1902, only a year after Wilde's death—and with the publication of *De Profundis* (brilliantly 'cut' by Ross to make it seem like something by Thomas à Kempis, instead of what it really was: a 50,000-word hysterically self-pitying scream of one spiteful queer against another) in 1905, one might well say that Ross had contrived Wilde's re-acceptance into 'polite society'. Ross, then, might have felt that it would not hurt if he attended to his own affairs: the decision to open the Carfax Gallery in the year that saw the publication of *De Profundis* indicates that he was laying the foundations of what we may call his 'non-Wildean' plans.

With the death of Wilde's Wife in 1898, of spinal paralysis, his two sons, Cyril and Vyvyan, now, respectively, thirteen and twelve, were left orphans—Mrs Wilde had reverted to her maiden-name, and given that surname—Holland—to her sons. It is ironic that there was no-one to protect Constance Wilde and her two innocent boys as Wilde, the cause of all their shame and agony, had Ross to 'mother' him. The elder boy, Cyril, volunteered for the British Army, and was killed in the First World war—"He was glad to go," his younger brother, whom I came to know well, told me; as he told me on more than one occasion of the cruelties that the 'respectable British' put upon Mother and sons—telling the proprietor of Continental hotel after hotel that 'either we went or they would go', and thus sending the Wildes running around Europe, trying to find a place in which to live at peace, until they did eventually did find one where no British ever came....

Ross, curiously enough, was on good terms with Mrs Wilde-Holland, and was (I should say rightly) trusted by her. He it was who acted as intermediary between the self-pitying Husband and the justly bitter Wife, and when she died, some of the responsibility for the two Wilde boys was uncomplainingly assumed.

Now, what follows here is, I admit, of the stuff of purest surmise; for the opinions offered here, I have no documentary or, indeed, other proof, save that what I do suggest here invokes behaviour, on the part of two principal actors, consistent with what we know of their characters from amply documented sources.

I suggest that, among the several persons asked by Ross to help the Wilde boys was Arthur Conan Doyle, known to be sympathetic, not merely to the orphan lads' Father, but, generally, to all victims of undeserved ill-fortune. It is too late now to ask Captain Vyvyan Holland (as Wilde's younger son became) to confirm or reject my theory; but if matters had turned out so, then both Ross and Conan Doyle would not have been behaving out of character. Ross would surely have asked the help of Wilde's old friend and (if not helper, then assuredly) non-condemner. And, asked, Conan Doyle would have responded as generously as he was to respond, not many years later, to the need of one of the most unpopular men of the day: Sir Roger Casement, double-damned both as a 'pro-German traitor' and a self-condemned corrupter of youth.

But for the strong *possibility* that Conan Doyle, approached by Ross, might have helped the Wilde boys; and for the *certainty* that, had Ross asked him, Conan Doyle would have done so; there is evidence of a different kind.

Conan Doyle has always—during his life and after his death—been accepted as a man rigidly dominated by his unwavering respect for what he considered to be his duty; duty, of course, being the acknowledgment of responsibilities willingly and fully undertaken. Now, both Wilde and Conan Doyle had become linked in a fraternalism that had nothing to do with a tolerance of Wilde's sexual perversions, or even, as some have uncharitably (and on no evidence whatever) hinted: that Doyle might have had an inclination towards Wilde's tastes.

The link between them—apart from the fact that they both wrote for their living—was forged when both became Freemasons, in an age when the privileges and *responsibilities,* the chief of which, in Masonic theory, is Benevolence, were taken far more seriously than they are taken now—at any rate, in England.

Wilde had become a Mason while he was still up at Magdalen, inducted into the 33rd Degree, Scottish Rite (Oxford University Chapter), and Conan Doyle, some years later, in 1882, at Portsmouth, becoming a member of Phoenix Lodge there.

The Mason who takes his oath seriously—and Conan Doyle, we may be sure, took his Masonic responsibilities as seriously as he took all those other responsibilities that he had accepted—is under a moral obligation to help any Brother in the Craft (and, no less, that Brother's widow, wife, *or children*) when seeing the need for that help, and having it in his power to offer that needed assistance.

Conan Doyle would have helped the children of any brother Mason; I submit that, in Conan Doyle's Masonic obligations alone, we may look for the near certainty that he did, in fact, help Wilde's boys when Ross pleaded for them. As a practising mason, he could not have refused.

———

It has now been well established, notably by my friend, Donald Redmond, the Canadian Sherlockian scholar, that not only did Conan Doyle use the names of those met in the course of his day-to-day living, but that he almost never used a name that had not come to be known to him personally. (I did my own share of this type of nomenclature-research in my book, *A Study in Surmise.*)

And here are several names that, taken as a group, surely indicate Conan Doyle's familiarity with them, for the reasons that I have hypothesized.

If Conan Doyle did not meet Robert Baldwin ROSS in 1890, he must certainly have known (as everyone in the London 'know' did) that Wilde was rarely seen without Ross.

The name, ROSS, is used by Conan Doyle in one of the earliest Holmes stories of all, *The Red-Headed League*, written only a year or so after Doyle had met Wilde at the Lippincott dinner in 1890. That story was written in August 1891; in December 1892 the name crops up again in the character of Colonel Ross, in the tale of *Silver Blaze*, and again, as half of the name of a business-firm, Mangles & Ross, in *The Hound of the Baskervilles*, published in *The Strand Magazine* over the period, August, 1901-April, 1902...Wilde having died five months before publication of *The Hound* began, and (I suggest) Robert Ross's activities on behalf of the Wilde boys—fifteen and sixteen on their Father's death—vividly present in Conan Doyle's consciousness. Though not until *The Valley of Fear* (*Strand Magazine*, September, 1914-May, 1915) does Conan Doyle use Robert Ross's middle name, Baldwin—doubtless reminded of it by the disastrous libel action that Ross brought against Lord Alfred Douglas in the previous year, 'only', as Sheridan Morley writes, 'to have his own homosexuality established publicly in a way that echoed horribly the events of 1895'. Robert Ross's *Carfax Gallery*, opened in 1905, was in Ryder-street, the narrow thoroughfare connecting St James's-street with Duke-street, St James's. In *The Three Garridebs* (1925) we find a '*Little* Ryder-street'—and some precisian has pointed out that, though there is a *Ryder*-street, there is no *Little* Ryder-street. Not officially, perhaps, but anyone who knows narrow Ryder-street knows that it is a decidedly little street, as Conan Doyle had in mind when he used the name. It may be that the capital letter of 'Little' is a typographical error, and that the street was originally written thus: 'little Ryder-street'.

———

Now I do not withdraw my suggestion that it was from the likeness of the *frette*, in the Churchill coat-of-arms to the plan of a *carfax* that impelled Conan Doyle to call his rather silly heroine—hers 'echoing' the case of Frances, Lady Gunning, of the Churchill family—Lady Frances *Carfax*, but I do suggest that it was Robert

Ross's use of the name for his new gallery that, as it were, reinforced Doyle's decision to use it. Ross's gallery opened, as I have said, in 1905; *The Disappearance of Lady Frances Carfax* appeared in *The Strand* in 1911. If we assume that Doyle had occasion to write to Ross after 1905, any envelope addressed to Ross must have borne, for Doyle, a most evocative superscription:

> Robert Baldwin Ross, esquire,
> The Carfax Gallery,
> Ryder-street,
> St James's,
> London, S.W.

Ὁ μαστήρ

Yes, the Greeks had a word for him...
the Seeker-out...

One of the strangest phenomena to be encountered in even the most superficial study of modern psychology is that tendency which allows to the better-known psychologists—Freud, Adler, Jung, Maslow, and the rest—the credit for having *invented* those human weaknesses that they have gained world-renown in examining.

Sex, acquisitiveness (nicer word that, than 'greed'!), possessiveness, cruelty, masochism, ambition (that Shakespeare called 'vaulting'), forgetfulness—intentional or 'accidental'—with vindictiveness, sloth, anxiety, and all other faults that mar the image of Perfect Man—why, to listen to the starry-eyed worshippers of our 'liberating' psychologists, you'd think that Freud and company had invented all those troubles to which, as we are told in *Job*, 5:7, 'man is born as sparks to fly upward.'

It is the same, no less, with the phenomena of that world in which trouble-endowed man finds himself; and it is with one of these phenomena, 'invented' by Jung—because he gave a decidedly imprecise name to it—that I am concerned here. Jung's 'synchronicity' is but our old experience, 'coincidence', writ large; and what is imprecise in Jung's definition of the coincidence is that the 'meeting-of-facts' (which is all that 'coincidence' means) is that there's a great deal more to 'coincidence' than mere 'matching-in-time, contemporaneity' (which is all that Jung's coinage, 'synchronicity', means). It is true that a coincidence forces itself upon our attention when the two or more 'matching' facts that combine to form the coincidence occur within a short period of time. Indeed, it was a decidedly non-scientific writer, the late Edgar Wallace, who detected what seems to be a law in the matter of the verbal coincidence, and stated as a fact that any never-before-encountered name will be met with again within twenty-four hours.

That this is generally true almost anyone will be able to confirm from his own experience; my own view is that the second (or third) appearance of the never-before-encountered name is not a matter of chance: that we come across it because we *seek out* the second encounter, by either some exercise of extra-sensory perception or by remembering subconsciously where that odd name is to be found. That is my view. I find that, looking for a book 'at random', I'll very often pick up a book that will have one of the odder names to be found in the book that I have just read. Jung, in his well-known study of 'synchronicity', appears to be about to adopt this theory (of *deliberate* 'matching') but never quite gets there.

But there are coincidences that appear to have little to do with that 'meeting-in-Time' that so fascinated Edgar Wallace and that is implicit in the phrase of Jung's coining—and it is with one of the oddest (and least explicable) of these coincidences that I shall deal in this article.

The Sherlockians' 'Master'

Several years ago, in a really excellent short-story in the old *Astounding*, an atom-bomb-shattered future is imagined in which a handful of regenerated humans are rebuilding civilization; and, as in all civilizations, simple or complex, the reconstructors are living by the principles and tenets of their Sacred Writings. In the story, those Sacred Writings—as all sacred writings do, and must—concern the age-old battle between the Light and the Darkness; but they do not tell of the battle in heaven between Michael and Lucifer, between Ormuzd and Ahriman...but of the triumph of Good over Evil in the destruction, by Sherlock Holmes, 'The Master', of his malignant adversary—who symbolizes the destructive Power of Darkness: Moriarty. The Canon—the stories that tell of the conflict between Holmes and Moriarty are the only 'sacred writings' that have survived from Western civilization's atom-blasted past.

Now it is clear that the author of this fine story derived his inspiration from the fact—and fact it is—that the 'deification' of Holmes, begun in a jesting fashion, but now no longer a jest, must now not improbably (inevitably, one feels) progress to that point at which Sherlock Holmes will join—if he has not already joined—that semi-divine and exalted company that includes Hercules, Arthur, Charlemagne, and the Cid: all originally no more than human, but now heroes of myth and symbols of Mankind-the-Grown-Divine.

One might say that this deification of Holmes has already happened.

His soul goes marching on

In quoting Watson's tribute to Holmes in *The Final Problem*, I wonder how many realize that the deification of Holmes had begun, not with the jesting academics of the post-1900 years—Monsignor Ronald Knox, Miss Dorothy Sayers, Sir Sydney Roberts, Christopher Morley, Alexander Woollcott, Edgar Smith and the rest—but with Watson hiimself. For, as that fine Sherlockian scholar, Mr Morris Rosenblum, wrote in his 'Foreign Language Quotations in the Canon', "Watson's words are an echo of Plato's *Phaedo*, describing the death of Socrates: 'such was the end, Echecrates, of our friend, who was, as we may say, of all those of his time whom we have ever known, the best and wisest and most righteous man'."

It's no great step from a comparison of Holmes with the already half-deified Socrates to a tentative and then, inevitably a definitive, deification of Holmes himself. The complete collection of the sixty long and short stories that make up the corpus of 'the Canon' are not called 'The Sacred Writings' for nothing....

I feel that there is nothing completely accidental in the employment of words and phrases made familiar through a different sort of Sacred Writings: the employment of these words and phrases

176 / IMMORTAL SLEUTH

in the context of Sherlockian scholarship. No-one familiar with the Sherlockian use of them would be at all astonished to know (as I recently discovered) the Mr H.V. Morton's best-seller of the early 1930's, *In the Steps of the Master*—which traces the journeyings of Jesus through the Holy Land—should have been thought to have been the imprecisely described work of mine, *In the Footsteps of Sherlock Holmes*. It is in no blasphemous or even irreverent sense that Sherlockians have come to designate their superhuman hero by a title that a more religious age reserved for Our Saviour.

And yet, what, in its essence, is that quality that men, from the dawn of human consciousness, have identified as 'divinity'? Surely it is no more—but no less—than the possession of talents (and the power which *must* be generated by them) superior to those possessed by the normality of mankind. Superiority always commands admiration—'We needs must love the highest when we see it'—and it is the most natural impulse in the human psyche to permit that irresistable admiration to turn to worship. We too often forget that most of mankind's gods or god-like heroes started off as no more than exceptional human beings. Hercules, that hero who has left his name over so wide an area, from Herculaneum to Monaco (the town of Herakles Monoichos) from Hartland Point to the Hartlepools (in which the old name 'pools' is a corruption of original Greek 'polis', 'city, town, settlement'), was a real man, and so was Arthur; and so—as I have argued elsewhere—was Sherlock Holmes. He was a private detective named Wendel Scherer, who gained a momentary fame by appearing in the case of a missing German *baker*. Conan Doyle, adding to Wendel Scherer's real personality, some of the spectacular detective talents of Dr Joseph Bell, one of the lecturers at the Edinburgh Medical School in Doyle's time, had already begun the process of glorifiying the obscure private detective, Scherer, who, as 'Sherlock Holmes', was to acquire, over the years, a greater glory little short of divinity.

'The Master'

The reader may now ask if I have not drifted somewhat far from my introductory remarks, which had to do with coincidences, especially as viewed by two men of such different and contrasted background: Edgar Wallace and Carl Jung. No, I have not drifted.

All which has been written since has been specifically relevant to the *very* odd coincidence concerned with that now most commonly used title of Holmes's: 'The Master'.

In modern usage, the word 'master' derives, through old French *maistre*, from Latin *magister*, which originally meant 'the greater of a contrasted pair'; the other element of that contrasted pair being *minister*, 'the lesser'. Of course, none of us needs to fly to a dictionary to know what 'master' has come to mean now—or even what 'The Master' (with capital letters) signifies. Sherlock Holmes, who, as he told Dr Watson, started out as the world's first private consulting detective, is well on the way to deification as 'The Master'—and it is here that quite the most extraordinary coincidence must be mentioned and explained.

We have seen what modern 'master' was in the original Latin, but there was also, in classical Greek, a word *master*—I dislike writing Greek words with Roman letters,[1] but, things being as they are, I suppose I must resign myself to doing that—and...what do you think that *master* meant? Why, a *detective* appointed and paid by the municipal authorities of the most famous city-state of the ancient world: Athens.

Now this Greek word, *master*, means literally 'a seeker, a searcher, one who looks for something', and in Athens, the *masteres* were officials appointed to pursue and discover those who owed money to the state—by fines or otherwise—or to ascertain the extent and location of exiles' fortunes—so as to confiscate them. The *masteres*—the Greek word *masterios* (nothing to do with our 'masterly', for all the outward resemblance) means 'skilled at searching, adept at finding out'—were the first officially appointed detectives of whom history holds record; specifically they were also the first Inland Revenue Investigation Service.

I find all this quite extraordinary—and extraordinary both Wallace and Jung would have found it, too. Over the centuries, the ancient Latin word, *magister*, changes into modern 'master'—and is applied, as a title of honour, to the world's greatest fictional detective. The Greek word, *master*, 'city-authorized detective', has not, one would say, survived.

---

[1] But I did manage to use Greek characters in the title of this article.

But is that really so? I objected to Jung's term, 'synchronicity', for the coming-together of facts—demonstrating their perhaps not-before-perceived relationship by the very fact of their coming-together. For Jung's word is derived from the Greek *synchronos*, that means 'contemporary', and there must be a way of looking at the coming-together of related facts that either takes no account of 'contemporaneity' or treats it, at best, as a very secondary element in the 'coincidence'. I suggest that a better word to describe the 'coincidental' pairing-up of facts, irrespective of the time element, would be the Greek *synemptosis*, 'a falling (*ptosis*) together, a happening together, a coincidence'—giving us rather 'synemptoticity' than Jung's 'synchronicity'.

For this is what we have here: a true 'synemptotic' falling-together of two facts that, despite entirely different origins—I talk now of English 'master' (from Latin *magister*) and Greek *master*—forced, one may say, their coming-together over many centuries and by many a devious path. In other words, Holmes has come, after two millennia, to bear that title 'Master', that the Greeks would naturally have given him. The Greeks, as I have written, did have a word for him.

But that he should bear the *Greek* title is fitting, and, I maintain, not by chance. Surely, not by chance....

THAT 'PATH LAB' MEETING

Was Holmes expecting Watson...?

In the account that Dr Watson gives of his first meeting with Sherlock Holmes in the Pathological Laboratory of St Bartholomew's Hospital, he makes no suggestion that, brought into the 'Path. Lab.' by 'young Stamford', Dr John H. Watson, was completely unknown to the world's first private consulting detective. In the light of what I am about to produce, it may be now surmised that each man had his own and very special reasons for suppressing the fact that Mr Holmes *had* heard of Dr Watson, and (though possibly not on that day; and not introduced by 'young Stamford') expected him to call, with details of an astonishing story that both men decided afterwards to leave untold.

Maiwand and After

'In the beginning of August, 1880, England was startled with the news that the British troops in Afghanistan had been defeated, and terrible slaughter inflicted on General Burrows's army at Maiwand.' So runs a contemporary reference to a military action that seems small enough to us—934 British killed in a force of 2,476 men engaged—and whose disgrace was quickly wiped out by the brilliant generalship of General (later Field-marshal Lord) Roberts.

Old soldiers, as Shakespeare reminded us, love to recount their tales of battles fought; and Dryden recalls that kindly warrior who 'fought all his battles o'er again; and thrice he routed all his foes, and thrice he slew the slain'. One may sympathetically concede that ex-Surgeon-lieutenant Watson ordinarily preserved a discreet reserve in discussing his wartime experiences. Yet those wartime experiences—or, rather, his immediately post-wartime experiences—made him the witness of such extraordinary happenings that these he could, and did, discuss. I shall now explain why I believe that it was to discuss certain of these extraordinary happenings—one in particular—that Dr Watson put himself in communication with Mr Sherlock Holmes (or, it may be, was approached by Mr Holmes for information), and, no matter who initiated the correspondence, promised that he would call upon Mr Holmes as soon as military transport should return Dr Watson to England. It was certainly an unusual story that Dr Watson had to tell; and we may not doubt that Mr Holmes was most eager to hear the facts from a man who had been an almost unbelieving witness of their happening.

Brought Back to Life

Wounded and unconscious, Dr Watson, as is well known, was carried off the field of battle by the *sauve qui peut* impulse and prompt action of his orderly, Murray. Out of range of further jezail-bullets fired by 'murderous Ghazis' (though rumour then had it that the really murderous elements of Ayub Khan's army were the 3,000 Turcoman cavalry supplied as 'volunteers' by the Russian government), Dr Watson joined the columns of sick and wounded, making their slow and uncomfortable way to the base- hospital at Peshawar. Over the unmade roads of India's farthest north, British and British-Indian casualties groaned the seemingly endless journey either from the waggons of the bullock- train or from the even more comfortless 'palki' or 'doolie', a litter carried by four native bearers at a curious swinging pace. It should be borne in mind that the war of 1914–1918 was the first in which British casualties from wounding exceeded those from disease. And for the sick and wounded who travelled the nightmare journey from Afghanistan to the hospitals of Rawal Pindi, Peshawar, Deolali, Nowshera, and the rest, a cholera epidemic awaited them at journey's end. It was with cholera, even more than with wounds, that Dr Roger G.S. Chew, of the Bengal Medical Service, and his brother military surgeons, were having to contend.

Dr Chew was a medical man of a type far more common in past centuries than it is to-day. Educated in India, at the Bishop's High School, Poona (of which the Reverend Mr Watson, Rector of St Mary's Church, was the chaplain), Chew, on passing his finals, joined the Bengal Medical Service, was sent to the North-west Frontier, served throughout the two Afghan Wars (1878–1880), joined the staff of the Calcutta Medical College, and served there for two years until being sent to join the Anglo-Egyptian Expeditionary Force in 1882. Dr Chew was a man of insatiable curiosity; and one of the principal objects of his curiosity was a then very widespread preoccupation: Premature Burial. In India, especially whilst serving with the armed forces, Dr Chew had had some unusual opportunities of studying, at first hand, his preoccupation—one might almost call it his obsession: that apparent death whose fearful result is too often the victim's premature interment.

Dr Chew has left us detailed notes of an extraordinary precision, even for the careful observers of a century since. The earliest case in Dr Chew's notes concerns Sergeant J. Clements Twining, of H.M.'s 109th regiment of British infantry, located, in 1876, at Dinapoor.

(The sergeant) was brought in an unconscious state to the hospital, supposed to be suffering from *coup de soleil*. Everything that could be done was ineffecutally tried to rouse him from coma, and he was removed to the dead-house to wait *postmortem* next morning. At two a.m. the sentry on the dead- house came rushing down to the dispensary (about four hundred and fifty yards off) declaring that he had seen and heard a ghost in the dead-house, to which myself and the compounder and dresser on duty at once proceeded, to find that Clements Twining, who was now partially conscious, was lying on the dead-house flags groaning most piteously—he had rolled of the table on to the floor. He returned to health, and in 1877 accompanied his regiment to England, where I met him at Woolwich in 1883, and he asked me to corroborate his story of 'returning to life' to certain of his acquaintances who had refused to believe him.

Two years later, 'when the East Norfolk regiment was out cholera-dodging in 1878', two more cholera-casualties, Colour-sergeant T. Hall and Corporal Bellomy (*sic*), were sent into cantonments for burial in the Nowshera cemetery. That the men were not buried at once was due to the happy accident that there was no wood immediately available for their coffins. Whilst wood was being found, the bodies were placed in the dead-house, where first Hall and then Bellomy regained consciousness, and were returned to duty.

In the same year, a sowar—native trooper—of the 7th regiment of cavalry, was carrying despatches at Nowshera when he was thrown from his horse, hitting his head violently upon a sharp stone, which became 'wedged in between the temporoparietal suture'. He was found some seven hours after the accident, and conveyed to the morgue of the European Depôt Hospital.

> Nothing would have convinced anyone that the sowar was still alive, and Surgeons-Major Hunter, Gibson, and Briggs, Apothecary S. Pollock, Assistant-surgeon J. Lewis and myself *verily* believed he was stone-dead. As 'cause of death' is what the army is exceedingly particular about, Surgeon-Major Hunter removed the impacted stone and lifted out portions of the fractured bone (prior to holding a proper *postmortem*) when to the surprise of us all 'the corpse' deliberately closed its eyes (which were staring open when the body was first brought in), and there was a slight serous haemorrhage. On (our) noticing this, the sowar's head was trephined—no chloroform or other anaesthetic being used—some more fragments of bone and a large blood-clot that pressed on the brain were removed, and as the sowar repeatedly flinched under this operation, a stimulant was poured down his throat, and he was removed to his regimental hospital, from which he was discharged 'well' some six months and a half later. After this he did good service in the Afghan and Egyptian campaigns.

—in the former of which, I suggest, he and his remarkable experience became known to Surgeon-lieutenant John H. Watson, MD.

The 'Resurrection Man'

What gave Dr Roger Chew this unusual—not to say abnormal—interest in 'miraculous' resurrections from the dead was the fact that he himself, as a schoolboy, was brought back to life as he lay in his coffin, awaiting interment—saved at the last minute only because 'my eldest sister, who was leaning over the head of my coffin, crying over me, declared she saw my lips move'.

Dr Chew, like most men who ride a hobby, was not at all reticent about his obsession—and it would have been impossible for any member of an Afghan campaign officers' mess to escape Dr Chew's reminiscences. One case in particular had excited his interest: that of the apparent death, from 'strong symptoms of cholera' of Assistant-surgeon H.A. Borthwick, who, in March, 1877, was proceeding under orders by bullock-train from Rawal Pindi to Peshawar, accompanied, not only by Chew, but also by Assistant-surgeons S. Blake and H.B. Rogers. Borthwick certainly seemed to have died, and 'the apparent corpse—he was cold, stiff, and seemingly dead—was lifted out of the bullock-train and carried into the hospital dispensary...preparatory to papers' being signed and arrangements made for its final disposal'. However, as with so many other cases coming to the attention of the Indian Army—and civilian-medical authorities, Assistant-surgeon Borthwick's 'corpse' came to life. 'We *do know* that Borthwick recovered consciousness while lying on the bed in that dispensary, and that he whom we mourned as dead returned to life. He served in the same military stations with me in the North-West Frontier till 1880....'

Dr Chew collected—mostly first-hand—details of resurrections from apparent deaths attributable to many different causes, though by far the commonest cause was that cholera that was pandemic in the Indian Empire of the last century. That many living persons were interred under the supposition that they had actually died of cholera was a fact that Dr Chew and his colleagues had reluctantly to admit; and that proper sanitation could abolish this terrible disease was known to all who had the welfare of India at heart. Dr Chew pays tribute to one of the most earnest workers towards this noble end: 'Though a layman, still it would be hard to find a more indefatigable sanitarian than my late commanding officer, Lieutenant-Colonel R.C. Sterndale, of the Presidency Volunteer Rifle Battalion, and for many years vice-chairman of the municipality of the suburbs of Calcutta'.

Indeed, the most striking of all the 'resurrections' noted and recorded by Dr Chew was a cholera case; a case which has a special significance in the matter of Dr Watson's meeting Mr Holmes.

'Shortly after the Afghan war of 1878, Surgeon-Major T. Barnwell and I were told off to take a large number of time-expired men, invalids, and wounded, to Deolali on their way to England.'

> Some of the wounded were in a very critical state, necessitating great care; one man in particular...who had an ugly bullet-wound running along his left thigh and under the groin.... When we got to Nowshera, he seemed on a fair way to recovery, but the swinging of the doolie seemed too much for him, and he grew weaker day by day (the soldier was suffering from cholera as well as from his terrible wound) till we got to Hassan Abdool, when we could not rouse him to take some nourishment before starting on the march, and to all appearance he seemed perfectly dead; but as there was neither the time nor the convenience to hold a *post-mortem*, we carried the body on to 'John Nicholson', where, the same difficulties being in the way, and no facilities for burial, we were obliged to put the *post-mortem* off for another day, and convey the corpse to Rawal Pindi rest camp, where we laid him on the floor of the mortuary tent and covered him over with a tarpaulin. This was his salvation, as next morning [*i.e.*, the third day succeeding his 'death'], when we raised the tarpaulin to hold the *post-mortem*, some hundreds of field mice [these tracts are *noted* for them] rushed out, and we noticed that (the soldier) was breathing, though very slowly—five or six respirations to the minute—and there were a few teeth marks where the mice had attacked his calves. To prevent a relapse by the jolting on further marches, we handed him over to the hospital staff, who pulled him round, and then forwarded him to the headquarters of his regiment at Meerut.

That regiment was the crack 10th (Prince of Wales's) Hussars, and the important relevance of this episode from the Afghan wars will be apparent to all my readers when I mention that the soldier brought back from the dead by the malign attentions of field-mice was...Trooper *Holmes*, almost certainly known personally to Dr Watson at Rawal Pindi Base Hospital.

The 'Grave' Preoccupations of Mr Holmes

That the strange tale of Trooper Holmes would have excited his more famous namesake's lively interest, we may not doubt. I am convinced that it was to tell Mr Holmes of his first-hand knowledge of Trooper Holmes's escape from *post-mortem* and burial that Dr Watson called on Mr Holmes, and that Mr Holmes expected the ex-Surgeon-lieutenant to do so. That chance meeting with 'young

Stamford' in the American Bar of the Criterion may have reminded Dr Watson that he owed Mr Holmes a call; and when 'Stamford' gave Dr Watson the opportunity to meet Mr Holmes, the medico leapt, as they say, at the chance. So the two men met in what is now seen as one of the most significant encounters in history. Why, then, have both men, to this day, suppressed the strange story that brought them together—a story that must have mentioned, in passing, the numerous other cases of resuscitation that Dr Watson had seen or had learnt about from other army surgeons, notably the remarkable case of Captain Young, 'dreadfully mauled while tiger-hunting in Madras', and pronounced dead by the then regimental surgeon, Dr Colin S. Valentine, LL.D., later Principal of the Medical Missionary Training College, Agra?

The reason or reasons for the suppression are, I think, easily surmised: they are to be found in the average Victorian's vivid and often only too uneasy awareness of his culture's social values. Kipling has put on record what that average Victorian thought of the 'gentleman-ranker'—the man of superior birth or education (or both) who 'joined the ranks'. A man of no birth and little education could find promotion from the ranks: on 27 September, 1879, the Kabul Field Force, under Major-general Sir Frederick Roberts, was attacked by a body of some two thousand Afghans, who were 'put to flight without their being able to do much damage'. In this relatively small but militarily most important battle (for Roberts was hurrying to join the British camp at Kushi, and engage the Amir Ayub Khan), the son of a Scottish ploughman, Colour-Sergeant Hector Macdonald, so distinguished himself by his bravery that he won for himself promotion to commissioned rank, and ended, before proof of a moral lapse drove him to suicide, as Major-general Sir Hector Macdonald, one of the 'great names' of the South African War—'Fighting Mac'. But no such promotion might be expected by any gentleman-ranker....

Now, even by the beginning of 1881, Mr Holmes had already laid, not merely the sure foundations of his chosen and created profession, but also those steps to social patronage and social preferment upon which all his ambitions must rest for their achievement. More than one person of importance had already learnt of Mr Holmes's discretion, no less than of his efficiency. Whether or not Trooper Holmes was related to Mr Sherlock Holmes, even the supposition that such a relationship might exist would do irreparable damage to what the jargonauts of advertising have taught us to call his 'image'. And, since Dr Watson, who had met Mr Holmes to tell him of the trooper's strange experience, had stayed to share diggings with him, it was to Dr Watson's advantage, as much as to that of Mr Holmes, that the name of Trooper Holmes, late of the mortuary-tent at Rawal Pindi and now of the Tenth Hussars' depôt at Meerut, be forgotten.

The Evidence of the Names

The use by Dr Watson or the Agent of pseudonyms of the real names of the *dramatis personae* has been the subject of much comment from many dedicated Sherlockianalysts over the years, including the present writer. Sometimes it is clear that it was Dr Watson who selected the replacing name, sometimes the Agent. Sometimes the pseudonyms have an allusive significance; sometimes they are patently suggested by recollection alone—names that were once familiar to either Dr Watson or to the Agent. I invite the reader to study the following list of those *real* names which became familiar to Dr Watson either during his service as an Army surgeon or in listening to the reminiscences of Dr Chew and other brother-officers. I should add that Dr Watson's interest in the grim subject of Premature Burial, aroused by actual experience of such 'near misses' as that of Trooper Holmes, persisted after Dr Watson's forcible retirement from the Army. In the ancient church of St Giles Cripplegate (once the temple of Semo Sancus Dius Fidius), there was, in the doctor's day, an imposing monument to the memory of Constance Whitney, who, dead and coffined, was restored to a long life through the criminal cupidity of the sexton, who disinterred her body to gain possession of a valuable ring with which she had been buried. And that Dr Watson maintained his interest in the subject through reading that included even the American physiologist and psychologist, Professor Dr Alexander Wilder, MD's *The Perils of Premature Burial* is indicated, I suggest, by the inclusion of that name in the list that follows:

Joshua Duke, medical officer to General Roberts
Constance Whitney
Professor Alexander Wilder

Dr Roger Chew
Assistant-surgeon S. Blake
Assistant-surgeon H.B. Rogers
Colour-sergeant T. Hall
Corporal W. Bellomy (*sic*)
Surgeon-major T. Barnwell
Surgeon-major Hunter
Surgeon-major Gibson
Surgeon-major Briggs
Apothecary S. Pollock
Ebenezer Milner, MD Edinb, LRCSE (Author: 'Catalepsy or Trance',
in *Edinburgh Medical & Surgical Journal*)
Sir Donald Stewart, General
Sir Frederick Haines, C-in-C, India
Dr Brewer (Lecturer on the dangers of Premature Burial)
Major (afterwards Sir) George White (led 92nd Highlanders at taking
of the Baba Wali Kotal)
Lieutenant-colonel R.C. Sterndale
Dr Colin S. Valentine, of Agra

Those familiar with the nomenclature of the Canon will already
have detected what I am about to set out below: the use of all the
above names in the Sacred Writings. *This cannot be by chance.* The
names, though never extraordinary, are still not at all usual—the
Smiths, Joneses, Browns, and Robinsons of normal character-nam-
ing are strikingly absent. Look at the names!

Joshua Duke	Rev. Joshua Stone	WIST
Constance Whitney	Elisa, Isa, Kate Whitney	TWIS
Alex. Wilder	Jas Wilder	PRIO
Roger Chew	Roger Baskerville; Morse (play	HOUN
	on word 'chew') Hudson	SixN
H.B. Rogers	Rodger Baskerville (the other	HOUN
	one)	
S. Blake	Blaker	VALL
T. Hall	Hall Pycroft	STOC
W. Bellomy (*sic*)	Maud, Tom, William Bellamy	LION
	(*sic*)	
T. Barnwell (*sic*)	Sir Geo. Burnwell (*sic*)	BERY
S/Major Hunter	Ned Hunter	SILV
	Violet Hunter	COPP
S/Major Gibson	Neil Gibson	THOR
S/Major Briggs	The *Matilda Briggs*	SUSS
S. Pollock	Pollock	STOC

Ebenezer Milner	Godfrey Milner	EMPT
Sir Donald Stewart	James Stewart	CROO
	Mrs Stewart, of Lauder	EMPT
Sir Frederick Haines	Haines-Johnson	3Gar
Dr Brewer	Sam Brewer	SHOS
Sir George White	Wm Whyte (*sic*)	STUD
	White Mason	VALL
Colonel R.C. Sterndale	Dr Leon Sterndale	DEVI
Dr Valentine of Agra	The Great Agra Treasure	SIGN

Eliminating the Impossible

Now it is true that all the names listed above (even the Agra Bank Limited had its fine offices in Nicholas-lane, City) could have been found, either by Dr Watson or by the Agent, in any Post-office London Directory. What is not true is that a collection of names, become significant in Dr Watson's consciousness *only* by reason of their having been associated with one particular phenomenon, Apparent Death, on one man, Trooper Holmes—should be chosen to name various characters in the Canon. The link between Dr Watson's military service in Afghanistan or at various base-hospitals becomes even more patent when we perceive that all the names of the medical men associated with the case of the resuscitated sowar, are, with the possible exception of one—Lewis (though Lucas, of SECO, may echo the name here)—*all* used in the Canon...and what makes that use all the more significant, are used as surnames: Hunter (twice), Gibson, Briggs, and Pollock. As it might have been dangerous to call attention to the Sherlock Holmes-Trooper Holmes link, Dr Watson avoided the use of the name, Chew, a fairly unusual one in Britain.

But he could not avoid a rather laboured punning change of that to-be-avoided name. The supine of the Latin verb, *mordeo*, 'I bite', is *morsum* (whence our 'morsel', 'a thing bitten off')—and this word supplies his distinctly unusual Christian name to *Morse* Hudson. I also think that we may see that same punning reference to 'Chew' in the name, *Morstan*, with its close links with British

India and, especially, Agra (to which Dr Valentine had gone to train medical missionaries).

It is clear, too, that these names were the choice of Dr Watson and not of the Agent, who had neither served in India nor had even visited the sub-continent. The choice of names reflects Dr Watson's own experiences, and his alone.

CAPTAIN HUDSON AND THE TRULY GRATEFUL SEPOY

An advertising fantasy in one act....

From my earliest years; from long before I could read, even; I have been greatly attracted to the advertisements in every kind of reading matter, of which our house had always a plentiful supply. Perhaps that deep interest—it would be no great exaggeration to call it 'fascination'— may have been the cause why I, many years later, and by a somewhat circuitous route, 'got into' Advertising, taking to that Skill (that some pretentiously like to call an 'Art') as, in the popular phrase, a duck takes to water. So much immersing myself in the moral convolutions of that 'Art', as to write a text-book on the theory and practice of Technical and Industrial Advertising, which was received as, and remains still, a 'classic' in its highly specialized field.

———

As a boy, I 'collected' things: stamps, that I could buy and stick into the 'King George the Fifth' stamp-album that my Father bought me as a ninth-birthday present; the makes of every car and motor-cycle and aeroplane—these not to be 'collected' in the material sense, but detected, memorized, and listed. More than usually observant in respect of those things that interested me, I not only 'knew' every advertisement to be studied in the pages of the many magazines and newspapers of those days, but I 'knew', too, the name of every artist who signed his or her work legibly. And, like any other art-connoisseur who really has dedicated himself to his study, I came to a point at which I did not need the signature to identify the art-work: I came to recognize the 'touch', so that I needed no signature to distinguish, say, among the three prolific and constantly-employed Pagets—H.M., Sidney (of Sherlock Holmes fame), and Wal—whose work in so strikingly (and, often, puzzlingly) alike as to suggest the equal sharing of a common talent; the same being true of the three Brocks: H.M. (another 'H.M.', first known to me as the deft illustrator of my first French grammar), T.H., and C.E.

I don't wish to give the impression that, in the fascination that these advertisements' artwork had for me, I was insensible to the attractiveness of what Mr Marshall McLuhan has taught us to call 'The Message'—I particularly liked the 'Message' to be spun out, in the manner of a comic-strip, as with, say, the long decline, spun out over at least a dozen frames, of the Drunkard's family's pitiful decline into the most abject want; a decline halted (thank God!) only when the skeletal Wife, in rags, saves all by dosing her Husband's beer with what was supplied under the 'world-famed' Turvey Treatment; or, some years later, a first-person narrative, beginning with the statement that 'I was a ninety-pound weakling', discovers 'Dynamic Tension', and so pumps his flaccid muscles up to the Michelin Man standard that he is able to knock out the gorilla-like oaf who, contemptuously kicking sand into the Weakling's face on a Coney Island beach, shamed the Weakling and (only temporarily, thank Goodness!) deprived him of the company of his Girl.

What injected the irresistible element of fascination into almost all the advertisements, whether in such 'respectable' journals as *The*

Illustrated London News, The Graphic, and such equally 'respectable' magazines as *The Windsor, The Strand, The Quiver, Nash's,* and some others, as 'respectable', but not quite so expensive; or in such outright 'Mob-reading' as *Answers, Tit-Bits;* the boys' school stories—*The Gem, The Magnet, Chums*—and the servants' hall literature: *The Family Herald, Women's Weekly, Home Notes;* was that *all* the advertisements, in all the papers and journals and magazines, of *all* social classes, were embarked upon by the copywriters in the free-and-easy spirit of Anything Goes. No claim was too wild as not to be able to find a place in the most 'respectable' journal—it is obvious that, though (naturally) Obscenity and even Indelicacy were excluded from all but the *Police Gazette,* Plain Lying, the Grossest Misrepresentation and Deliberate and Calculated Fraud were decidedly not.

On my desk, at the side of my typewriter is a rather tattered copy of that most 'respectable' organ of news and opinion, *The Illustrated London News,* for the week ending 5th September, 1896. The title-page sets the tone of the journal by shewing a full-sized wash-drawing of the 'Visit of the Czar and Czarina to Vienna: The Two Emperors Riding Through the Prater Strasse'—and though Trouble is not overlooked:

THE MASSACRES AT CONSTANTINOPLE
THE TROUBLE IN CRETE
THE ADVANCE TOWARDS DONGOLA: THE SHADOW OF DEATH
THE CRISIS AT ZANZIBAR
A BRITISH NAVAL BOMBARDMENT

—and so on:

The real and expected 'Family' tone of the journal is set by such paragraphs as:

Her Majesty the Queen, accompanied by Princess Henry of Battenberg, with her children, and Princess Victoria of Schleswig-Holstein, on Monday evening left Osborne for Balmoral, arriving there next day early in the afternoon.

In the United States, Mr M'Kinley has consented to be the candidate of the Republican Party at the Presidential election. Li-Hung-Chang, on his arrival at New York from England, was visited by President Cleveland, but not officially. He proceeds to the western coast, on his way to China.

The 'Family' tone is well supported in other paragraphs. The journal, reporting a fight 'with sticks and stones', between two rival groups of deep-sea fishermen at Scarborough, fought on through the Saturday night, 'even desecrating, it is to be feared, the early Sabbath hours'.

Alas! this pious 'Family' tone is obviously missing when we come to study the ads. Oh!, the pious tone is there right enough, but the basic morality is hard to find among the advertisments, which range from sheer catch-penny to downright fraudulent.

> ALLAN'S ANTI-FAT (*with the usual Before and After cuts*)
> PURELY VEGETABLE, Perfectly Harmless. Will reduce from two to five pounds per week; acts on the food in the stomach, preventing its conversion into fat. Sold by Chemists. Send stamp for pamphlet.

Presumably it also prevents food from being converted into energy? This is by no means the wildest, though even 'Himrod's', supposedly endorsed by 'the late General Sherman', and 'Miss Emily Faithful' [The Queen's 'Lady Printer-in-Ordinary', Miss Faithful was the victim of an indecent assault in a railway-carriage by Admiral Codrington], advertises itself as a 'Cure for Asthma', and not—as is now required by Law—as 'giving relief in cases of Asthma'.

But probably the most irresponsible of all the advertisements—though perhaps ignorance may be pleaded here—is the quarter-page for *Sozodont* dentrifice, of which it has this to say:

> Dr Van Buskirk applies the Röntgen Rays in his Dental Practice and finds that those habitually using SOZODONT have perfect teeth, hard Gums, and sweet Breath.

It isn't this bit of adman's copy that is so objectionable—the same claims, ninety years later, are still being made for almost all the dentifrices on sale to-day. No: what is terrifying is the illustration, which shews Dr Van Buskirk, standing reading, watched by a smiling lady-patient, reclining on the 'Queen Anne' dental-chair—and with both bathed in the full glare of the Röntgen lamp: a flood of lethal radiation calculated to send both out of the dental-surgery with terminal cancer....

All these patent nostrums claimed to *cure*—and all were panaceas, the list of diseases 'cured' being limited only by the dimensions of the ad. My most affectionately remembered were those offering to increase the height of the unhappily small—'Four to Six Inches Without Exercises or Appliances'; and the 'Vibro' Belts (I was too young to understand what these 'Electrical Stimulators' were *really* offering, but I was greatly taken with the sparks and rays and lightning bolts that coruscated around the 'Magnetic Belts').

So here we come to what, perhaps, was my favourite ad of all, which, differently from the 'comic strip' type of advertisement, told its story in words, not pictures. It had, in fact, one picture only, and that had a special attraction for me, since the artist, whose unsigned work I recognized, was a relative of my family by marriage: R. Caton Woodville. (An excellent drawing by this talented artist decorates my book, *I, Sherlock Holmes.*)

I have tried to get a copy of this advertisement of a time around seventy years ago, but, despite the fact that I am usually fortunate in tracking down the objects of my research, I have, so far, been unable to find an example of this. What I shall describe, then will be from my reasonably retentive memory. In any case, I could hardly forget the essentials of an ad that so took my young fancy.

———

Until the British public—the British non-combatant—was, willy-nilly, involved in 'hostilities'; first, in the Great War of 1914–1918, by aerial bombardment from the German *Taube* and *Gotha* 'planes, and by shelling of the East Coast seaside resorts by German cruisers; then, much more violently, during World War II, with the 'blanket-bombing' of the four-year aerial *Blitz* that ended with the assault by the V1 and V2 rockets; the British had always had a romantic eye for the soldier-in-uniform—especially the commissioned officer.

Now, R. Caton Woodville—as he always signed his work, when he did sign it—had himself been a commissioned officer before he bacame a professional artist; but it was evident that he had never been on a battle-field. True, the drawing that I am about to describe was intended to shew an 'incident' in the heat of battle, and to make this point, the artist had thoughtfully provided volleys of shells whizzing overhead. But the officer in question—Captain Hudson—had the sort of warlike appearance that one saw on the Victorian manoeuvers, of this sort, that I quote from that 1896 *Illustrated London News*:

> A Division of the troops at Aldershot Camp, under command of Major-General Kelly Kenny, marched on Friday from Pirbright to Frensham, in movement preparatory to the autumn military manoeuvres. The Duke of Connaught inspected other divisions at Aldershot, and those of Lord Methuen and Lord Seymour performed special operations.

There was no mud; no blood; no death; not even wounds. And no nasty shells—and all the officers were in their brilliant parade uniforms. It was with a memory of such spit-and-polish mock-battles that R. Caton Woodville painted his battle-scene for Mrs Hudson, of New Bond-street.

As I recall this example of Advertising flim-flam at its most romantically improbable, the drawing shewed a very smartly-turned-out British officer, in what then passed for battle-kit: well-cut tunic of khaki cord, with the old-fashioned double-Sam Browne; with the pistol-holster high on his chest, and a leather-scabbarded sword of the 'Service' type held in his left hand. To indicate that there is pretty rough fighting going on, the Captain, his Macassared hair quite unruffled, is bareheaded—in the heat of conflict, he has lost his cap. He is, in fact, the sort of British officer familiar to the tens of thousands of theatre-goers in that theatre-going age, who have thrilled to the hundreds of 'military' plays that were one of the 'hardy perennials' of the British stage.

Caton Woodville's wash-drawing shewed the Captain (a higher rank then, than it has become since) bending, in an elegantly theatrical pose, over an Indian soldier, who is lying on the ground while the Captain Sahib supports the Indian's head and shoulders with a tenderly protective arm.

Alas!, as the caption makes clear, nothing may be done for the wounded Indian:

THE DYING SEPOY

Even through the mist of retrospect, the advertising-copy retains for me all its old charm; but as I may no longer reproduce it *verbatim*, I shall give what I truly believe to be a not inaccurate paraphrase of what followed on that eye-catching drawing and caption.

Mortally wounded, the Captain's Indian orderly—a Sepoy— was tended by his English Sahib, who did his best to make the Indian comfortable in his last moments. Realizing that his end had come, but properly grateful for the sympathy that the Captain Sahib was shewing to a mere orderly (and a coloured one at that), the dying Hindoo wondered what gift he could make the Captain to shew his deep gratitude. Ah!—and he asked the Captain to bend lower, so that he could whisper a secret in the Captain's well-formed English ear. The poor Indian had nothing to give of material value; so, in his gratitude, he imparted a secret to the Captain—a secret so valued by the whole Indian race that never before had it been (no, *not* 'betrayed', but rather) 'imparted' to one of a foreign race: *the secret of how Hindoo women kept their bodies free from Unwanted Hair*! That was the priceless gift 'imparted' to the kindly British officer by the dying and properly grateful Sepoy....

Did the Captain, as the Sepoy fell back, dead, wonder to himself why, in death, the human mind, in its last cerebral effort, so often turned to the most trivial matters? I feel that the Captain did not— could not—appreciate the priceless value of the Dying Sepoy's last gift. It would have been a very odd military gentleman indeed who could have done so....

But, when he returned on furlough, and told his Wife of the singular death of the Hindoo, be sure that Mrs Hudson saw at once the rich commercial potential of her letting in abnormally hirsute ladies of Britain and the Empire on this priceless depilatory secret. Hence the advertisements in all the 'better quality' magazines—'glossies', as they are called to-day—inviting ladies troubled with superfluous hair to communicate with Mrs Hudson, at an address in New Bond-street, when full particulars would be sent to them under 'plain, sealed cover'.

I suppose that what I should have done—should, in fact, do now—would be to check the Captain's name, rank, regiment, and details of his active service with Army Records.

I am reluctant to do this; besides, one would have to know in which Victorian battle it was that the Sepoy made his last precious gift to the Captain Sahib. (Better leave it, I think....)

Who Mrs Hudson was obviously might help to ascertain the identity of Captain Hudson, her husband. For she must have had an ascertainable identity; to pay for the placing of her advertisements; to pay the rent of her New Bond-street address. But...well, as I can't trace even one of those well-remembered ads, I imagine that it would be no easy task, even for a trained researcher (as I am) to track down the details of Mrs Hudson's tenancy of her West-end offices.

Of course, it must be inevitable that, on their learning of Mrs Hudson, Depilatrist-on-the-Hindoo-System, of New Bond-street, it will occur to the majority of Sherlockians to wonder whether or not they may identity Mrs Hudson, proprietrix of a 'Gentlemen's Furnished Chambers' business in Baker-street, with that other Mrs Hudson, who ran *her* profitable business a mile or so further east? Let us examine, if not altogether the likelihood, at least the possibility, of identity.

First, the tale of the Dying Sepoy does not mention to which regiment Captain Hudson belonged, or whether he was serving in the British Army, stationed in India, or in the Indian Army itself. Officers unable to live on their pay—something impossible in England under field-rank (Major), and even then it was a struggle to get by—went to India, where it *was* possible to live on one's pay even as a relatively junior officer. If Captain Hudson was serving in India, he must have applied for transfer to 'our Eastern Empire' because he lacked wealth of his own—and his Wife would not have lost him caste by earning a separate income as the owner of a respectable boarding establishment in nearly the best (and certainly one of the most respectable) districts of the Metropolis. (In England, this would have been unthinkable; any officer who sought to augment his insufficient pay by permitting his wife to 'take in lodgers' would not exactly have been drummed-out, but his Colonel would certainly have demanded that he send in his papers.)

———

That Captain Hudson's grateful benefactor was a Sepoy tells us that the campaign, whichever it was, was fought, wholly or in part, with Indian native troops; so that the battle took place, in all probability, somewhere on the northern borders of India, there having been no fighting inside India itself since the suppression of the Mutiny in 1858. Considering all the evidence—though one must admit it isn't much—one would suggest that Captain Hudson and his Sepoy were engaged in conflict with the Afghans, not so much in the earlier disastrous campaign that included Maiwand, but in the later, successful campaign under General Sir Frederick Roberts. (*See* page 152.)

The long attempt to 'stabilize' the North-west Frontier kept British and Indian troops in continuous active service, long after the Afghan War, as such, was 'officially' over. The Afridi tribesman, as the Russians are painfully finding out to-day, are not to be 'pacified', 'stabilized', and Captain Hudson, even had he been with the victorious Roberts Campaign of 1880, might well have stayed on in India to finish a specified tour of duty. I mention this because 'our' Mrs Hudson seems to have taken leave of absence round about the year of the Golden Jubilee—1887—when an impressive parade of troops from all parts of the Empire might well have given Captain Hudson the motive and opportunity to pay a Government-subsidized visit Home.

Elsewhere I have argued for March, 1888 as the date at which the (real-life) events of *A Scandal in Bohemia* reached their climax; and when these events were taking place...Mrs Hudson was away from Baker-street, a Mrs Turner having been appointed to stand in for her. If we accept the order in which William Baring-Gould lists the Canonical Cases, and if we accept (though we need not do) that failure to mention Mrs Hudson *may* imply her continuing absence, then, from *The Second Stain*, when she was definitely at Baker-street, she is 'missing' during

· *The Man With The Twisted Lip*
· *The Five Orange Pips*

· *A Case of Identity*
· *The Red-Headed League*

—but has definitely returned (on Captain Hudson's rejoining his Indian posting?) to look after her star-lodgers in *The Adventure of the Dying Detective*: a period of absence that I estimate as somewhat short of two years, but covering the two half-years—1887–1888—of the Queen's Jubilee (an historic date for Sherlockians, as the year 1887 marks the date of Holmes's First Bow).

Meeting her husband, the Captain, did then Mrs Hudson hear from him the tale of the Dying Sepoy, and did they, together—but always on her initiative—discuss the commercial potential of the Sepoy's great Depilatory Secret; resolving to wait until she could profitably dispose of the Baker-street 'connection' before embarking on what *might* be the even more profitable business of making English ladies as hairless as chichahuas or female Hindoos? It is noticeable that the 'Dying Sepoy' ads begin to appear only after Mr Holmes has retired to his bee-keeping on the Sussex Coast....

———

My Uncle had a job under the Colonial Office, designing the trunk roads that seemed the provision of a miracle when, thirty years later, the Far Eastern Command, faced with the menace of the Japanese advance into Burma and, perhaps India, moved its headquarters to Ceylon. On one of his leaves, I shewed the Captain Hudson-Dying Sepoy ad to Uncle Percy, who laughed.

"The poor old Sepoy," he commented, "must have been in the last stages of delirium—but it looks as if your precious Captain had caught the infection, too. My goodness!—what absolute tosh! Yet I suppose there are damnfool women who are taken in by this."

"But, Uncle," I persisted, "*is* there a secret that the Indian women have for—well," I quoted the ad, "'removing Unwanted Hair'?"

"Yes—though there's no secret about it. It's what the Romans did: tweezers and pumice-stone. Painful, but effective.... No, it's the preposterous situation here that gets my goat. I can imagine that when a man's had it, he'll talk the most utter tripe...but would the Captain listen, with all those Archies[1] whizzing about over-head? I wonder what's wrong with the Editors of these magazines, to permit this catchpenny stuff room in their pages."

———

So much for Captain and Mrs Hudson—but, not so many years after, about the time that Count Zborowski, the racing-motorist, killed himself in his *Chitty-Bang-Bang*, a lingering memory of that contemptuously dismissed drawing of the Dying Sepoy matched up with a tragic reminder of the artist. Caton Woodville took his own life; and, because, as I have said, he was a distant relative of ours by marriage, my Father inevitably noticed the charitable obituary, and—being my Father—could not resist 'pointing the moral', without, as matters were, having to 'adorn the tale'.

As the need for 'Our Artist's Impressions' were replaced, in the news-magazines, by the photographs taken by ever-more-active and ever-more-daring photographers (and ever-more-speedy emulsions), the artists whose work had filled the pages of *The Graphic*, *The Illustrated London News*, *The King*, *Army & Navy*, *Black & White*, and so on, (not forgetting *The Strand*) fell into neglect. Among these now forgotten artists was old Caton Woodville, now fallen into the most desperate poverty. This and the appalling loneliness of a friendless old age had driven him to the brink of despair—and his old Service revolver had taken him over that Dark Divide....

———

When they found him, it was obvious that he had spent his last sad days in this bedroom, through the open door of which he could hear, after the postman's double-knock, the letters falling, each hopeless day, through the letter-slot—mail that he dared not open, since every letter (he knew) contained some demand for the money that he no longer had.

---

[1]"Archies"—'H.E.s' = High Explosive (shells) in World War I battlefield slang.

But—and this was the point that my Father almost passionately emphasized—among those many unopened letters that the police, forcing the front-door, found piled on the hall-mat, was one that did *not* demand money. And, said my Father, had he had the courage to open them all, he must have found this letter from a firm of Solicitors, telling him of a legacy that would have relieved of all his debts and ensured for him an income sufficient to maintain him, in some degree of comfort, for the rest of his life.

So, my Father pointed out, the moral is this: One *never* may say 'This is the end. There is no more hope....'

"That," said my Father, "is something of which we may never be sure. Poor old boy...if only he'd had the nerve to open those letters.... Well: he's gone, but remember this: whatever troubles you have—and no life's ever free of them—HANG ON! Don't *ever* give in. You never know what God, after he's sent you perhaps a lot of suffering, hasn't in mind to send you for comfort...."

———

Well, I've had a lot of advice in my long life—advice good, bad, and uselessly indifferent. Some I've taken, and regretted it; some I've not taken, and regretted that, too. But the lesson that my Father read me after he'd saddened over the unnecessary suicide of R. Caton Woodville, I have never forgotten. I've had a lot of trouble; but, I'm *happy* to say—rather than *proud* of saying—that, so far, I've never given in. I have, as my Father advised all those years ago, found the strength (or, perhaps, no more than ordinary common-sense) to hang on....

So, because of that, the lesson of Caton Woodville is never far from my mind. And because I remember his tragic end, I remember, too, the advertisement for which he did the unsigned artwork: the fanciful picture of the Captain and the dying Sepoy....

BIBLIOGRAPHY

It is now many years since my friend, the late Frederick Dannay (the collaborator with the late Manfred Lee in the most successful of all literary partnerships: 'Ellery Queen') was moved to remark that the bulk of the commentaries on the Sherlock Holmes stories far outweighed what his creator had left for our enjoyment. I suppose that that remark is getting on for its half-century, and the then incredible mass of Sherlockian commentary has doubled and trebled and quadrupled, and possibly increased by tenfold, if not more—I myself having added to the mass with no fewer than six full-length books, one Sherlockian anthology of my editing, and eight monographs, not all of which have yet been published. The total of the commentaries—books and articles—must run now to several *thousands*: unique testimony to the relentless hold that Conan Doyle's Immortal Sleuth has taken on the world's fancy. Of no other character in fiction has so much commentary been written.

———

The two most nearly complete Bibliographies of Doyle's work—no such Bibliography may ever hope to achieve completeness, so long as Sherlockian comment and commentary are being published by the week, or even the day—run to hundreds of pages; so that I could not hope to give anything but the smallest sampling here.

What I do list following are the Sherlockian books that I have read, consulted, quoted from, and, in all cases, judged them among the most worthy of their class. I would like the reader to consider them, not only as my source-books, and, generally, my inspiration, but also as books that I recommend for 'further reading'. A point to notice is that the publication-dates cover essentially the whole growth of Sherlockian study and scholarship, from the late Monsignor Ronald Knox's tongue-in-cheek *ballon d'essai** of more peaceful days a decade after the first world war: that fascinating mock-serious study which, one may justly say, 'started it all'. Thereafter, with more seriousness—or, at any rate, the well-contrived appearance of scholarly sobriety—such scholars as the late Dorothy Sayers, and such wits as the late 'Archie' Macdonnell—to name but two of those who took up the Knoxian torch to illuminate some of the more foggy parts of the Canon—were joined by many others, not one of them lacking in scholarship, and many, such as (oh dear! this dreadful and inescapable adjective!) the late Bernard Darwin and the equally late A.A. ('Winnie-the-Pooh') Milne, true wits as well. Such Sherlockian scholars as—no, I shalln't say it again!—Harold Bell and T.S. Blakeney and Gavin Brend laid the solid foundations on which later Sherlockian exegetists such as Sir Sydney Roberts and James Edward Holroyd raised enduring monuments to their so highly specialized scholarship; that scholarship including, in the case of my greatly lamented friend, 'Bill' Baring-Gould, excursions into fiction as well as into the knottier problems of chronology and geography: *when* the sixty Cases were likely to have happened, and *where* they might well have taken place.

So here, for further reading, are what I consider the pick of Sherlockian theorizing, together with some other books, not specifically Sherlockian, but giving some wonderful glimpses of that world of a century and more ago, in which, to quote Vincent Starrett's inspired sonnet, *221B,* 'it is always 1895'; that far-off and more romantic world in which, in the pages of a Christmas magazine, the Immortal Sleuth made his First Bow....

———

Altick, Richard D. *Victorian Studies in Scarlet.* New York: W.W. Norton, 1970.

Annual Register, The. July, 1861; pp. 119–27, inclusive.

Anonymous. *Handbook to London as It Is.* London: John Murray, 1879.

———. *London: A Complete Guide.* London: Henry Herbert & So., 1876.

———. (i.e., J. Osgood-Field). *Uncensored Recollections.* London: Eveleigh Nash & Grayson. 1924.

———

*'Studies in the Literature of Sherlock Holmes'. from *Essays in Satire.*

Baring-Gould, Wm. S. *Sherlock Holmes of Baker Street: A Life of the World's First Consulting Detective.* New York: Clarkson N. Potter, Inc., 1962.

Bell, Harold W. *Baker Street Studies.* A Miscellany, with contributions by Dorothy Sayers, Helen Simpson, Vernon Rendall, Vincent Starrett, Monsignor Ronald A. Knox, A.G. MacDonnell, (Sir) S.C. Roberts, and H.W. Bell. London: Constable & Company, 1934. *Note*: This is one of the most important works in the whole corpus of Sherlockian scholarship; one to which the adjective, 'seminal', most justly applies. No serious student of Sherlockismus should neglect this joint effort by eight leading Sherlockian thinkers to elucidate some of the more knotty problems of the Canon. I wholeheartedly recommend it as 'required reading' for all students of matters Sherlockian.—M.H.

————. *Sherlock Holmes & Dr Watson: The Chronology of their Adventures.* London: Constable & Co., 1932.

Blakeney, T.S. *Sherlock Holmes: Fact or Fiction?* London: John Murray, 1932.

Booth, J.B. *London Town.* London: T. Werner Laurie Ltd, 1929.

Brend, Gavin. *My Dear Holmes: A Study in Sherlock.* London: George Allen & Unwin, Ltd, 1951.

Carr, John Dickson. *The Life of Sir Arthur Conan Coyle.* London: John Murray, 1949.

Christ, Dr Jay Finley. *An Irregular Guide to Sherlock Holmes.* New York: Argus Books; Summit, N.J.: The Pamphlet House; both 1947.

Churchill, Sir Winston S. *The World Crisis* (4 vols). London: Thornton Butterworth, 1923–27.

Clunn, Harold P. *The Face of London.* London: Spring Books, n.d.

Collins's Illustrated Guide to London. 1883.

Dakin, D. Martin. *A Sherlock Holmes Commentary.* New York: Drake Publishers, Inc., 1972.

Darwin, Bernard. *Every Idle Dream.* London: Collins, 1948.

Dilnot, George. *The Real Detective.* London: Geoffrey Bles Ltd, 1929.

Encyclopaedia Britannica: Article: *Lighthouses.*

Guedalla, Philip. *Mr Churchill: A Portrait.* London: Hodder & Stoughton, 1941.

Hall, Trevor H. *Sherlock Holmes: Ten Literary Studies.* London: Gerald Duckworth & Co., Ltd, 1969.

Hardwick, Michael and Mollie. *The Sherlock Holmes Companion.* London: John Murray, 1962.

Harper, Charles G. *A Londoner's Own London.* London: Cecil Palmer, 1924.

Harrison, Michael. *Painful Details: Twelve Victorian Scandals.* London: Max Parrish, 1962.

————. *London by Gaslight, 1861–1911.* London: Peter Davies, Ltd, 1963.

————. *In the Footsteps of Sherlock Holmes* (Revised edition). Newton Abbot: David and Charles, 1972; New York: Drake Publishers, Inc., 1972.

Harrod's Catalogue. 1895. Reprint. Newton Abbot: David & Charles, 1975.

Haydn's Dictionary of Dates. London: W.H. Allen, 1910.

Holroyd, E.J. *Baker Street Byways.* London: George Allen & Unwin, 1959.

————. *Seventeen Steps to 221B.* London: George Allen & Unwin, 1967. Yet another fine miscellany: seventeen Sherlockian essayists making their (on the whole) valuable contributions to Holmesian theory and scholarship.

Jerrold, Walter. *Field-marshal Earl Roberts, V.C.: The Life-story of a Great Soldier.* London: W.A. Hammond, 1913.

Knox, Monsignor Ronald A. *Essays in Satire.* London: Sheed & Ward, 1928.

London Post Office Directory.

Morgan, Robert S. *Spotlight on a Simple Case, or, Wiggins, Who Was That Horse I Saw You With Last Night?* Wilmington, Delaware: The Cedar Tree Press, 1959. Of this unique Sherlockian item, William Baring-Gould had this to say in admiration: 'In brief, a tour-de-force—simply not to be missed'.

Morton, H.V. *Ghosts of London.* London: Methuen, 1939.

'Queen, Ellery', (Ed.). *The Misadventures of Sherlock Holmes.* Boston: Little, Brown & Company, 1944. Not an easy book to find, since it was suppressed in circumstances which are not easy to explain; but well worth the finding. A fine miscellany, memorable for containing Vincent Starrett's 'The Unique Hamlet', described by William Baring-Gould as 'the single greatest Sherlockian pastiche ever written'.

Roberts, Sir Sydney. *Dr Watson: Prolegomena to the Study of a Biographical Problem.* London: Faber & Faber, Ltd, 1931. One of the directors of this publishing firm was the American-born poet, T.S. Eliot, himself a dedicated 'addict' of the Canon.

————. *Holmes & Watson: A Miscellany.* London: Oxford University Press, 1953.

Simpson, A. Carson. *Simpson's Sherlockian Studies.* Philadelphia: International Printing Company, 1953–60. Eight studies by one who, in Baring-Gould's admiring words: 'combines prodigious scholarship with wit'.

Simpson, Colin. *Lusitania.* London: Longmans, Green & Co., 1972.

Simpson, Professor Keith. *Forty Years of Murder.* London: George G. Harrap & Co., Ltd, 1978.

Smith, Sir Sydney. *Mostly Murder.* London: George G. Harrap & Col., Ltd, 1959.

Starrett, Vincent. *The Private Life of Sherlock Holmes.* London: Nicholson & Watson, 1934.

Thackeray, Wm. Makepeace. 'On Two Roundabout Papers Which I Intended to Write'; *Cornhill Magazine*, IV (1861), pp. 379–80. *The Times* (London). Issues of 13th-23rd July, 1861.

Thornbury, Walter. *Old and New London* (4 vols). London: Cassell, Petter & Galpin, n.d. (but circâ 1890).

Turner, E.S. *May It Please Your Lordship*. London: Michael Joseph, 1971.

Whitaker's Almanack for 1882.

Zeisler, Ernest Bloomfield. *Baker Street Chronology: Commentaries on the Sacred Writings of Dr. John H. Watson*. Chicago: Alexander J. Isaacs, 1953. Again I can do no better than to quote the opinion of that most percipient Holmesian, William Baring-Gould: 'A volume of prodigious scholarship, by a man who is a celebrated doctor, lawyer, mathematician, Shakespearean scholar, and social and political commentator—as well as an esteemed Sherlockian'.

INDEX